CW01497156

Black Dog Publishing

Visionary Landscapes

The Films of Nina Danino

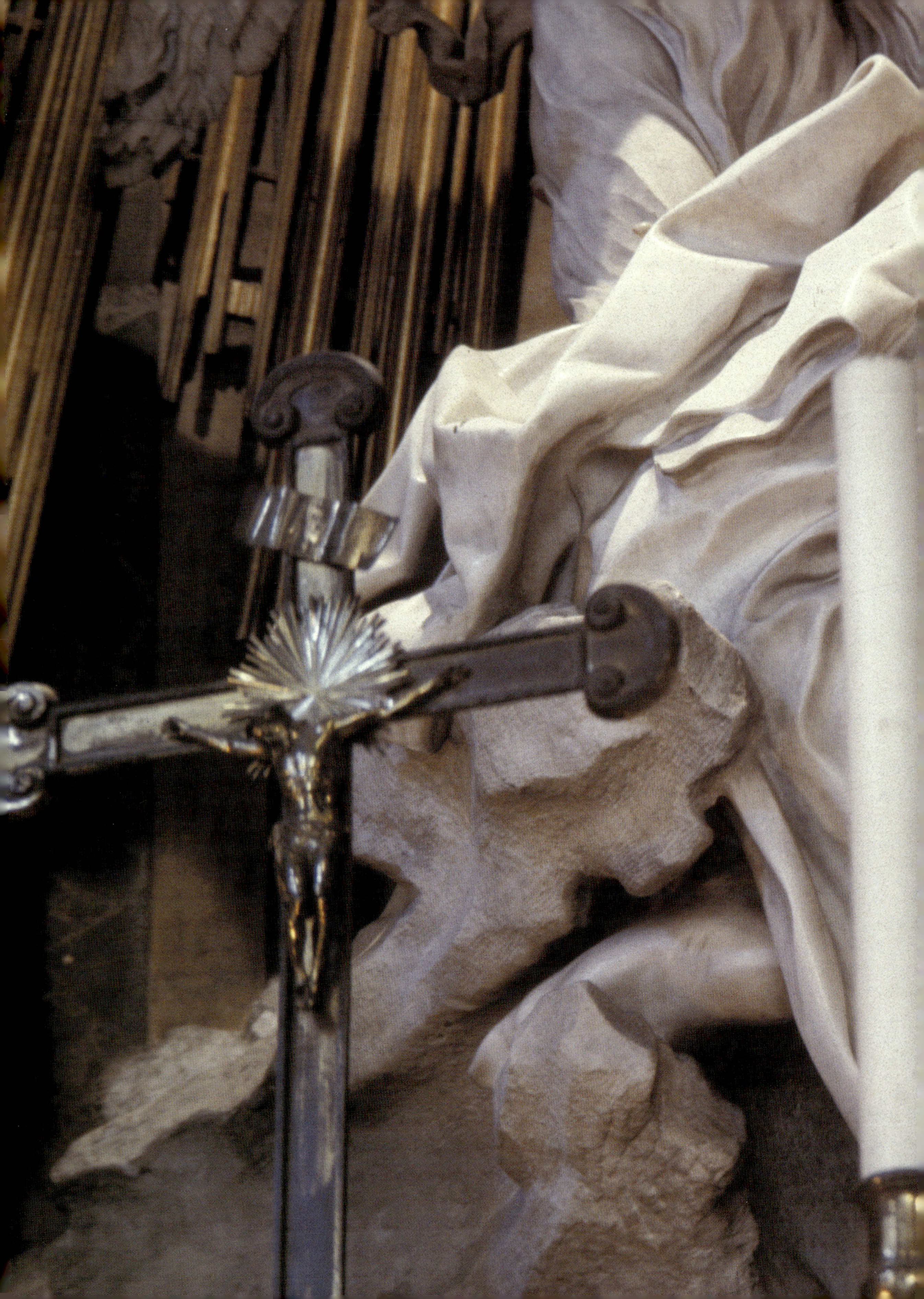

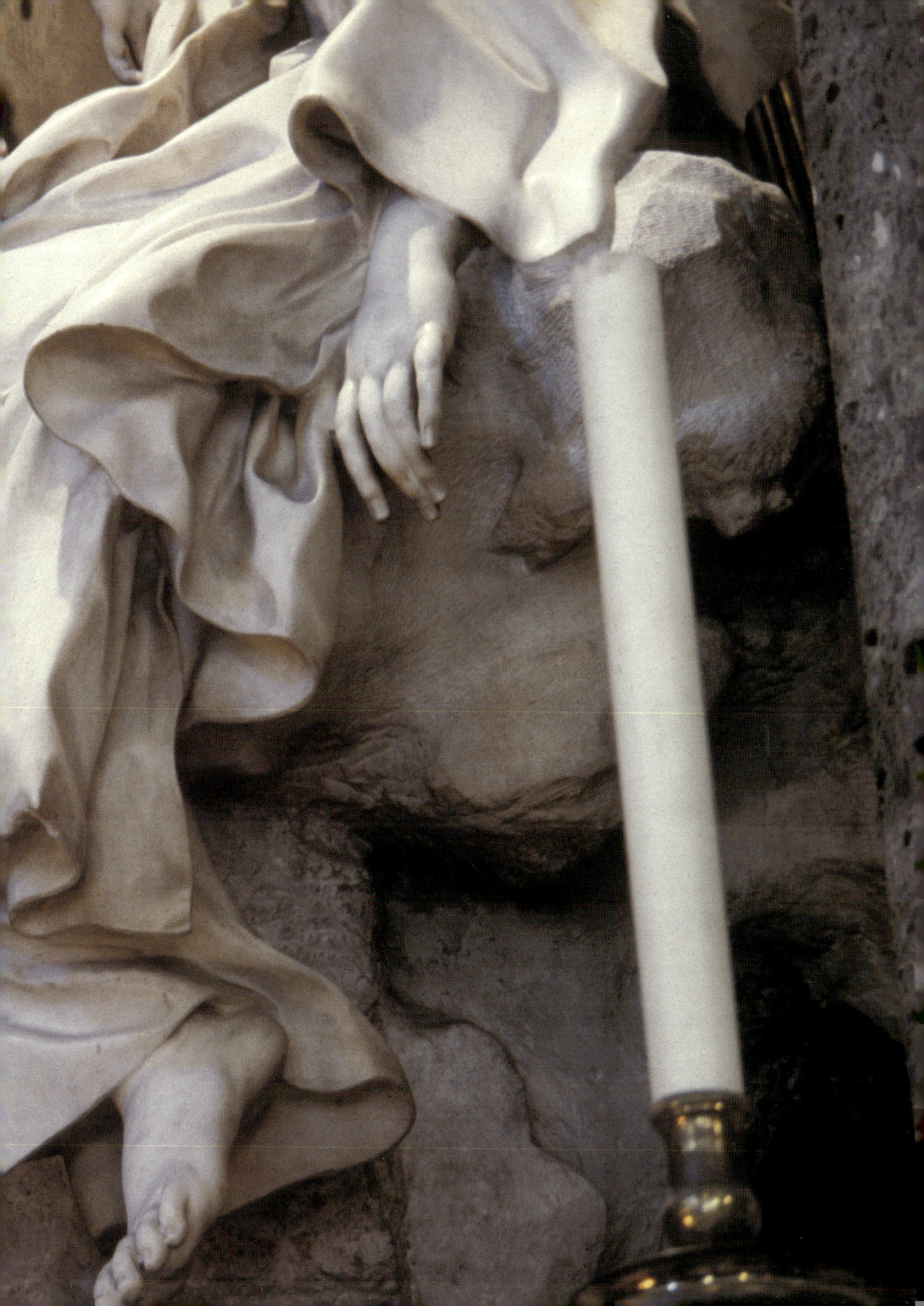

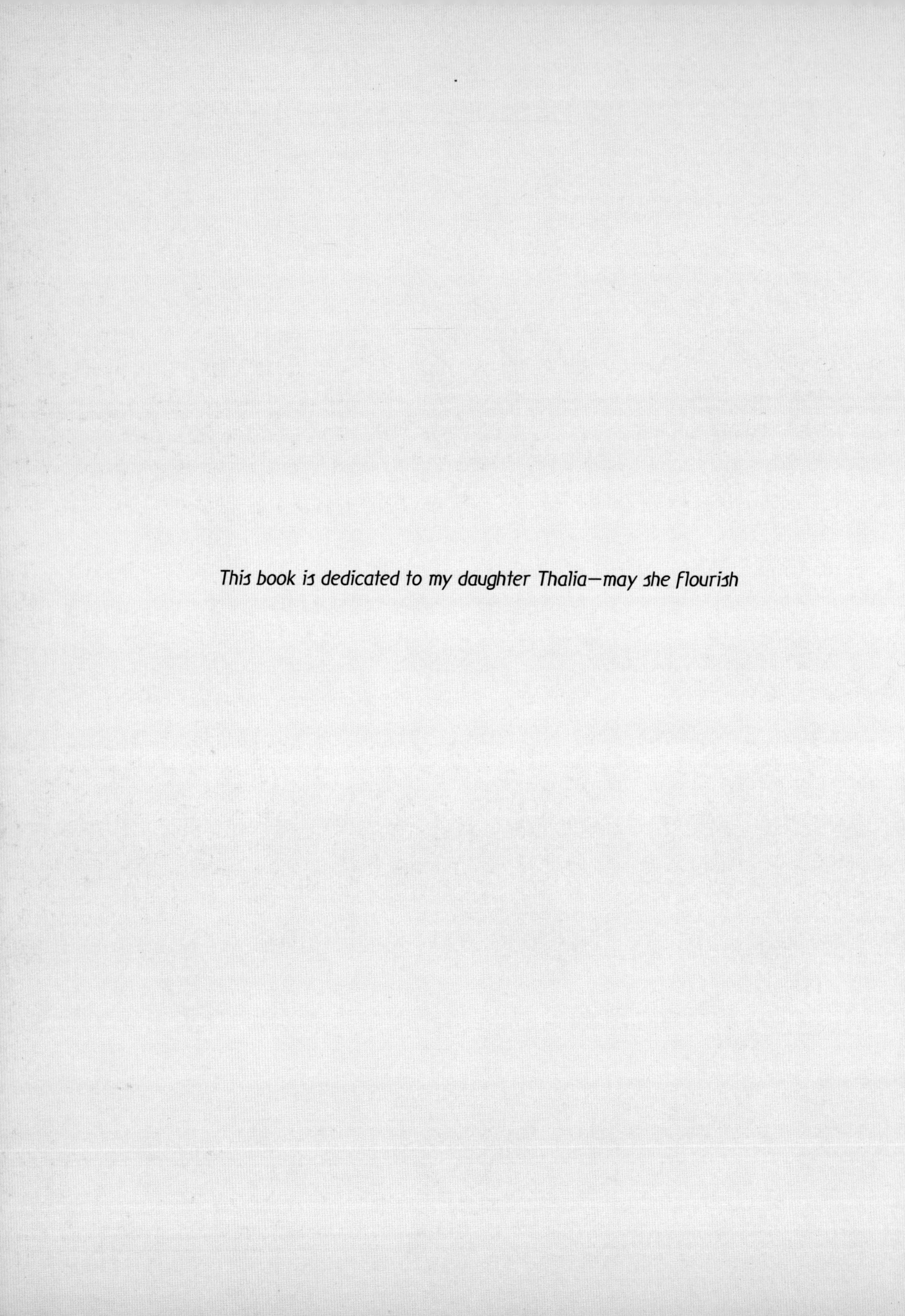

This book is dedicated to my daughter Thalia—may she flourish

Ritualising Images: The Frames of Space, Time, and Aesthetics

S Brent Plate

> To recycle, reuse, archive and recall, to perform in order to be included in an archive (as a lot of performance artists do), to seek roots, explore and maybe even plunder religious experiences, expressions, practices, and liturgies to make art is to ritualise; not just in terms of subject matter and theme, but also structurally, as form. Ethologists and psychologists have shown that the 'oceanic feeling' of belonging, ecstasy, and total participation that many experience when ritualising works by means of repetitive rhythms, sounds, and tones which effectively 'tune' to each other the left and right hemispheres of the cerebral cortex.[1]

As a theorist of religions who examines the visuality of religious practices, I approach Nina Danino's films from a particular point of view. I am interested in the intersection between art and religion, when and where the two converge, and at the points where delineations become impossible. Nevertheless, part of my vocation is to analyse, to show forth differences, and in the following essay I approach Danino's filmmaking activity (especially *Temenos*, 1998) through a few heuristic categories if only to show where the lines of demarcation between art and religion become hazy. As I will point out, there are a number of formal and structural parallels between rituals and the operations of filmmaking: both work with the raw materials of space and time, re-creating these substances and making them perceivable for an observing community. Then I turn to rethink some of the ideas of creation itself, making clear its intricate relations to destruction, and the importance of the divisions that take place between one thing and another—an idea brought out through the very term "temenos". Filtering these divisions briefly through the psycho-linguistic theories of Julia Kristeva, I highlight the operations of the human subject who is her or himself structured through these divisions. Kristeva theorises a subject who is 'in process', who is not simply constituted by a symbolic regimen, but is always shot through with the more heterogeneous impulses of the material world. This leads to a reviewing of Danino's audio-visuality with reference to mystical experience. Finally, I suggest the avant-garde tactics of Danino's filmmaking offers a vital understanding of ritual-making as revitalising to religion itself. Religions continue to exist because of their ritual practices, and rituals endure because they are artistic, and constantly susceptible to change.

The Content, Form, and Frame of Religious Art

When I tell people that I teach "religion and the visual arts" they tend to believe that I spend a lot of my time looking at Renaissance images of Mary. Or for those who understand there is more to religion than Christianity, they might include Tibetan Buddhist mandalas or

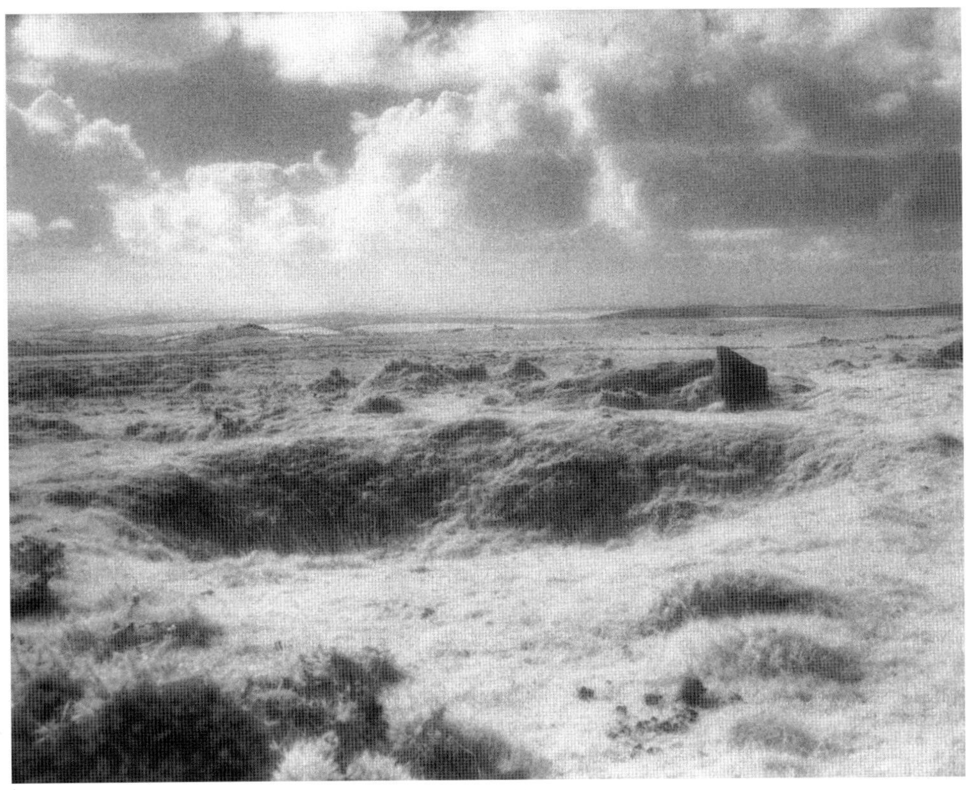

Temenos, 1998

Islamic architecture. In general, however, the assumption is that 'religious art' is that which contains a recognisably religious content or subject matter. So, Bernini's *Ecstasy of Saint Teresa* is religious art, and for that matter so is Chris Ofili's *Holy Virgin Mary*—which is exactly why it was thought to be offensive when it was displayed in the Brooklyn Museum of Art—and so is Mel Gibson's film *The Passion of the Christ*.[2] This is what I would call the first level of religious art.

Such a view of what constitutes religious art is certainly not wrong, just incomplete. A second level view of religious art includes the reception, the engagement and interaction, with the visual work. In this way, Mark Rothko's abstract expressionist paintings may be considered religious, particularly when we take into consideration Rothko's own words on the experiential interaction with his canvases. Here, the experience of viewing becomes a religious experience and, while triggered by the visual object itself, nonetheless becomes religious because of the interrelations between viewer and object. From another angle, the religious dimension to film form and style can also be seen in relation to the contemplative emphasis of various religious traditions, and here film becomes a new medium in a long list of visual media, from icons to yantras to thangka paintings, designed to facilitate meditation.[3]

We can take this interactive, receptive dimension even further and suggest that any bodily and mindful interaction with a work of art is ultimately a religious experience. This is what I would call the third level of religious art. What I mean to suggest here is that art viewing and appreciation is parallel to—if not in fact the same thing as—the activities of religious ritual. Consider Goethe's 200-year old comments, first written with the dawn of the art museum in Europe:

> That salon turning in on itself, magnificent and so well-kept, the freshly gilded frames, the well-waxed parquetry, the profound silence that reigned, created a solemn and unique impression, akin to the emotion experienced upon entering a House of God, and it deepened as one looked at the ornaments on exhibition which, as much as the temple that housed them, were objects of adoration in that place consecrated to the holy ends of art.[4]

Goethe later realised, as Carol Duncan paraphrases him, "that the very capacity of the museum to frame objects as art and claim them for a new kind of ritual attention could entail the negation or obscuring of other, older meanings."[5] Formally speaking, the art museum and the temple/church/mosque are not hollow and neutral receptacles that are filled by various religious and artistic substances and activities, rather the spatial environment itself is responsible for creating the meaning of the objects within that space. The structural environment is itself religious.

More explicitly, regarding the medium of film, the feature that is common to museums, ritual making, and filmmaking, is that of 'framing', a boundary-setting activity that separates, even as it allows the possibility for focused attention. As with museum rituals, film engages the viewer at a number of intellectual, emotional, psychological, and physical levels, and they both achieve this through very specific aesthetic devices that correspond well to religious rituals. Compare the following two descriptive quotes:

> A ritual provides a frame. The marked off time or place alerts a special kind of expectancy, just as the oft-repeated 'Once upon a time' creates a mood receptive to fantastic tales.[6]
>
> Whatever its shape, the [camera] frame makes the image finite. The film image is bounded, limited. From an implicitly continuous world, the frame selects a slice to show us.[7]

The first quote is by anthropologist of religion, Mary Douglas, the second by film scholars, Kristin Thompson and David Bordwell. Note, in each instance and in totally separate contexts, how the activity of framing stands at the heart of ritualised seeing. Framing provides a "marked off time or place" that "makes the image finite," meanwhile retaining, as Goethe says, the power to negate or obscure "other, older meanings". Thus, in the very process of selection, of boundary marking, meaning is generated and regenerated. Boundary marking, line drawing, frame making, all these are the activities of art and religious ritual. Thus, religious art happens on a number of levels, and we are not bound merely by content.

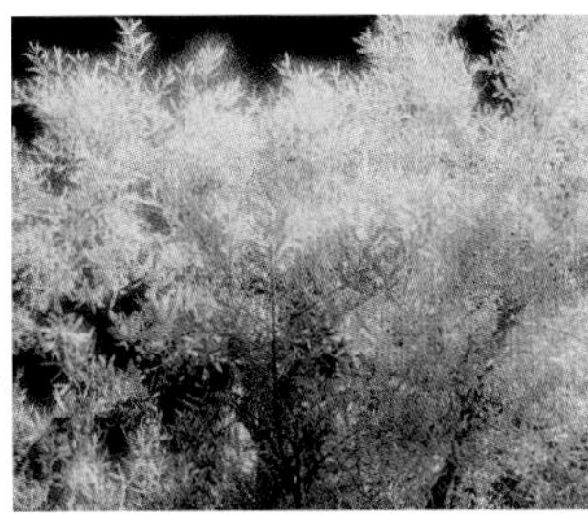 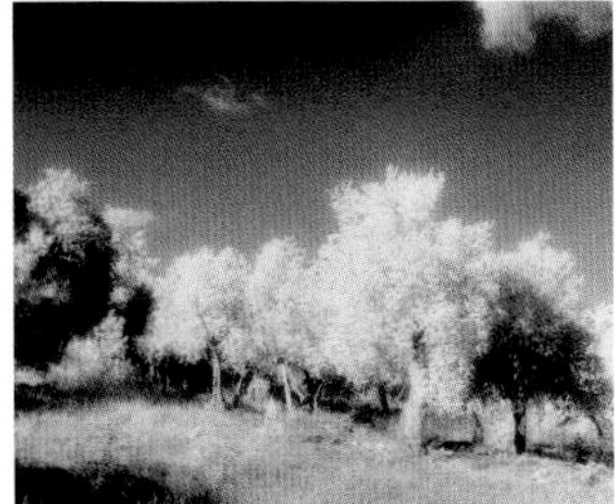 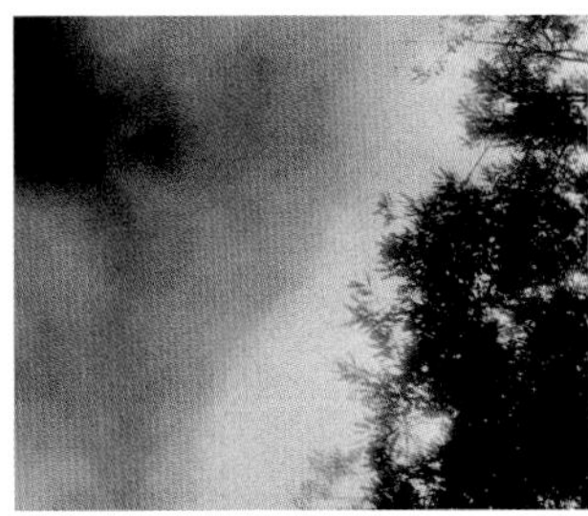

Temenos, 1998

Ritual Re-creations

With the preceding frame in place for this essay, I now turn our attention inward, to some of the specifics of Nina Danino's films, and how she has used the frame in her work, most especially in *Temenos*. *Temenos*, like any well-done ritual activity, offers us a re-created world. The viewer is shown the space of nature, the world 'out there': forests, trees, deserts, sand, water, et al. The natural world 'glows' as if imbued with an aura, as if spirits lived in the very leaves of the shimmering trees. Everything from the effect of the wind on grass, to overexposed film, to use of a hand held camera, to an interspersing of black-and-white and colour film, creates a natural world that is alive. Even without the presence of humans, the landscape has some agency—if a tree fell in this place without anyone to hear it, it would surely make a sound.

Yet it must be clear that this is not the world-as-it-is. It is a framed world. The landscape is framed spatially in the first instance and most obviously by the rectangular shape of the camera frame (the world-as-it-is does not have perfectly straight lines around the edges of its existence). In the second instance the world is framed temporally by the duration of the shots, edited and juxtaposed with other images of nature. In the third instance the images are framed conceptually by intertitles, which both undergirds a classification of *Temenos* as a 'silent' film, even as these words tend to interrupt the images and shift our perspective. In the fourth instance the world viewed is framed aesthetically by sound: by shrieks, monologues, chants, natural sounds, electronic blips and cuts.

Most assuredly, *Temenos* presents viewers with sacred space, and as far as subject matter goes—what I noted above as the first level of religious art—we understand that what we are seeing are several sites called "temenos", or ritual precincts, spaces that have been deemed sacred because of what has occurred in that very place. In these places, the sacred has been manifested. Explicitly here, these natural landscapes are sites where humans have encountered apparitions of the Virgin Mary, and so the ordinary, 'profane' space is turned into sacred space. Sacred is the landscape in which the Virgin has appeared; profane is everything else. But just what is the difference? Why is this tree/rock/mountain/dirt sacred, and that over there is not? Sand is just little bits of rocks, mountains simply shifted tectonic plates in

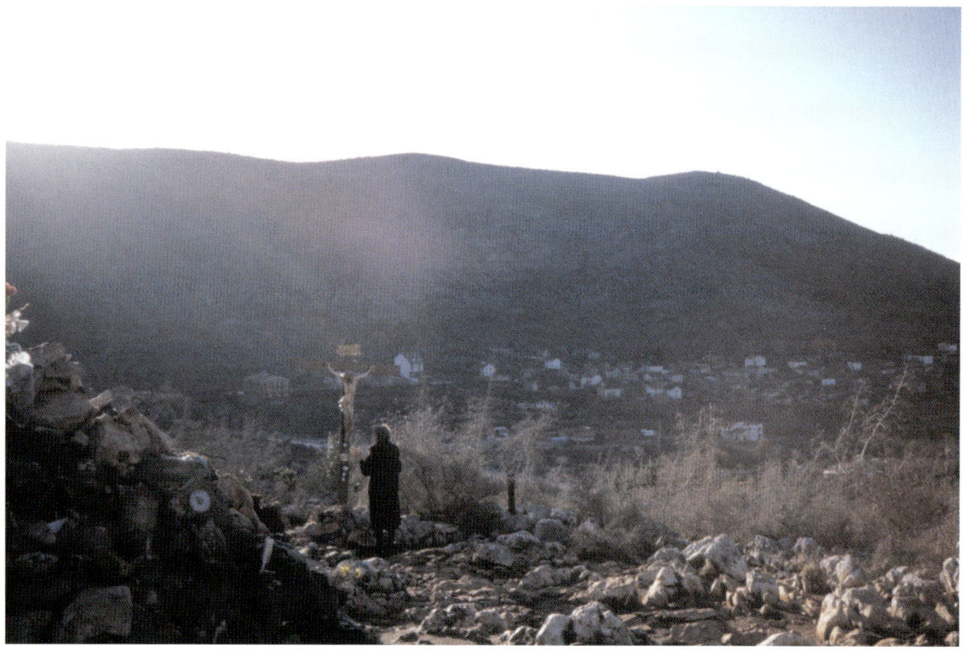

Temenos, 1998

geography, a river nothing but channelled water. So why take some mountains over others? Why claim one river—the Ganges for instance—over another as the residence of deities?

The first and foremost answer to such questions is that certain spaces have been invested with more power than other spaces, and that investment is instilled by believing, behaving, meaning-making humans. Even if a divine presence has made itself felt/seen/heard at a certain point, there must be a being to perceive the presence. A landscape is not sacred unless it is believed to be such. Here we come to the heart of the sacred: the sacred, in its most basic form, is that which is 'set apart', differentiated from the profane. Lines are drawn, boundaries set, and from that instance forward, human behaviour changes when one crosses that line.

In the cases of the spaces represented in *Temenos* we have people from Lourdes, Fatima, and Medjugorge who have experienced visions of the Virgin. They have responded to these visions by telling others who, in turn, also believed and, as a result, consecrated the space. This space is now made sacred; the woman at the end of the film, with rosary in hand, is standing on dirt that is more special than the dirt 'over there'. She knows it, and that is why she prays here and not over there.

And Nina Danino knows it too. Her camera, the images she takes from this sacred space, also invests the place with aura, consecrating the land. Space is caught in her lens; the world is framed. In this way, Danino is not simply recording something out there. Instead, she participates in the religious activity of setting apart.

But we need to redraw our lines of vision slightly before we can understand the sacred, and before we might realise the full impact of *Temenos*. While the theological implications of visions of the Virgin have valence, I am most interested in Danino's film in terms of the second and third levels of religious art, outlined above. That is, I wish to think about the framing activity itself as a religious activity. If the activity of setting apart is at the heart of making sacred, then the activities of filmmaking (like all artistic creation) might function religiously by revealing the very processes of framing. Working in a certain avant-gardist filmmaking style, Danino presents viewers with a created work. Yet it is a creation that always threatens to unravel because the viewer is continually made aware—through rough cuts, shaky images, chopped up sound, dissonant voices—that the film is, in fact, a creation. The goal of commercial filmmaking is to allow the viewer a sense of escape, of forgetting that they are watching a film, by relying on standard techniques to which many of us have grown accustomed. Avant-garde filmmakers tend to shake this up, to make viewers aware of their own space of reception, of the lines that are drawn between the object of film and their own subjectivity. There is always a divide; the medium of film is always present. There is no im-media-cy.[8]

The Greek meaning of the term "temenos" indicates its relation to sacred space, as it designates an area that has been made sacred (consecrated), and is sometimes used in the case of apparitions of the Virgin. Yet significantly, the roots of temenos (Gk. *temn-*) reveal that it encompasses connotations such as "cut, divide, sever, cut down, cut into shape".[9] In other words, there is an emphasis not simply on the 'content'—what is inside that sacred space—but more importantly on the very boundaries at the edges of that space: the frame. Regarding space, etymological relations of temenos also show it relating to the surroundings of a temple or altar.

The religious relevance of dividing or cutting is deeper than one might first imagine. Temenos might be usefully understood alongside the Hebrew term *karath*, which also means "cut down, cut off" and even "destroy". The term is found throughout the Hebrew bible, particularly in Genesis 15 at the point where God comes to Abram and creates a covenant with him. The language used here is that God "cuts" (*karath*) a covenant. The implication is that to create is to cut, to divide; to strike up a deal, a unity between two parties, means this unity implicitly entails a division. If this seems strange, we can back up 15 chapters to the beginnings of the cosmos, finding in Genesis One how a spirit of God creates the world. On close inspection, the world is not created simply by some divine finger-snapping or magic spells, but through separation and dividing: "God separated the light from darkness" (1.4), "... separate the waters from the waters" (1.6), "Let there be light in the dome of the sky to separate the day from the night" (1.14), etc. (The term used throughout Genesis 1 is *badal*, which is different from *karath*, but the implications are parallel as they both indicate this dual process of cutting and creating, of divinely dividing.) The very activity of creation, in a religious context, is an activity of cutting, of framing, of separating one thing from another.

As should now be obvious, the stress here is on this in-between point, the border, the limit, the frame, between one space (time, person, thing) and another. It is logical to see an altar or shrine as sacred, but the surroundings are what are intriguing here. Indeed, the great psychoanalyst and theorist of religion, Carl Jung, reappropriated the spatially related term temenos to designate a kind of protective container for the human psyche:

> The symbol of the mandala has exactly this meaning of a holy place, a *temenos*, to protect the centre. And it is a symbol which is one of the most important motifs in the objectivation of unconscious images. It is a means of protecting the centre of the personality from being drawn out and from being influenced from outside.[10]

Temenos is a 'magic circle', a boundary that separates, marking what is inside from what is outside, even as it protects and simultaneously enables a much greater power of focus. It is no little coincidence that Jung discusses the temenos in the context of both the human psyche and a visual ritual object, the mandala. The power of visual focus, hence of psychic stability, is rooted in the human's ability to meditate using the body.

Danino translates, or better, transmediates, these ancient mandala forms into an entirely modern medium, thereby remaining true to the tradition while moving it forward, providing an intervention into contemporary life. Yet, this is an avant-garde work, make no mistake, and the Jungian notion of the ordered, quaternary images with harmonious, symmetrical squares and circles, does not fully translate. What we must come to terms with is the liminal status of temenos, the ways in which it leaves us betwixt and between. To see in this ritualised way means the viewer must herself enter into a liminal space, a place neither here nor there, neither inside nor outside, in and out of time. Speaking of the film, Danino herself calls the temenos an "unlocatable geography", and suggests how she "wanted to clear a space".[11]

I believe Danino's work operates at what I will describe below as the aes-thetic level, a bodily-sensual experience that stimulates the re-creation of the world. As with any film, her films are an audio-visual medium, affecting primarily two of the senses. Yet this strict separation of the senses strikes of a too-scientific view of the world, an objectified categorisation that seeks to make strict, permanent boundaries. In reality, all sensual interaction is multisensual. Food does not taste as it tastes without its smell (wine enthusiasts know the importance of the aroma for the taste), and interrelations of sound and sight have their affects on the other. Through the employment of two contrasting sensual stimulations, *Temenos* leaves the viewer in-between.

Perceiving the Aes-Thetic

> [O]nce words come to dominate and occupy flesh and matter, which were previously innocent, all we have left is to dream of the paradisiacal times in which the body was free and could run and enjoy sensations at leisure. If a revolt is to come, it will have to come from the five senses![12]

How do these cuttings, these boundary lines of division relate to the arts, and to the body? As I have explained in more detail elsewhere, I have sought to revive the Greek roots of the term aesthetic as a way to bring us back to the bodily basis of artistic production.[13] Rather than the modern day assumption that aesthetics are about judgments of beauty and/or theories of art—and thus intellectual exercises—I am interested in bringing to light the material basis of art. Stemming from the Greek *aisthesis*, aesthetics have to do with 'sense perception'. Its focus is on how we perceive (and, simultaneously, create) our worlds through vision, taste, smell, touch, and hearing, among other possible senses.[14] Sensations emerge when stimuli from the world around us are received through bodily sense organs such as the ears, skin, eyes, nose, etc.. These sensations are then interpreted and made meaningful by a conscious brain that is guided by learned and biologically inherited structures of the mind, most notably memory. Sense perception changes due to geographical and chronological circumstances, as well as by age, race, class, gender, sex, and religion; it is crucial to identity formation, both individually and socially, based on how we sense and are sensed by others; it is a primary component of our interactions with religious myths, rituals, symbols, and memories; and it is the fundamental nexus for understanding both religion and art, and particularly the dividing line between the two. With sense receptors as the crux of the matter, perception also links the inner world to the outer world, the body to the physical stuff around us, the body to the mind, bodies to other bodies, and ultimately the activities of perception are responsible for the formation of community and society.

This reviving of the materiality of aesthetics is parallel to the work of Julia Kristeva who, in *Revolution in Poetic Language* and followed up in later books, outlines her version of "semanalysis", a mixing of psychoanalysis with semiotics. She is concerned with the linguistic and artistic construction of subjectivity, particularly with regards to its gendered dimension, and understands that there is no stable subject. Rather, what we find is a "subject in process", most especially put into motion through poetic language (she includes "visual art" in her definitions, but is ultimately a linguist and literary theorist). While there is no space to fully outline Kristeva's theories here, there are a few related ideas that help draw the connection to the bodily basis of aesthetics.

Most significantly, Kristeva contrasts two realms of subjectivity: the semiotic and the symbolic. Briefly, the semiotic is related to (though not identical with) Freud's pre-Oedipal phase and Lacan's Imaginary register. It is a place of archaic relations between the infant and the mother. Noting the term's Greek etymology, Kristeva psychosomatically relates the semiotic's sense of "distinctive mark, trace, index, precursory sign, proof, engraved or written sign" to the body of the infant (Lat. in-fans, "without speech"). The energies and drives flowing through the infant leave their trace on the body, and these marks/traces/engravings, stay with the human throughout their lives. These primal charges are brought together in what Kristeva, borrowing from Plato, calls the *chora* (lit. "receptacle", or "womb"): "a non expressive totality formed by the drives and their stases in a motility that is as full of movement as it is regulated".[15] Developmentally speaking, the semiotic realm is a stage of 'pre-subjectivity', as the infant cannot yet speak, nor express his/her self in any symbolic manner, nor have the power of self-reflection. As she puts it in *Powers of Horror*:

> In that anteriority to language, the outside is elaborated by means of a projection from within, of which the only experience we have is one of pleasure and pain. An outside in the image of the inside, made of pleasure and pain. The non-distinctiveness of inside and outside would thus be unnameable, a border passable in both directions by pleasure and pain. Naming the latter, hence differentiating them, amounts to introducing language, which, just as it distinguishes pleasure from pain as it does all other oppositions, founds the separation inside/outside.[16]

To exist solely in this semiotic state of total fusion would leave the subject (who is not yet a 'true' subject) in an impossible world and make communication and hence society itself only a dream. So, at a certain point, the infant divides itself off from its mother in order to enter into what Kristeva terms the symbolic realm, an ordered world entailing relations between individual subjects. For the infant to become their own subject, they must strike their independence and enter that social contract in which symbols are agreed upon. This is how meaning is constituted in our lives and it is this that makes us able to communicate and makes signification possible. Because we agree on symbolic meanings, we are able to share ideas, desires, and fears with each other. It is the family and society (particularly that which is patriarchally structured) who establish this symbolic order and into this world we are thrown.

What is stressed in Kristeva, and forms the heart of poetic language, is the boundary between these two realms, even as that line cannot be definitively posited. The semiotic is not eliminated by the birth of the subject into the symbolic order—these two are not exclusory—rather, the semiotic continually lies in a nascent state and all language needs both the semiotic and the symbolic to function. The separation between the two reaches a climax in the formation of the "thetic" (which is connected to the Freudian Oedipal threat of castration): "the subject, finding his identity in the symbolic, separates from his fusion with the mother, confines his jouissance to the genital, and transfers semiotic motility onto the symbolic order. Thus ends the formation of the thetic phase, which posits the gap between the signifier and the signified as an opening up toward every desire but also every act."[17] The thetic phase is precisely the point of difference, where a space of between is enacted, an initial separation between the signifier and the signified that allows them to be put back together again in new ways. In artistic practice, the semiotic "transgresses" the symbolic order and in "the transgression breaks up the thetic, splits it, fills it with empty spaces, and uses its device only to remove the 'residues of first symbolisations' and make them 'reason' within the symbolic chain". The original positioning of the thetic is altered, making way for a new position. Thus, art "does not relinquish the thetic even while pulverising it through the negativity of transgression".[18] The thetic is related to the body and the infant drives and thus it necessitates the materiality of the body.

Following from Kristeva's work, I wish to transpose the thetic here so that what was mentioned above about the aesthetic becomes the aes-thetic, a boundary line through which art becomes significant even as it stands as a place that is under continual threat from the drives of the *chora*. As aesthetics are based at the cusp of the body—the site of sense perception—and therefore stand to reconfigure both inside and outside, so does the thetic

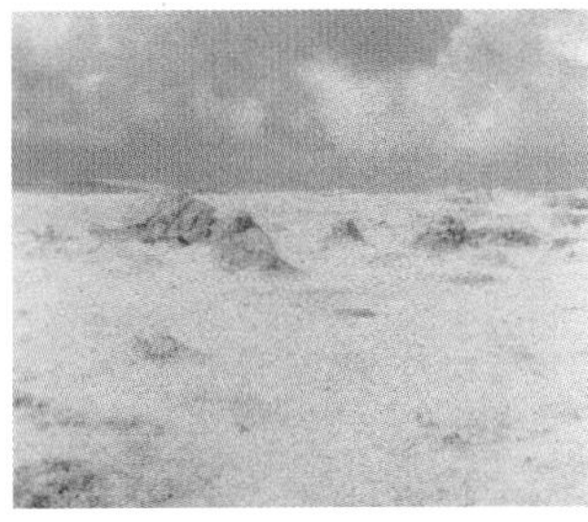
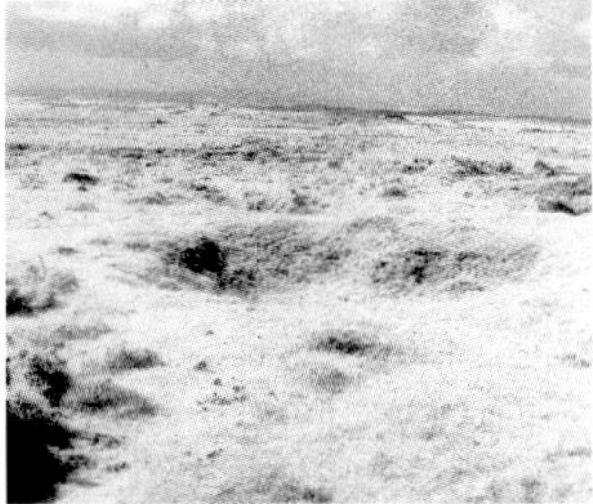
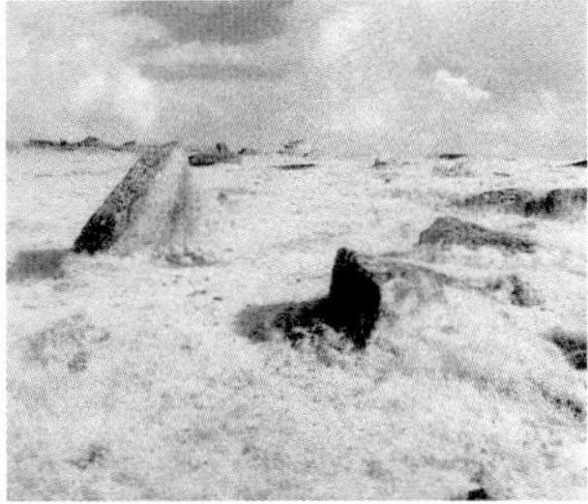

Temenos, 1998

stand at the boundary of semiotic and symbolic, and initialises the difference between signifier and signified. The aesthetic perception of art is what Kristeva believes will allow a transgressive flash to manifest itself, the semiotic to rush through the thetic and manifest itself in the symbolic order, thereby offering a re-creative aesthetic.

Mysticism, Experience, and Its Incommunicability

One of the more abiding issues in religious studies today is that of experience. We scholars can observe religion from the outside, phenomenologically, in terms of its activities, trends, histories, political valence, economic impact, etc., but what of the intensely experiential? How to discuss those moments of psychological/spiritual *in*-sight that are so difficult to share, to communicate, to represent, to others?

For example, Hildegard of Bingen, 1098-1179—doctor, theologian, musician, mystic—had a series of mystical visions in her forties. These visions were not intended to be merely personal, for they came with the charge that they were to be shared—not unlike the visionary imperatives to St John on Patmos, "Now write what you have seen" (Revelation 1.19) or Muhammed on Mt. Hira, "Recite!" (Quran 96.1). In the tradition of John, Muhammed, and others, Hildegard set about trying to share her visions and eventually came to produce her famed *Scivias*. Yet it is critical to note that her retellings took her over ten years to complete. Throughout the work, Hildegard gives a description of the vision, and then spends pages and pages trying to interpret what these visions meant. There is no simple correspondence of mystical experience, no simple way to communicate.

The aes-thetic exists at a point of in-between, linking oneself with the world outside, and thus allowing for social bonds. We speak, show, give off smells and tastes to each other, providing interrelations in the world. But there are events like the mystical experience where this symbolic realm breaks down, where the incommunicable strikes the core of our being. Such was one of Georges Bataille's consistent struggles throughout his writings: the problem of communication and the abilities and inabilities of poetic language to communicate. When he makes a comment like the following, we begin to see how Bataille was influential on Kristeva: "If poetry introduces the strange, it does so by means of the familiar. The poetic is the familiar dissolving into the strange, and ourselves with it. It never dispossesses us entirely, for the words, the images (once dissolved) are charged with emotions already experienced, attached to objects which link them to the known."[19]

I think this too is what we get with Danino's film: the strange introduced by means of the familiar, leaving us suspended, in-between, attached to known and felt objects, even as their meanings do not remain stable. Perhaps the means through which Danino best achieves this type of what we might call a 'filmic mysticism' is through her insistence on film's multimedia, particularly the interventions between sound, images, and words. And this is where I believe the performance of art brings us somewhat closer to the communicability of experience, and to an understanding of an other's experience, even as we simultaneously recognise the utter uniqueness of the other and the very real incommunicability.

Temenos brings the viewer into a recreated world, a world of the desert. A subject also brought up in *"Now I am yours"*, 1992, where an intertitle suggests: "A stone, a tree, a flower: imperfection and loss." The desert is the place where we lose our senses, become anaesthetised, yet it seems to be the place where, precisely at the moment of ultimate loss, the sacred is manifest. Jesus, Moses, the Buddha, Muhammed, all wander in the wilderness, denied of sustenance, surely at the point of death all, and then the revelations come: words of God, temptations overcome, insights into the reality of the cosmos.

Such mystical events cannot merely be re-presented, in the way a documentary might show us around Fatima, replete with interviews of those who saw the apparitions of the Virgin. Instead, these experiences, through Danino's lens, are re-created, given over to the viewers in order to also re-create something of that experience. And in this way we realise we can hear, speak, touch, and share with another across time and space. Danino herself suggests how she "wanted to clear a space. The landscape is empty and yet something happens.... Listening, stillness and quiet predominate but there is a sense of being drawn in and an unseen aspect which creates suspense."[20] Without that clearing and those divisions, we would miss the invitation to be called in and to cross the border into another place.

Revolution in Ritualising

I brought Kristeva into my account in part because Danino herself has noted her influence (through her film *Stabat Mater*, 1990) but also because Kristeva, I believe, allows us some aesthetic terms with which to rethink the activities and theories of ritual. I wish to conclude by returning to ritual, and briefly suggesting how the avant-garde work of Danino suggests new forms of ritual that "break the frame" of ritual. The framing dimension of ritual and film is what, in part, provides its symbolic structuring and allows for communication to occur. But there is more to signification than the symbolic realm, and the frame—the aes-thetic—is broken apart as the sensual materiality of the body posits a new articulation.

Ritual too needs both the stabilising function of the symbolic border, yet becomes static and merely repetitious if it remains there. What rituals need is their own reviving, their own revolution in aesthetic activity. One is here reminded of the famous parable by Kafka: "Leopards break into the temple and drink to the dregs what is in the sacrificial pitchers; this is repeated over and over again; finally it can be calculated in advance, and it becomes a part of the ceremony."[21] With a view toward inventive ritual, ritual theorist Ronald Grimes contends how "without constant reinvention, we court disorientation. Without rites that engage our imaginations, communities, and bodies, we lose touch with the rhythms of the human life course."[22] Danino's film brings us into unfamiliar territory precisely through the familiar, allowing us to get 'in touch' with human rhythms that have often been submerged under the surface of the symbolic realm.

Rituals provide a frame, giving us places and times to which we (the ritualising faithful/the film viewers) can return and find solace, comfort, familiarity, remembrance, community. The symbolic structures are provided, and they reaffirm us in our place and time. Yet, the motile, underlying drives of the semiotic pulse beneath the surface, and what is ultimately needed is a destruction of the symbolic ritual. A redrawing, reritualising, re-creative impulse that loosens the structuring forces of the symbolic, puts not only the subject but the ritual in process. And where this primarily occurs is at the in-between space of the aes-thetic, that sensual boundary between one's own body (*corps propre*) and that of the other. *Temenos* is a cut, separation, a mixture of word, sound, and image that is also nowhere itself, even as it opens up space for change, allowing the leopards into the temple.

Temenos, 1998

Notes

1 Schechner, Richard, *The Future of Ritual*, New York: Routledge, 1993, pp. 19-20.

2 I discuss the Ofili controversy and the *Sensation* exhibit in more detail in the introduction to my edited book, *Religion, Art, and Visual Culture*, New York: Palgrave Macmillan, 2002.

3 Francisca Cho, for example, has discussed the relation of Korean Buddhist films to a "cultic mode" of viewing heavily dependent on the aesthetic choices made in the making of film. See Cho, "Imagining Nothing and Imaging Otherness in Buddhist Film", in *Imagining Otherness: Filmic Visions of Living Together*, S Brent Plate and David Jasper eds., Oxford: Oxford University Press/ American Academy of Religion, 1999, pp. 169-196.

4 Quoted in Carol Duncan, *Civilising Rituals*, London: Routledge, 1995, p. 16.

5 Duncan, *Civilising Rituals*, p. 16.

6 Douglas, Mary, *Purity and Danger*, London and New York: Routledge, 2000 [1966], p. 64.

7 Bordwell, David and Thompson, Kristin, *Film Art: An Introduction*, sixth edition, New York: McGraw Hill, 2001, p. 216.

8 There are interesting relations to, on one hand, Stan Brakhage's works, and, on the other, to the slickly produced works of Godfrey Reggio (e.g., *Koyannsqaatsi, Powaqqatsi*) and Ron Fricke (*Baraka*). Unlike Reggio's and Fricke's films, however, Danino's camera disallows much of the overtly synthetic relations to piece together the world into something of a seamless whole. With Fricke's *Baraka*, we may not know what it is we are looking at, but it is all right because the music covers a multitude of cross cuts and the world is recreated as a whole. I find the experience of watching Danino's work somewhat more akin to watching Brakhage's films in which the viewer is confronted with what are at first disorienting images, while eventually there is a meditative calm that comes over the viewer. There are, of course, striking differences, most especially Danino's intricate use of sound.

9 Liddell, H G and Scott, R, *The Liddell and Scott Greek-English Lexicon*, ninth edition, Oxford: Oxford University Press, 1996.

10 Jung, Carl G, "The Tavistock Lectures", *Analytical Psychology: Its Theory and Practice*, New York: Vintage, 1970, pp. 200-201.

11 Danino, Nina, "Temenos and Other Places", *Filmwaves*, no. 5, Summer, 1998, p. 23.

12 Serres, Michel, *Angels: A Modern Myth*, Francis Cowper trans., Paris, New York: Flammarion, 1995, p. 71.

13 See my *Walter Benjamin, Religion and Aesthetics: Rethinking Religion Through the Arts*, New York: Routledge, 2004.

14 The notion that there are 'five senses' is not universal. In the West, the number was chiefly derived from Aristotle's philosophy, but many other thinkers in the West have had different ways of counting the senses, and other cultures continue to divide the world into two, three, or more senses. For interesting overviews on this, see David Howes, *Varieties of Sensory Experience: A Sourcebook in the Anthropology of the Senses*, Toronto: University of Toronto Press, 1991, and Constance Classen, *The Color of Angels: Cosmology, Gender, and the Aesthetic Imagination*, New York: Routledge, 1998.

15 Kristeva, Julia, *Revolution in Poetic Language*, New York: Columbia University Press, 1984, p. 25.

16 Kristeva, *Powers of Horror*, New York: Columbia University Press, 1982, p. 61.

17 Kristeva, *Revolution in Poetic Language*, p. 47.

18 Kristeva, *Revolution in Poetic Language*, p. 69.

19 Bataille, Georges, *Inner Experience*, Leslie Anne Boldt trans., Albany: State University of New York Press, 1988, p. 5.

20 Danino, "Temenos and Other Places", p. 23.

21 Kafka, Franz, *Parables and Paradoxes*, New York: Schocken Books, 1961, p. 93.

22 Grimes, Ronald L, *Deeply into the Bone: Re-Inventing Rites of Passage, Life Passages*, Berkeley: University of California Press, 2000, p. 3.

First Memory
1981

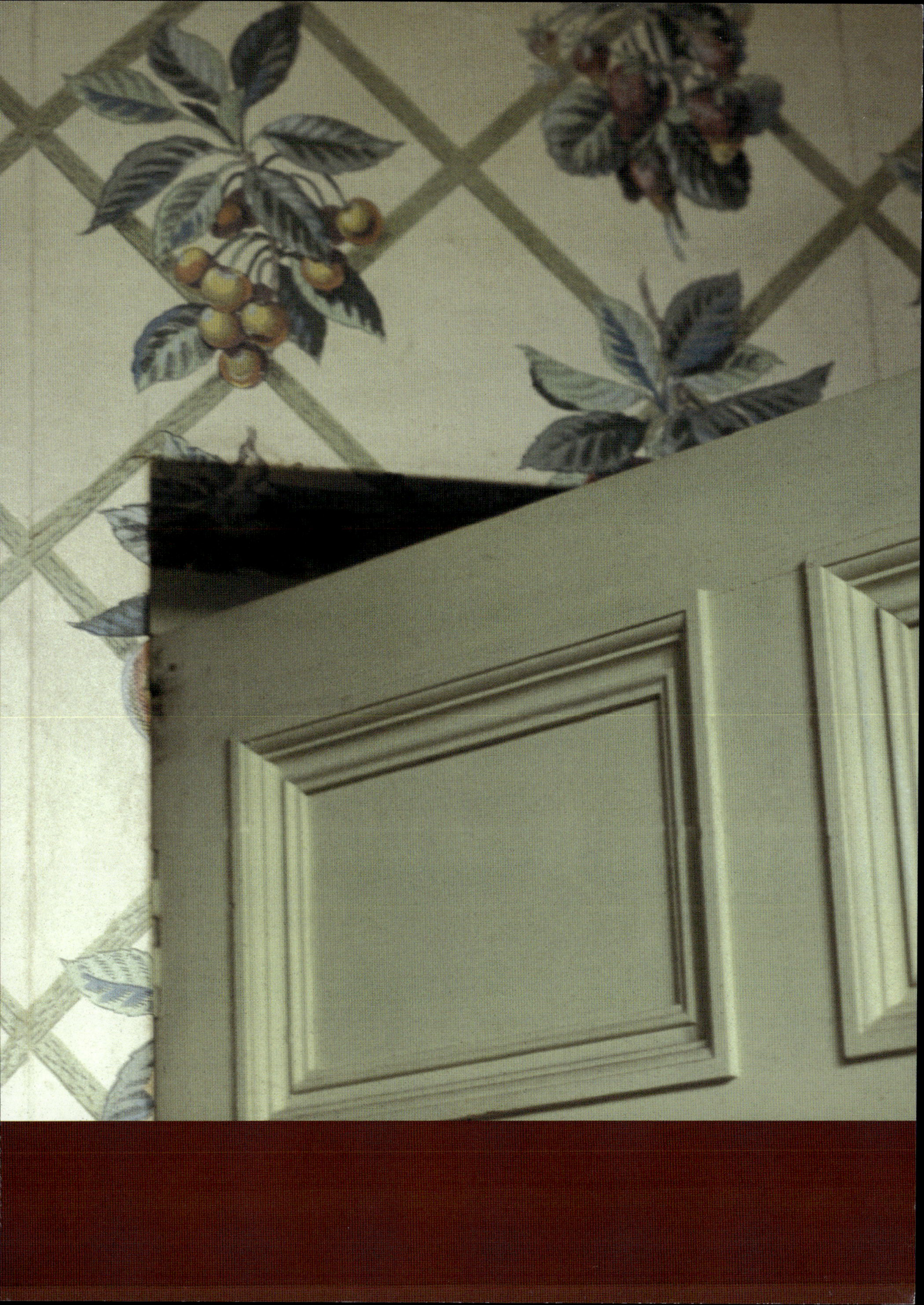

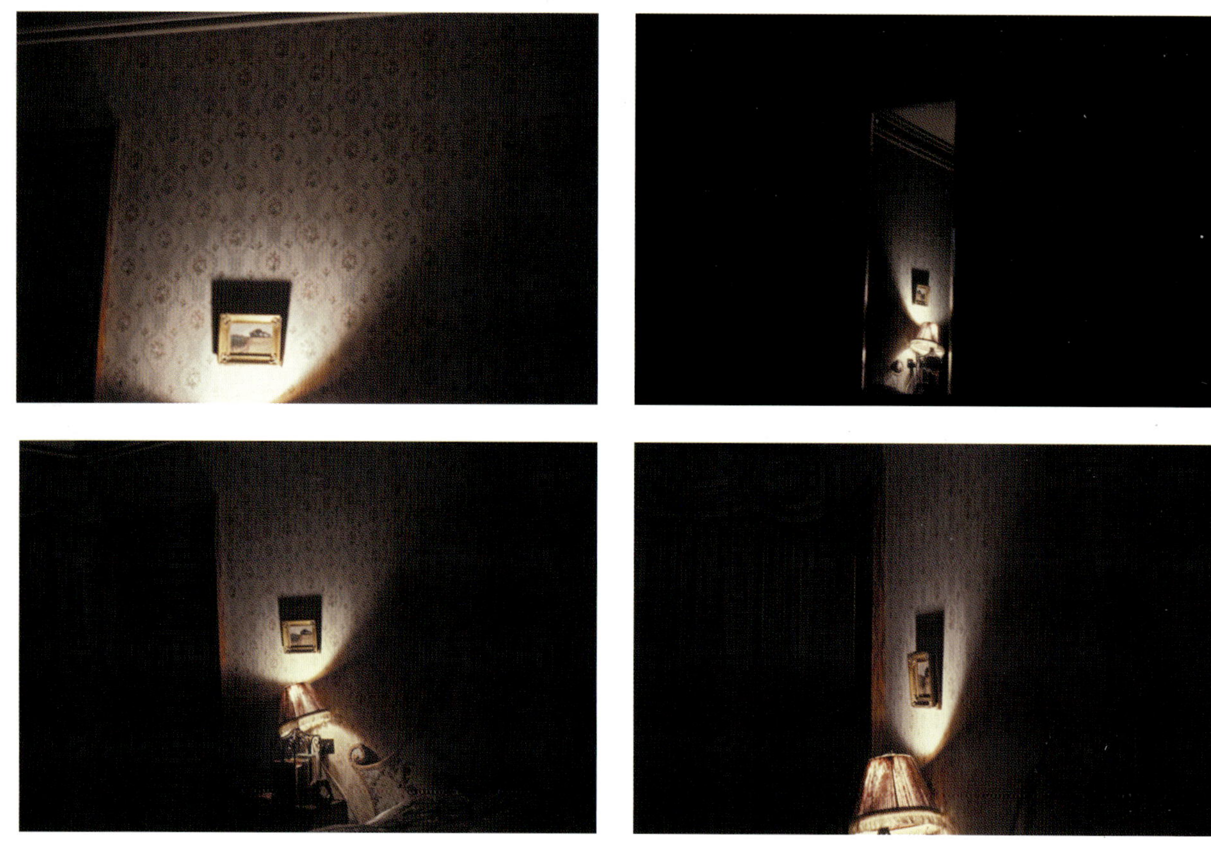

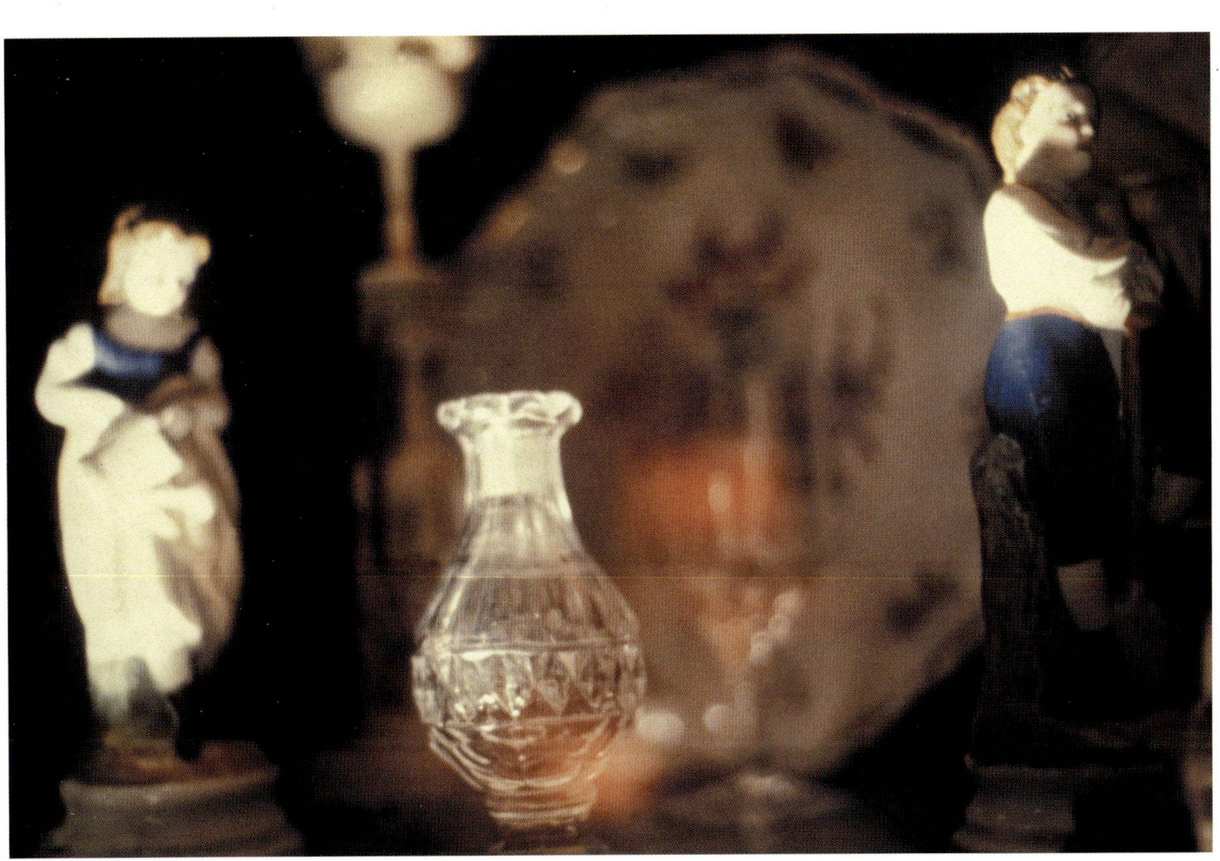

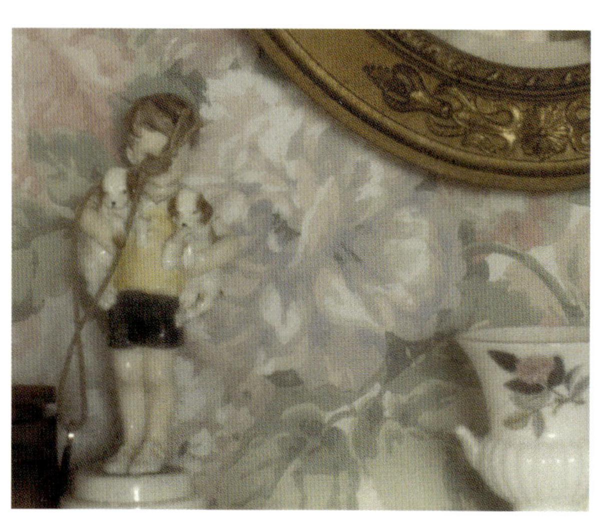

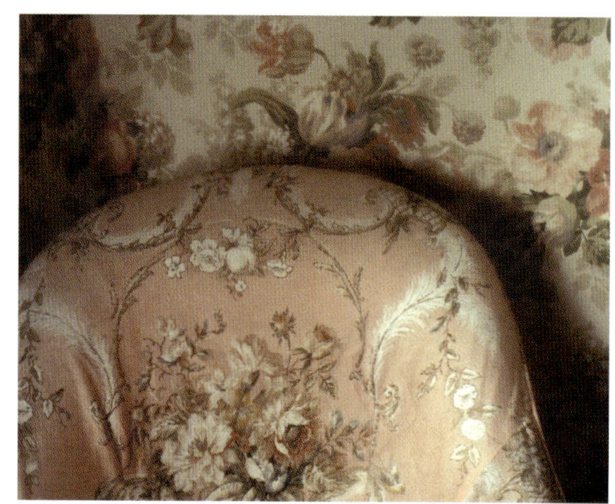

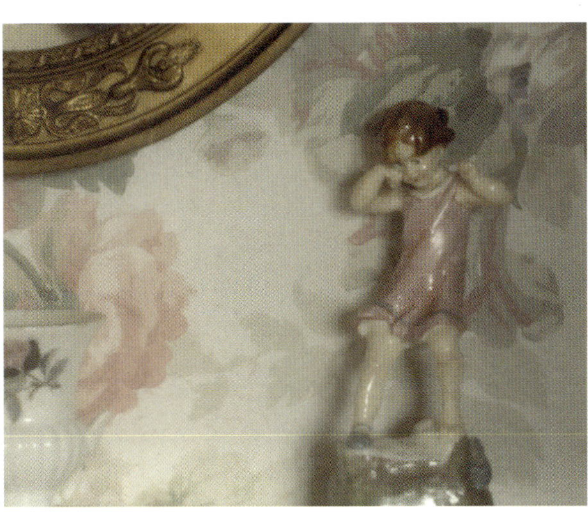

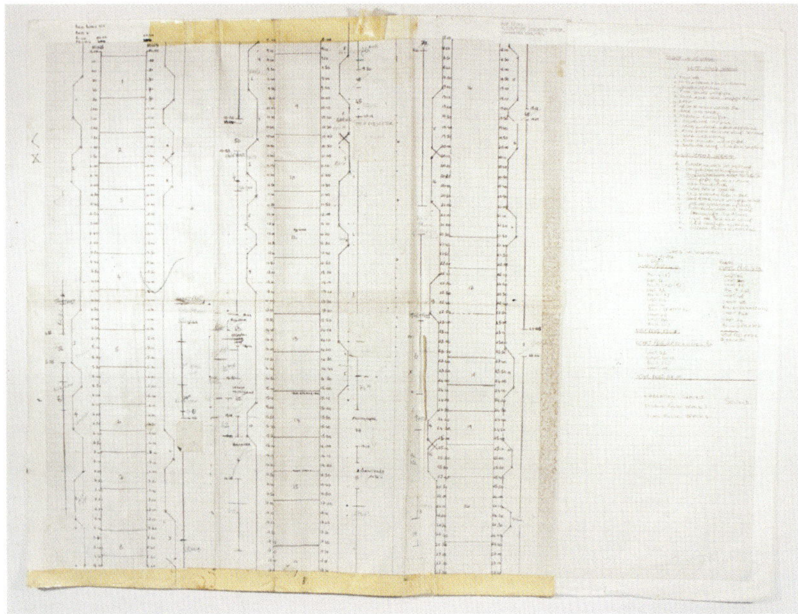

First Memory, 1980
Graph, Edit Two for Multi-Media Projection

The graph was used to time a live multi-media projection first presented as a special event in *About Time/Womens' Images of Men*, ICA, London, 1980. The multi-media piece used two screens, two Super 8 projectors, two slide dissolves, four slide projectors, a Teac time-pulser, a slide-dissolve pulser, and two sound amplifiers. The graph shows the sequence of slides, the fade-in and fade-out points, the length of hold on each image, and the projection of Super 8 images. The superimpositions of the slides and Super 8 could not be 'locked' but instead were timed through the lengths of film and black spacing on the spools which ran simultaneously. The central column of the graph shows the narration and silence, against the time-line of the whole assembly with a running time of 27 minutes 20 seconds.

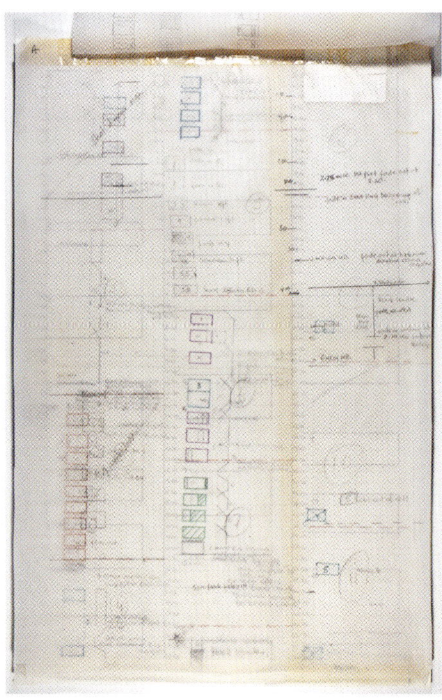

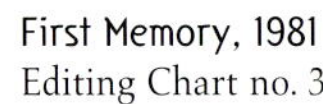

First Memory, 1981
Editing Chart no. 3

The chart shows the sequence of slides to be filmed, the duration of each shot, in-camera fade-in/outs and camera tilts and pans.

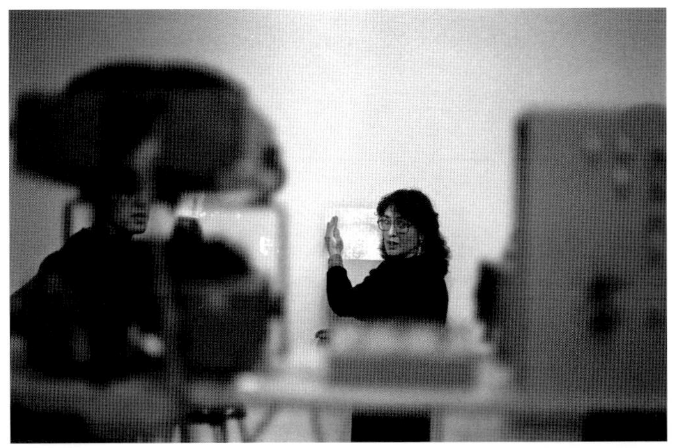

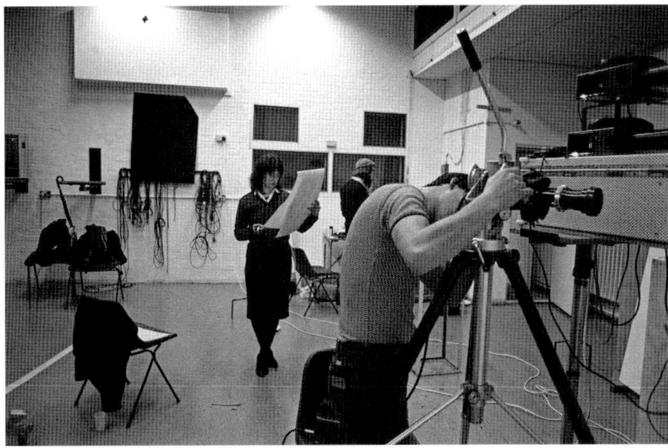

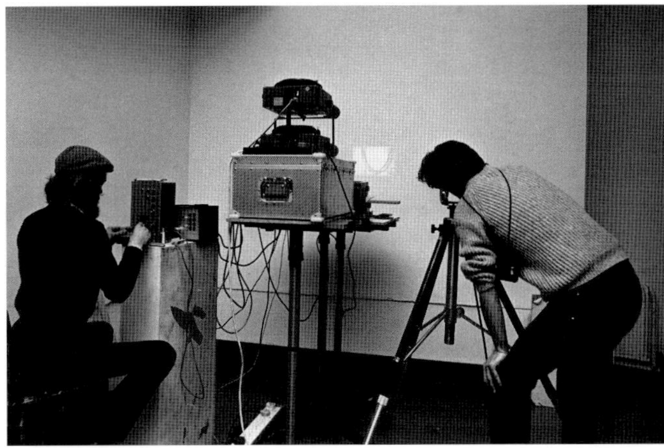

Filming First Memory, 1981

Filming on 16mm from the slide projections in the Audio/Video Studio, Environmental Media, Royal College of Art, London, 1981.
Central photograph with Editing Chart no. 3.

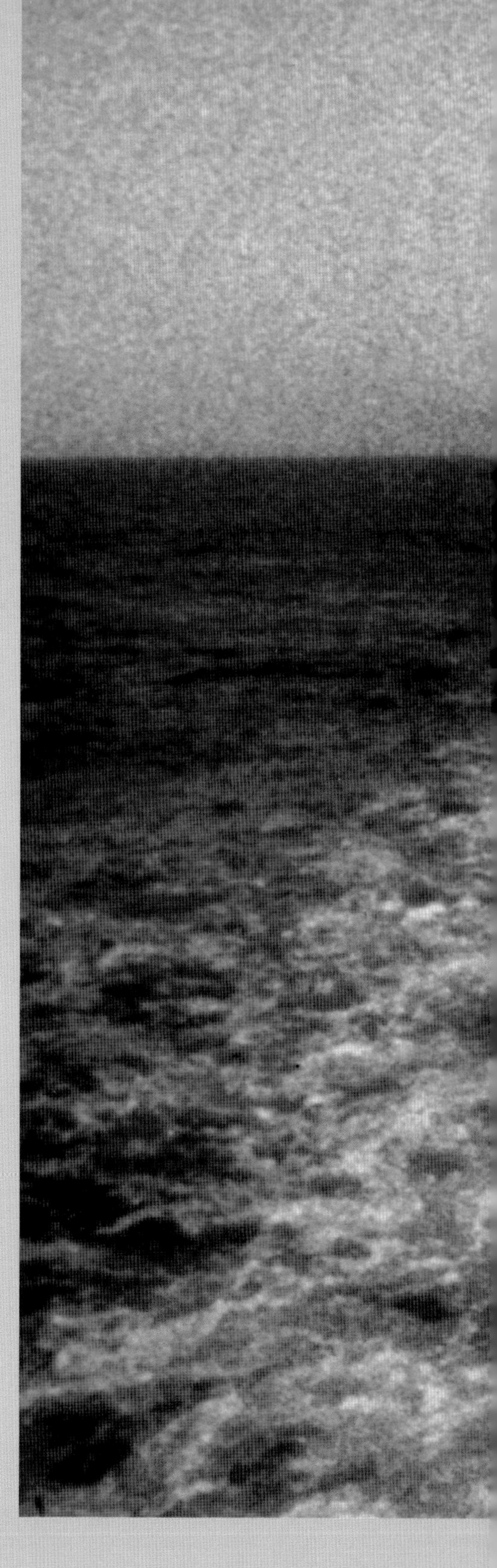

Close to Home
1985

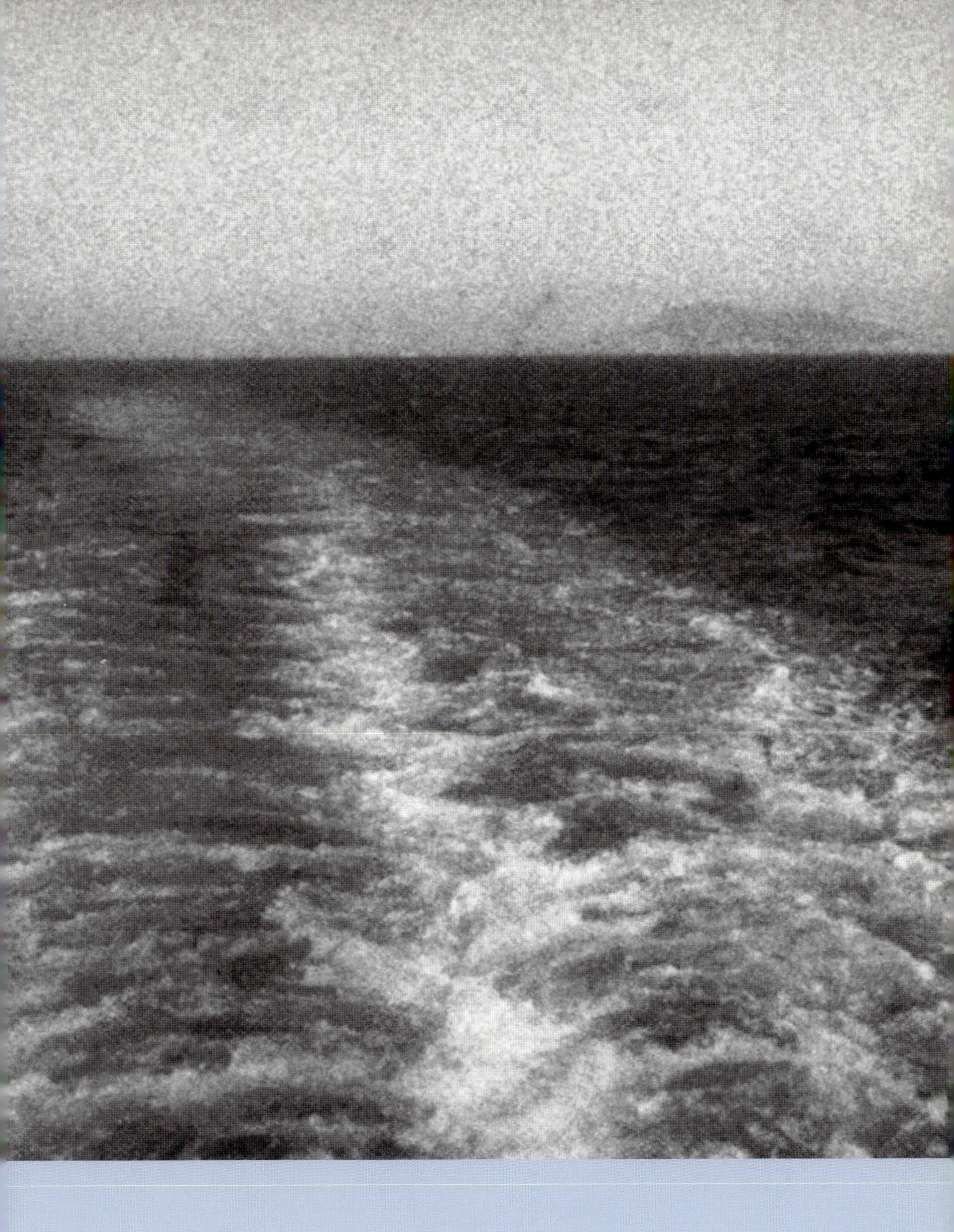

A Time of Frontiers

J J Tellez

From Gibraltar can be seen the frontiers of the new World Order: the Punto Euxino from which one can watch the barbarism of human misery on which the opulence of the First World is sustained.[1] From the Europa Point lighthouse, one can see perfectly clearly how Africa drowns in the Strait.

Also from there, from the very British shutters which punctuate the steep incline of Europa Road, to the port shot in black and white film in *Close to Home*, one can contemplate two close yet completely alien worlds side by side. On one side the world of grand avenues of the imperial monoliths, the sports grounds, the supposed green of its winters. On the other, religious processions which pass in front of the ice cream cafés and the baroque silence of Spain. Both worlds were closed off to each other in 1969, a year after the events in Paris the previous May. At that time I lived on one side of that frontier—does it matter which? Perhaps my world was similar to that within those rooms, china and patterned wallpaper which appear in the scenes in *First Memory*. Outside of childhood awaited a world in conflict. That too is Gibraltar and its region's military bases, with missiles positioned in the highest points of the mountain, atomic submarines and a road for traffic to Spain which crosses the airport.

The decades passed and these two territories remained permanently closed off to each other because of the whim of a dictator. In the summer of 1981 the poet Rafael Alberti came up to that other wall of shame, the old Customs House, where a group of people who were shouting greetings to their relatives on the other side less than 30 metres away opened a path for him. The presence of the poet with his white mane of hair caused an increasing wave of murmuring and soon the Civil Guard appeared to disperse the crowd. "Leave me alone, I don't bite" exclaimed Alberti, "besides if I did bite that Rock, only blood would come out".

For years people called out to each other over the high gates. That shouting was gothic: messages crossed back and forth in three languages: in English, Spanish and in a jostling mixture of both. All that lasted too long, but one by one, though often separated by the two states, there continued to circulate the vendors of pancakes and fried fish, women who smuggled tobacco, stuffy gentlemen, bolshy trade union leaders giving raised fist salutes and capitalists with closed fists, policemen and civil guards, business men and domestics, Moroccans with no passport other than that of survival or Hindus whose third eye is the shop windows of their bazaars.[2] At that time in the periphery of the city there were synagogues and cathedrals, but also mosques humbly housed in garages. Now the frontier is open, but not the soul nor the eyes either. The neighbours contemplate each other without understanding each other.

The Frontier is not an accident but a way of life, an attitude to history. One of these days we will have to cross it, we will have to cross each other.

1 Punto Euxino was the name that the Romans gave to the last frontier of the Empire. It is now symbolised by the Strait of Gibraltar.

2 *The Third Eye* by Longsan Rampa was a philosophical book about the eye of the human mind.

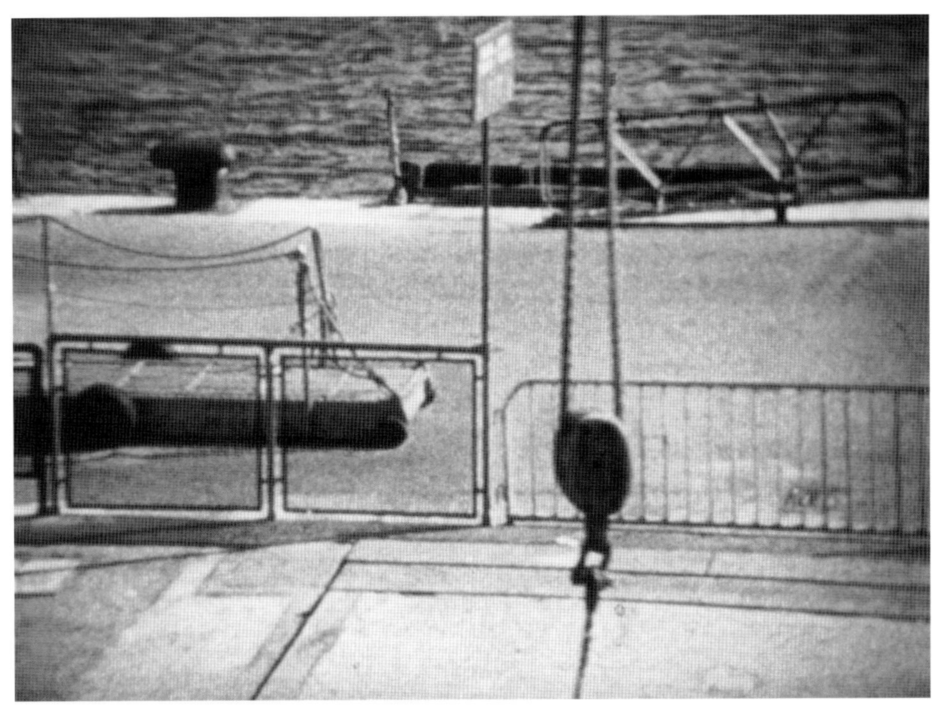

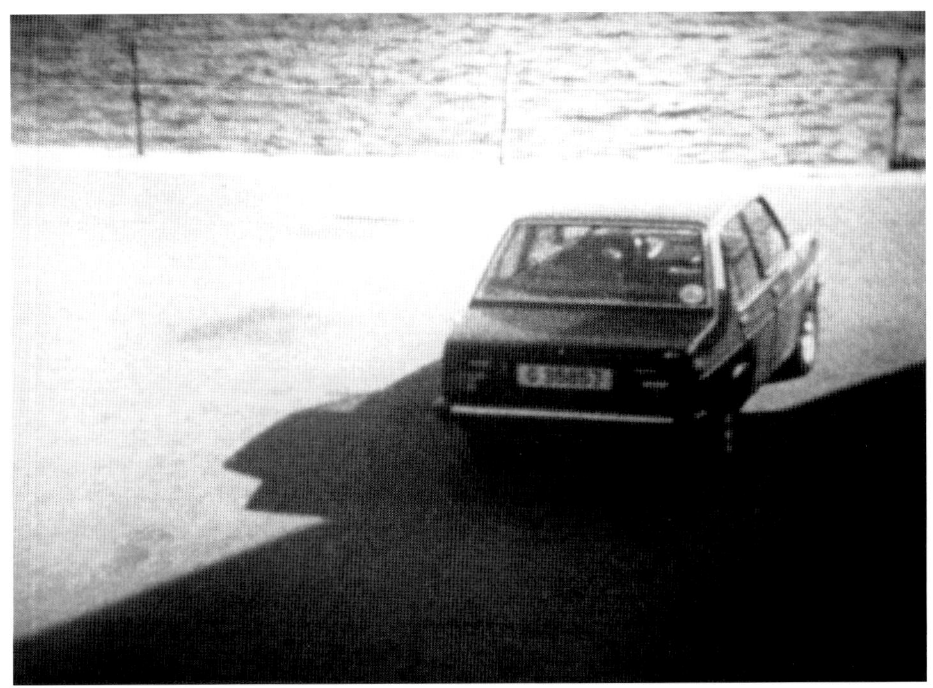

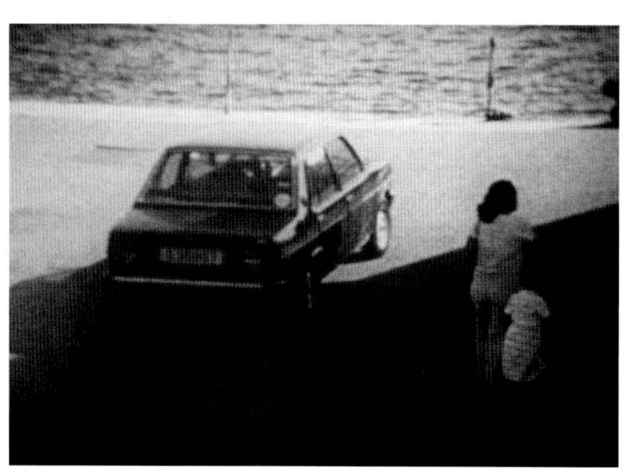

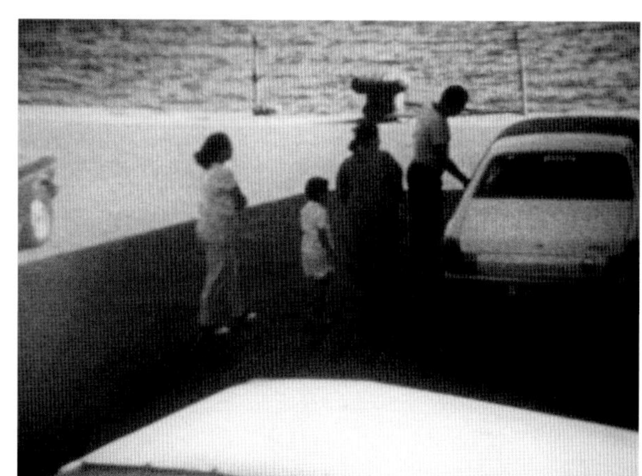

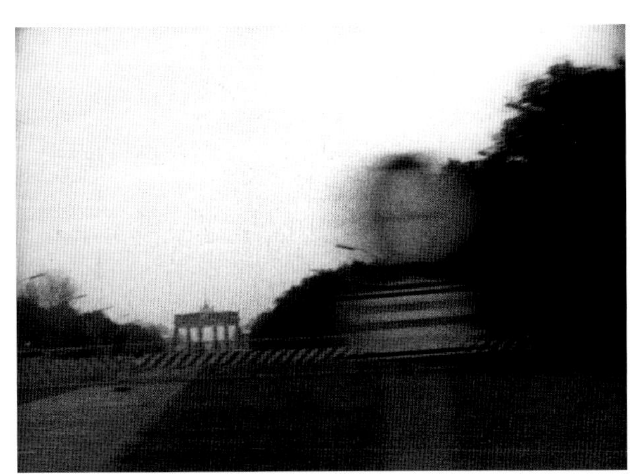

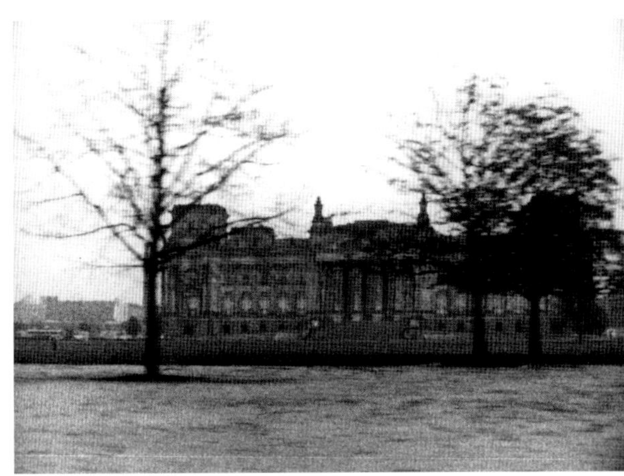

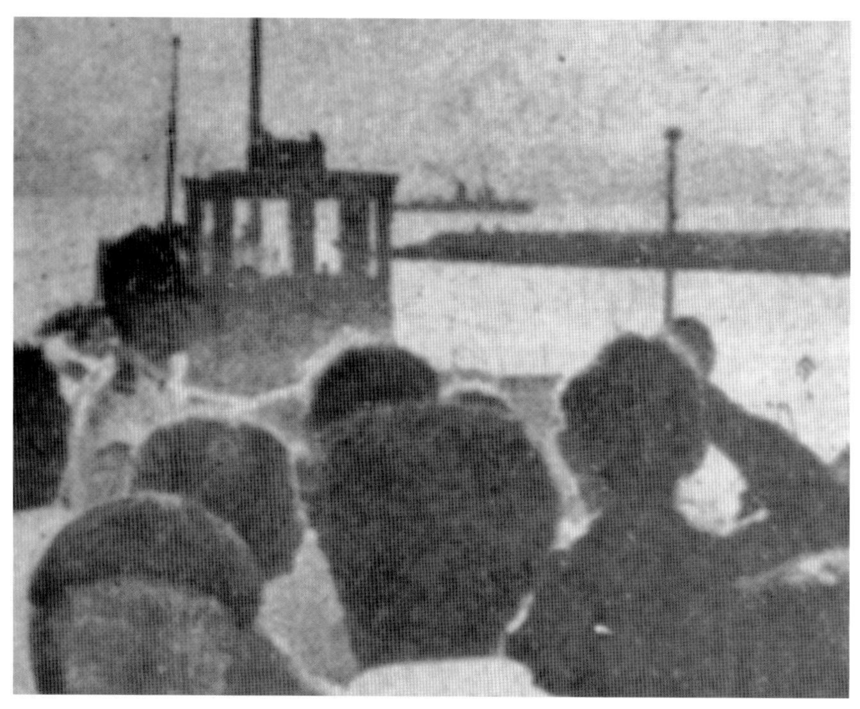

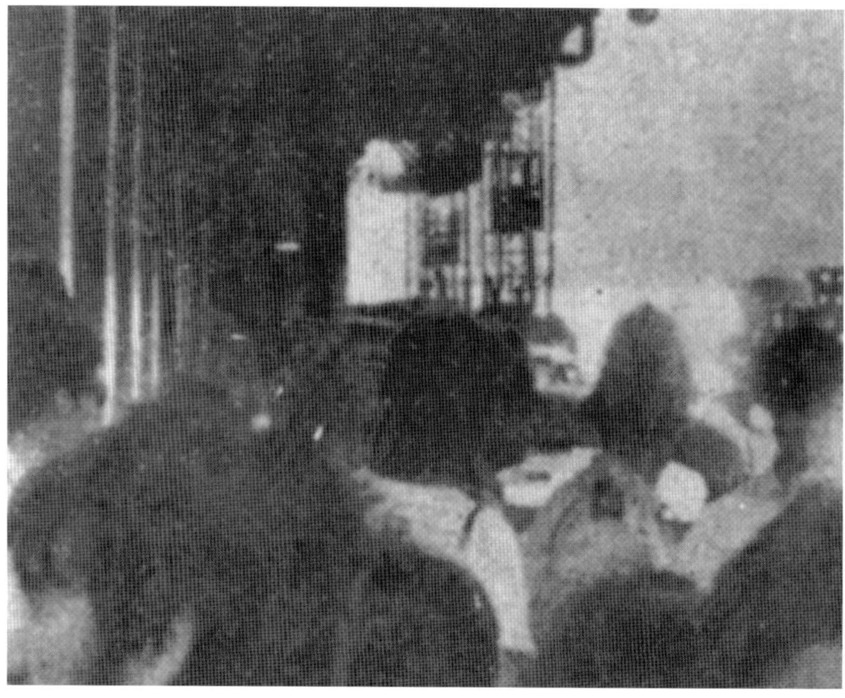

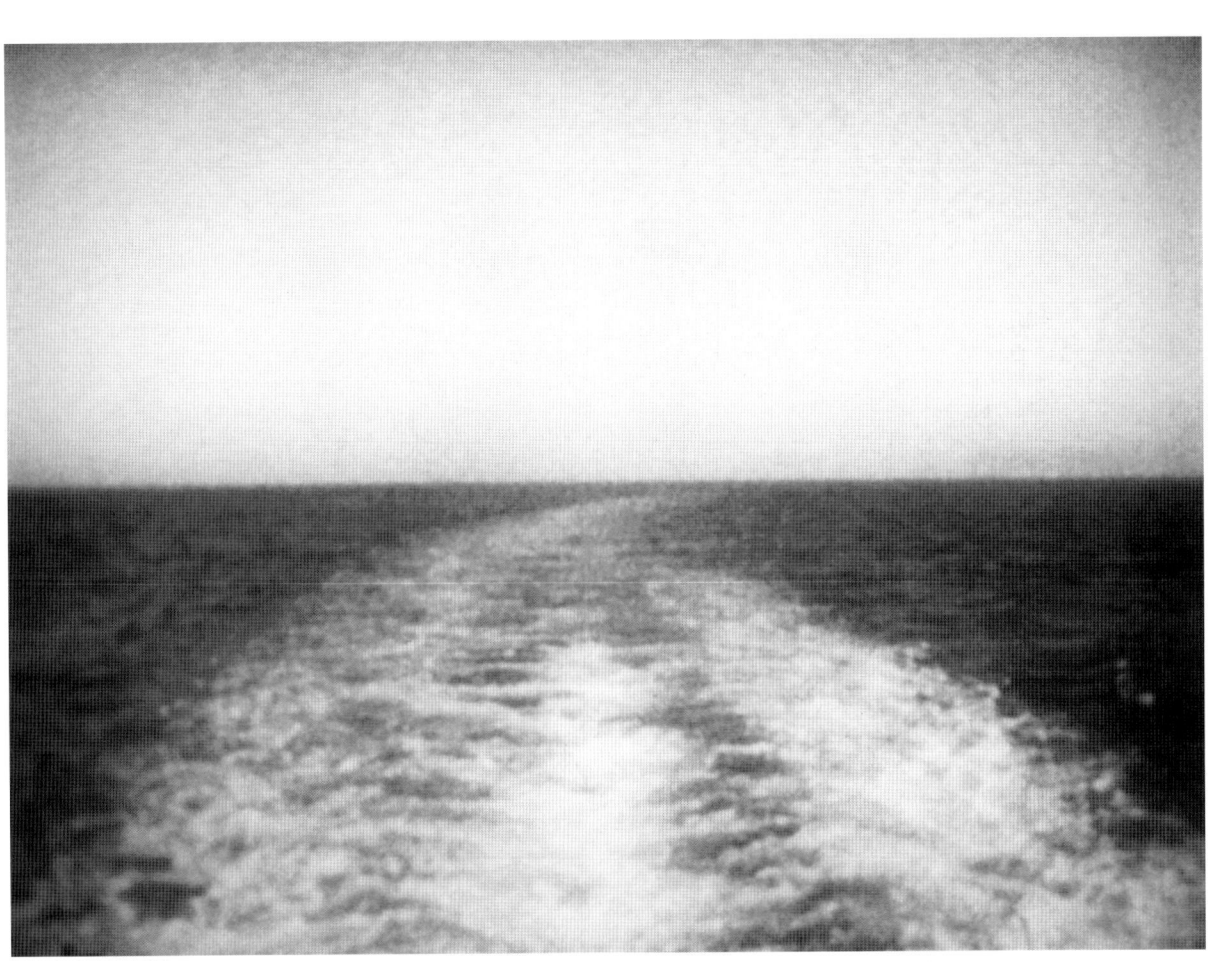

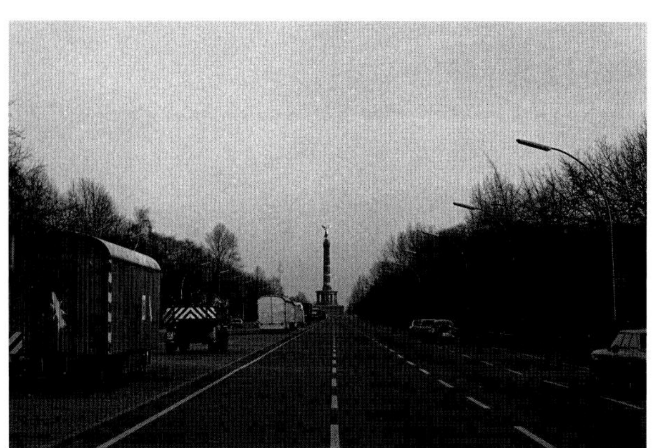
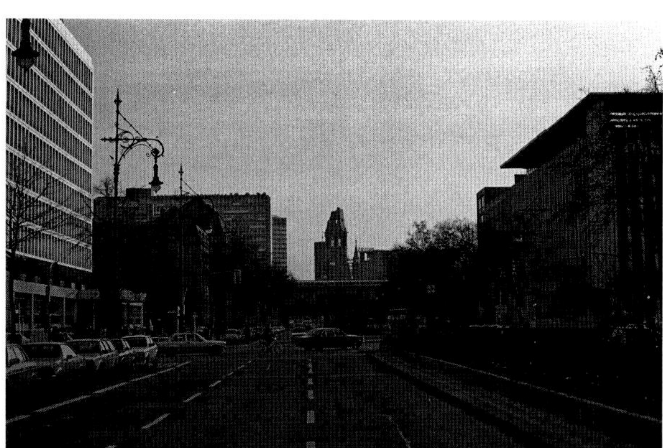
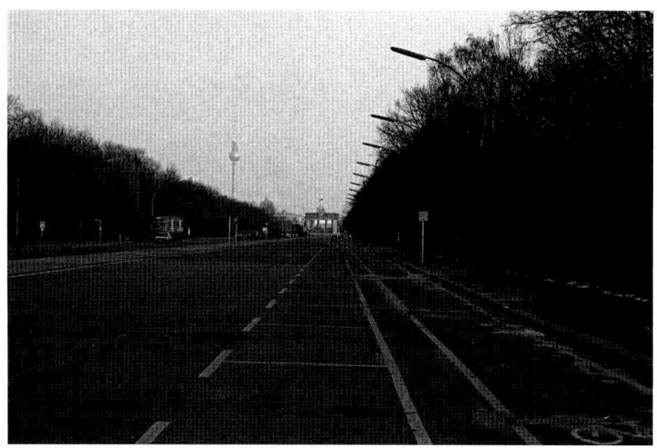
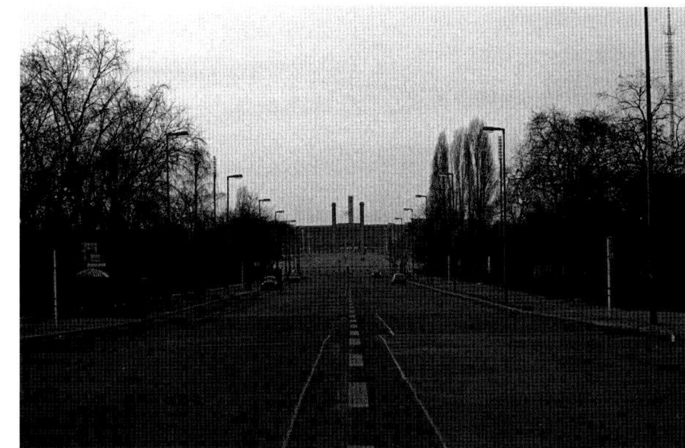

Close to Home, 1985

Location photographs used in the film

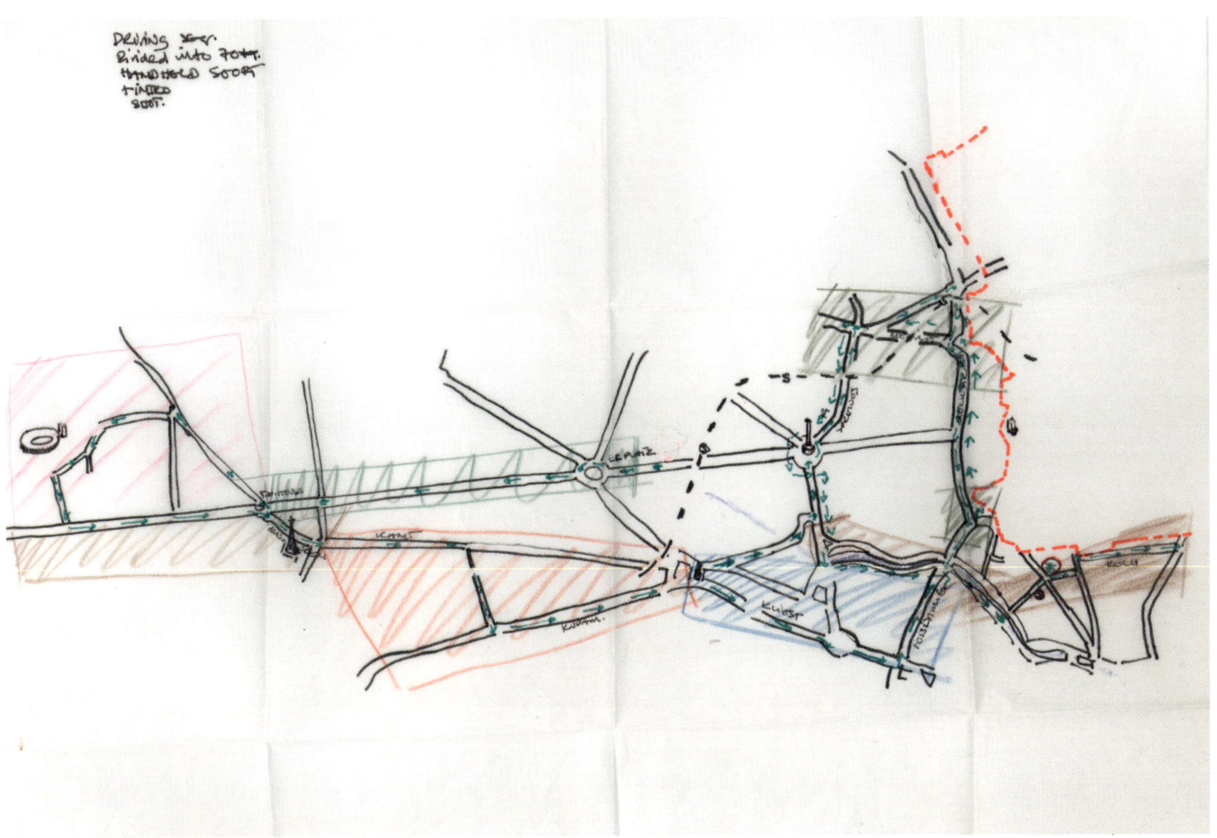

Close to Home, 1985

Hand drawn map for filming driving sequences. Each sequence was divided into 70 foot handheld shots of Berlin landmarks: the Olympic Stadium, Anhalter Bahnhof, Brandenberg Gate, Wall, Kaiser-Wilhelm-Gedächtniskirsche and Victory Column.

Transfiguration and Transmediation

Helen de Witt

> Only when the world, teeming with anonymous and nomadic, impersonal and pre-individual singularities, opens up, do we tread at last on the field of the transcendental.
> Gilles Deleuze

The films of Nina Danino come from one special place and transport you to another. Using dialectical movements, her films transcend the expected languages of both film and art to traverse a series of fascinating oppositions. These opposites attract, and move the viewer into an altogether different and mysterious space, one that film, as film, has hitherto not occupied.

Her work is, in itself, an exploration of the creative process and the urgency of personal expression that crosses the boundaries between film and art practices. Her films, although far from having a conventional narrative structure, do lure the viewer into a filmic time and space that carry a structural, or logical, development. In this sense, they share with dominant cinema the invitation to the viewer to willingly suspend disbelief. Yet unlike conventional cinema, Nina Danino's films do not draw the viewer into a fictive place through the projection of desire, instead the films are analogous to the meditations of St Teresa, transmediating us into an interior castle.[1]

In all her films, Nina Danino displays an intricate knowledge of how films are constructed. She uses her camerawork to take the viewer into a new place, whether that be a child's remembering of a set of interiors in *First Memory*; the streets of Gibraltar in *Stabat Mater*; a chapel, home to Bernini's famous St Teresa sculpture in *"Now I am yours"* or amidst the Holy Week processors in *The Silence is Baroque*. But this is a far too literal sense of place. These sites, although highly relevant for the subjects of the films, are both real and metaphorical sites. They are places of transformation, places of everlasting love that transcend death, and as such their permanent geographical existence sets up a paradox. Nina Danino resolves the paradox, through a refusal to fix the viewer within the film. The places we see are fleeting—street signs in *Stabat Mater*, bits of alcatrave in *"Now I am yours"*, and close-ups of the ornate enthroned Virgin in *The Silence is Baroque*. It is not possible for the viewer to establish themselves there, as these are not understandable spaces. They are uncomfortable and unfixed.

Her first feature film, *Temenos*, 1998, is different from the earlier films in that it begins with a vast empty wilderness. Open terrain replaces enclosed space but it is an equally unsettling place. Exquisitely photographed in high contrast 35mm, each twig and blade of grass appears hyperreal, linking the specific thing to its universal form. It could almost be a fairytale landscape. But it is eerily empty; the viewer now occupies a vast space, but despite

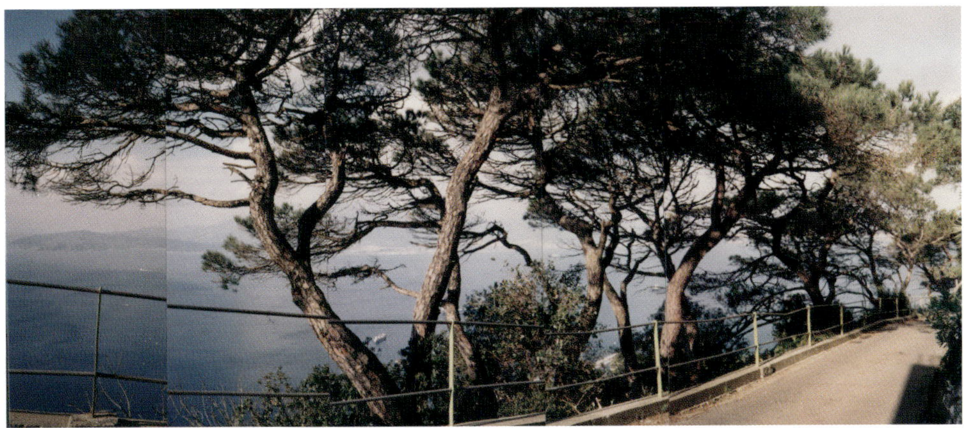

Composite photograph of the location for *Stabat Mater*, 1990

the difference in scale is equally dislocated in terms of feeling, with the same sense of disquiet as in the more enclosed environments of the earlier work. The high pitched sounds of birds and beasts are abstracted from their source, and as mysterious as the wind, they pierce the stillness of the silent landscape. In *Temenos*, it is through the film medium itself that the natural world becomes transcendental. The viewer comes to understand that these earthly phenomena have taken on an existence that takes them beyond their physical locale into a psychic, emotional place.

The navigational tools of conventional film language—identification through the gaze—cannot work. This is really because there is nothing easily identifiable, or, in the strictest sense, to look at. In *Temenos*, the viewer enters into an apparently empty landscape, but finds if full of visions and sounds that penetrate the mind. It is a synaesthesiac experience where boundaries between each sensory experience blur. It is akin to falling in love. Instead of projecting oneself into the film, the film locates itself within the viewer, as the transcendental presence of the Virgin locates herself on the earth. To truly participate in Nina Danino's films is transfiguring act, a leap of faith.

Nina Danino's two early works, *First Memory*, 1981 and *Close to Home*, 1985, differ from the later films in that, instead of an emersion in the interface between the human and the divine, they explore the fragile nature and fleeting connections between people—families, and lovers. At this point in the 1980s, women artists were drawing on the pioneering experiments of an earlier generation. Their work, much of it video or performance-based, privileged the artists' own subjectivity through personal narratives and experiences that were for the first time seen as political. This work took up subjects such as domestic work, motherhood and violence against women that were previously deemed unworthy as the subject of art. Not only did it raise awareness of these issues but also drew attention to the ways that patriarchcal discourse conspired to obscure them from the public arena. Nina Danino sought to get behind the time and pace of film language itself in order to create a

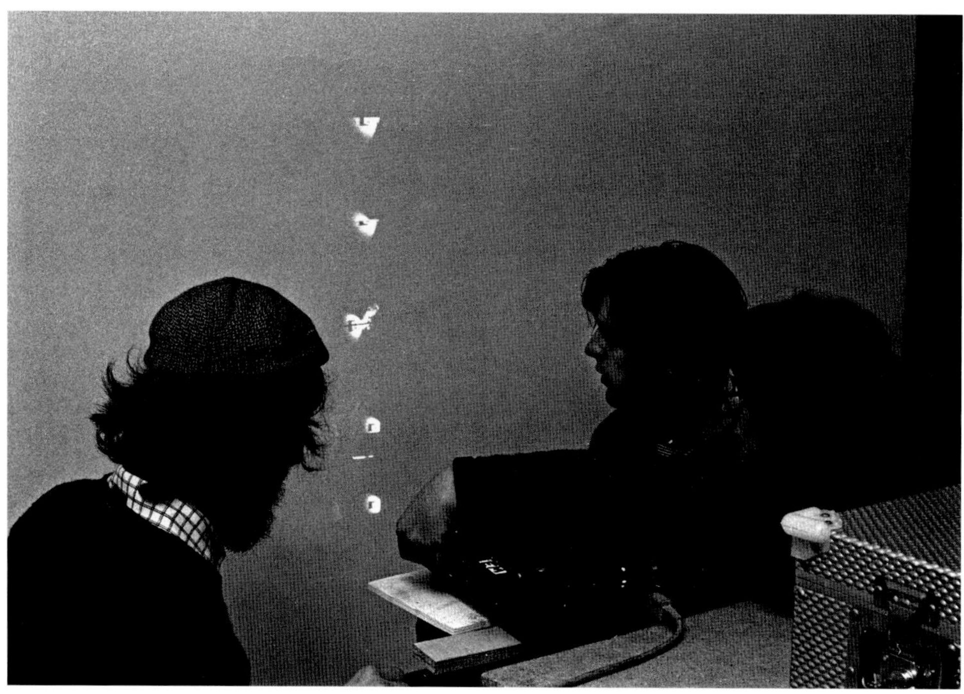

16mm filming of projected slides for *First Memory*, 1981, at the Royal College of Art, London

new aesthetic experience of the feminine. One that came from within, rather than looking at the condition of femininity as a social construct. To do this, she foregrounded the voice, and in particular her own voice.

Her first major piece, *First Memory*, was screened as part of the seminal feminist exhibition *About Time/Women's Images of Men* in 1980, at the Institute of Contemporary Arts, London. Made as a two-screen work that included Super 8, tape-slide and sound, it explores the many possibilities of audio-visual presentation. Later it was made into a 16mm single-screen film. In it, over shadowy images of household objects, faded wallpaper and darkened rooms belonging to a bygone era, the filmmaker's voice recounts the strangeness of the interior, its drabness, its decay. The images are disjointed, interrupted by black and then suddenly illuminated by shafts of sunlight entering the frame from the outside world. Tension in the film is created through the intercutting of these black screens and the images of the interiors, as the adult voice describes her childhood reactions to being on the threshold of womanhood.

Close to Home is also about division and separation in the family, and between lovers. The film's title sequence opens with footage of a boat leaving a quayside. In the first part of the film, the camera travels around West Berlin like a tourist, picking out historical monuments and describing them in terms of their significance to military history. The circling claustrophobia of the camera reveals the confinement of the walled-off city, and the commentary charts the bleak history of the blockade and the cutting of transport links. The filmmaker reads aloud a family letter. She is reading it privately to herself but it is the sound of her reading that forms the soundtrack of the film and makes the connection with the viewer. Like the people of the city, the writer and reader are kept apart by forces that they cannot control, connected only by a shared text. Later in the film, we are told in another letter that the reader has missed the excitement of a border being opened at midnight. The film then cuts to footage of a boat sailing into the open Strait. It is an image of freedom, and of closure, but it is also a melancholy image of parting.

All of Nina Danino's films are personal films. In a sense *Stabat Mater*, 1990, is one of the most personal. Like her later films, it is an attempt to transmediate the divine through culture. *Stabat Mater* begins and ends with sung laments, which like the film, seeks to locate something absent and unnameable. In order to convey fleeting glimpses of that which the camera cannot capture, the film is quickly edited to create a sequenced rhythm of hand-held images. In this way the Danino is able to convey time that is outside of human perception. For Deleuze:

> What amounts to montage, in itself or in something else, is the indirect image of time, of duration. Not a homogenous time or a spatialised duration... but an effective duration and time which flow from the articulation of the movement-image.[2]

Stabat Mater was filmed in a luminous Mediterranean light, but alongside the images of the sun-drenched city, parks, palm trees and the sea, there are also English road signs that look peculiarly out of context. The dominant image is that of a serene statue of a young Virgin. Her image is one of eternal presence. This permanence contrasts with the rapid female voice on the soundtrack.

The voice performed by the filmmaker recites fragments from Molly Bloom's meditations at the end of *Ulysses*.[3] The film shifts Joyce's stream of consciousness from (hetero)sexual love to maternal love, a shared female love. The film moves towards the Strait, the mythological site of the Pillars of Hercules that keep vigil at end of the classical world. It is the place where borders dissolve into the timeless dimensions before and beyond language. Joyce's disjointed prose matches the unpredictable cutting of *Stabat Mater*. The Joycian text is prefaced and ended by quotations from Hélène Cixous that enforce the sense of female love and loss at the heart of the work.

"Now I am yours", 1992, is a meditation on death, focusing on the ecstatic experiences of Spanish mystic and nun, St Teresa of Avila. Danino filmed Bernini's statue of *The Ecstasy of St Teresa* in the Cornaro Chapel, Rome, a magnificent Baroque sculpture showing St Teresa lying back in a state of rapture, about to be pierced by the arrow of God's love, held by an angel. Over a montage of images, showing the sculpture from every angle and in increasing detail, we hear the filmmaker recite her own meditations mixed with the saint's writings about her experiences of the divine. The words speak about being at the point of death.

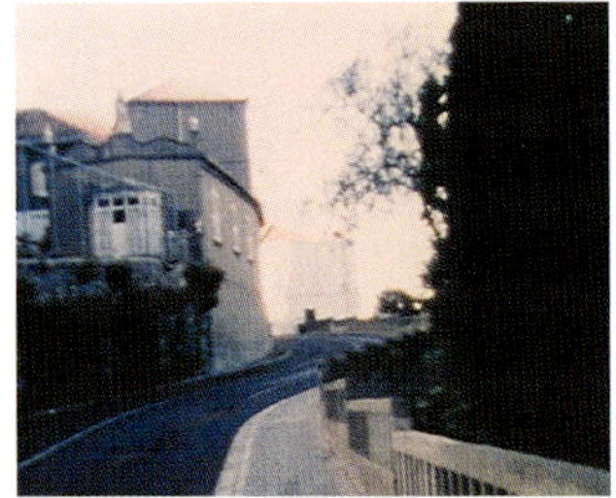
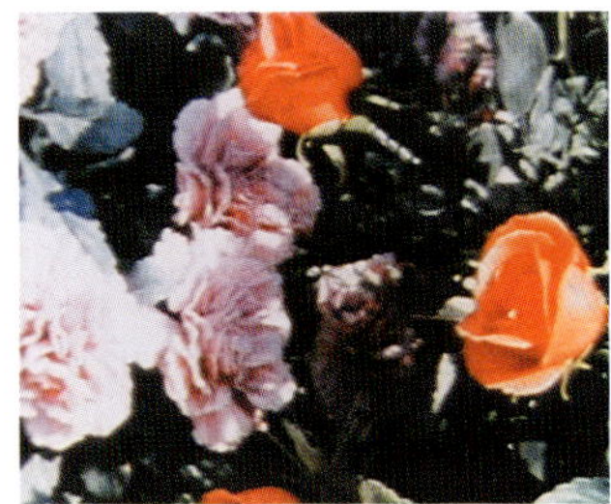

Stabat Mater, 1990

Although she doesn't die, she is unable to move and is wracked with pain, but it is a sweet pain leading her from longing to abandonment and rapture. The film unites the work of art which captures St Teresa, with her own words that are her own free expression. Deep and piercing sounds from Shelley Hirsch and Diamanda Galás are heard on the soundtrack and blend with the words spoken. The separation of sound and image create a notion of a female subjectivity that is not bound by representation, or even by the body, but that is timeless, uninterpretable, yet resonant with meaning.

Intercut between images of St Teresa are scenes from the Catholic Mass, images of a garden, and images of stones and flowers in a cemetery. Like the camera, Christ on the cross gazes down on Teresa—life and death co-existing at the same moment, like the flowers in the cemetery at the opening and closing of the film. The film is about that boundary between life and death. As Jutta Bruckner expresses this moment of transfiguration:

> The soul and the body, and the body and the world are therefore always the materialisation of inside and outside; and the body in its central position, is both at the same time. It is the place where the invisible soul can make itself visible and where the visible world can inscribe itself on the invisible.[4]

Religious experience permeates all of Nina Danino's films and she uses cinematic apparatus as a means of revelation.

The cinema is a ritualistic space. The audience arrives at the designated hour to partake in a transcendental experience as the image is projected onto the screen. The image at once reveals something real, but is simultaneously only a chimera, a ghost, a spiritual presence, or maybe distilled essence, of what is captured. Nina Danino uses this very ethereal element of the cinematic register as her material. It is this ghostly, or spiritual, dimension that she works with rather than the representational properties of the film. In this way, her work meshes emotional, sexual, and psychic energies into a transcendental subjectivity that is transmediated beyond language, formless but all pervasive.

Although the films are imbued with a Catholic understanding of spirituality, whether it is the Marian visionaries in *Temenos*, or St Teresa in *"Now I am yours"*, the transcendental is

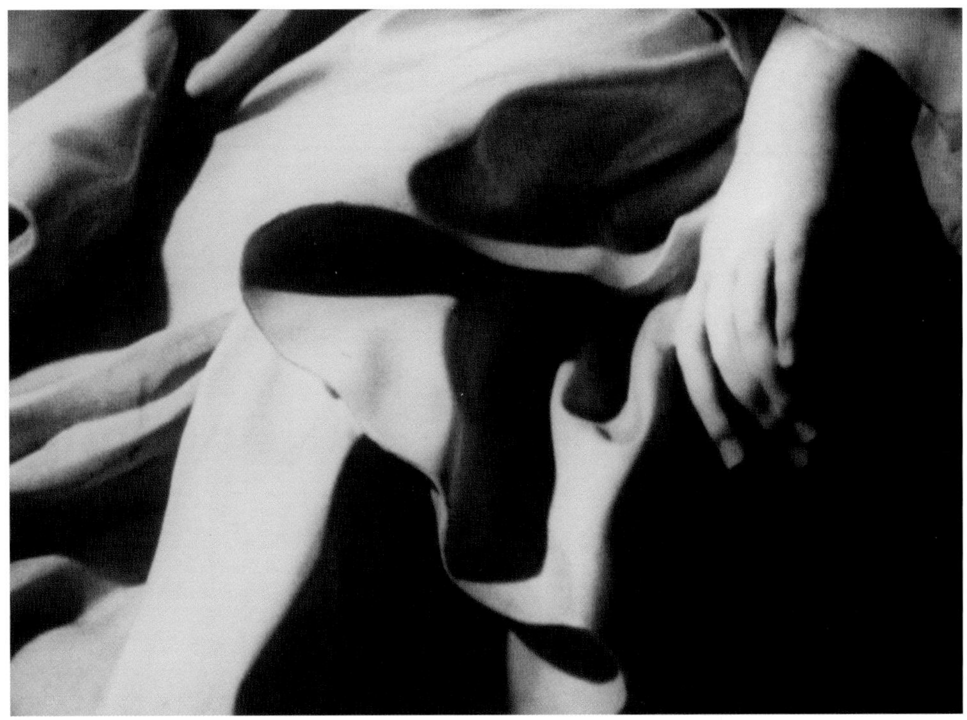

"Now I am yours", 1992

personalised through the experience of the women themselves. Here, the conformist Catholic interpretation breaks down and the power and pleasure of the feminine shines through. These women are visionaries, their sight cannot be controlled and neither can their minds. Their visions transfigure them to another realm, one of pure fulfilment and abandonment. The way that Danino portrays St Teresa through close-ups of the mouth and figure reclining backwards, leaves the viewer in no doubt that she is experiencing sexual ecstasy, with her body, as well as her mind being penetrated by divine force. This is jouissance—performed excess—a physical response to the performance of the camera and the performance of the voice. Here, it is an excess within the image that goes beyond the informational and the symbolic into meaning that cannot be contained by filmic time and space.

These films have a material presence, the filmmaker is keen to make the viewer aware that they are watching a film, a projection that is happening in time and space in which the film is unravelled from its spool and comes into presence before the viewer's eyes, akin to the rolling folds of St Teresa's robes. The progression of *"Now I am yours"*, like the saint's ecstasy, builds in waves into a state of orgasmic intensity. The film was manipulated in post-production to merge the mixed film and video formats that it was shot on, which were then transferred back onto 16mm to form a hybrid texture. This makes the image itself turbulent, it cannot hold the intensity of the experience it is struggling to encapsulate. Deleuze describes it as the overflowing excess of the sculpture that ruptures the rectilinear Renaissance space

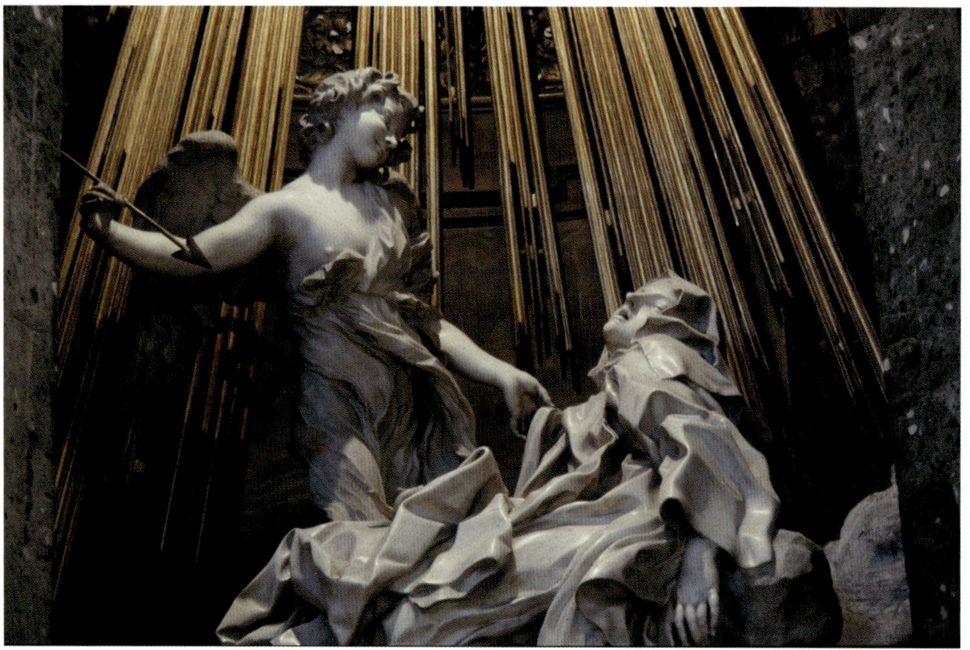

"Now I am yours", 1992, location photograph of Bernini's *The Ecstasy of St Teresa*

and erupts into infinite waves of space. In an analogous way the film image in *"Now I am yours"* is edited antithetically to the picture frame so it unfurls itself in the film's time beyond its usually confined space.

> Bernini endows [folds] with sublime form in sculpture, when marble seizes and bears to infinity folds that cannot be explained by the body, but by a spiritual adventure that can set the body ablaze.... And especially, is it not fire that can alone account for the extraordinary folds of the tunic of Bernini's St Teresa?... [who] does not find her unity in the satyr's little arrow... but in the upper origin of the golden rays above....[5]

The film itself unfolds, becoming its own object as it is projected onto the screen. It is an object created though the cinematic apparatus, but denying its language of representation. Instead the film struggles for its own enunciation of jouissance, through the performed excess of image and through the breathlessness of its voice.

> Pray to the giddiness of minute perceptions, they endlessly reach presence in illusion, in vanishment, in swooning, or by converting illusion into presence: Penthesilea-Teresa? The Baroque artists knew well that hallucination does not feign presence, but that presence is hallucinatory. [6]

The film is created out of its own material, the material of cinema. It brings into being its own body through time. It becomes its own matter through the plasticity of its unfolding through the literal projection onto the screen. It comes into presence as it unfolds in the mind of the viewer. The body of the film therefore comes into being and finds its own voice. The look of the viewer is never purely visual but also tactile, sensory, material and embodied.

> ... like dreams and hallucinations, cinema offers us perceptions (sound, image, movement) which are in fact representations, which allow us access in the same way to desire, keeping at bay the 'reality principle' which would repress desire.[7]

The recitation of the meditations on the soundtrack neither expresses nor represents an already given female identity; rather through stream of consciousness technique, identity is seen as the effect of a flow of speech. The voice makes present the transcendental dimension of the film. It takes flight, it is not bound by the material earth, or constrained by the visual image.

For Deleuze cinema is a surface of intensities. This means effects of colours and of movement that form an event that cannot be contained within the viewer's point of view. Therefore it demands a new way of looking. The movement in the image needs to be thought of in relationship to the viewer rather than just in relation to the apparatus. This is because the viewer does not see the succession of images on the film but an intermediate image. For Deleuze, this is not the illusion of movement but its reality.[8] Movement is also connected to colour and operates within it as a force. Each tone or modulation of colour exercises an impetus upon a corresponding body within the frame. It is colour and its effects within the image that provides a haptic world. This is where the seen and the felt collide creating an imbrication of experience across the senses. We can see this most clearly in *"Now I am yours"*. The turbulence of the image cannot contain the flux of colour and sensation that saturate it. The experience explodes in the mind of the spectator, taking it beyond the representational register into a new mode of perception that is not tied to a single act of perception. In this way, the transmediation of the image transfigures the experience of the viewer.

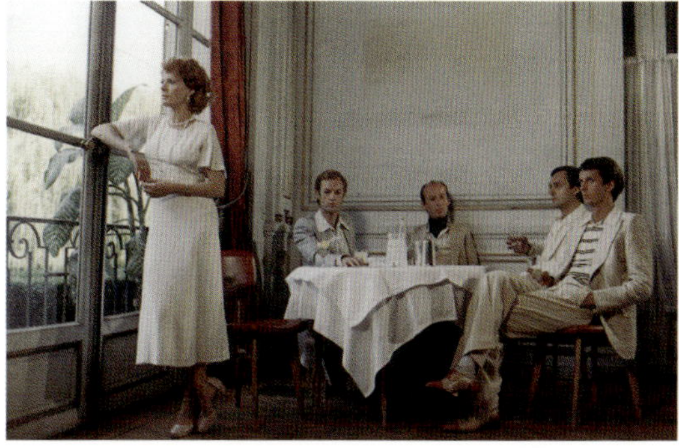

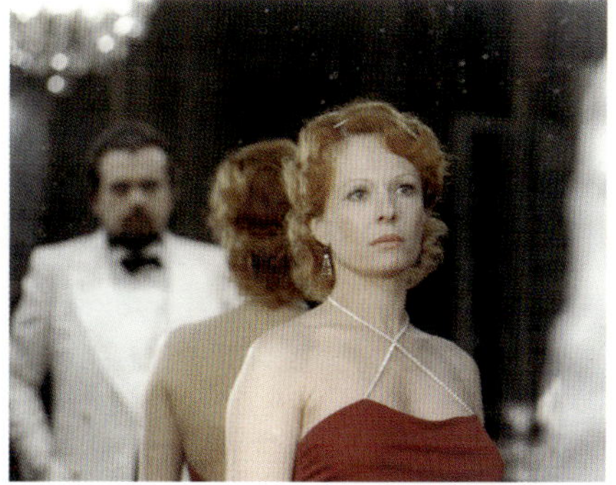

Marguerite Duras, *India Song*, 1975, film stills

Through Deleuzian ideas we can begin to present an 'aesthetics of sensation', where the cinematic experience is not necessarily one concerned with verisimilitude, subjectivity or with psychoanalytic configurations of desire, but one involving transversal and perspectival discourses, constructing the bodies of the spectators as a collection of disparate, complex and decentred perceptions.[9] It is this transformative and fluid experience of the cinematic that is present in all of Nina Danino's later films. Her work is redolent with meaning, but not in a strictly embodied or representational form, instead her work is a transmediation of material elements changed into spiritual form through the willing participation, or act of faith, of the viewer.

Beyond the visual register, Nina Danino uses the personal voice of the woman to create an intimate subjectivity. Her discourse displays the narrative qualities of immediateness and urgency. At the time this move was unprecedented in both fine art and avant-garde film, where the majority of feminist practices preferred a language-based semiotic method. Nina Danino is pioneering in her privileging of the voice as an essential aesthetic and sensory component of the film.

Defying the masculine conventions of avant-garde and experimental cinema, Nina Danino joins a number of women filmmakers, including Mona Hatoum, Jayne Parker, Jean Matthee, Lis Rhodes, Sandra Lahire and Lucy Panteli, who began to work with ways of representing their own experiences as artists and women using film and moving image. Nina Danino's work uses the voice as a central device that could foreground female subjectivity and counteract the tyranny of the cinematic visible image—the female as the object of desire, and therefore without a voice—through its concern with the cinematic processes of subject and narrative. Her work on the voice is revolutionary in that it is used very precisely to get away from the representation of gender in order to present the feminine as an unrepresentable concept in relation to narrative within the visual. A possible comparison could be the films of Marguerite Duras, such as *India Song*, 1975, in which Duras used her own incantory and somnolent voice, which nonetheless, like Danino's, carries a powerful erotic charge. The voice has an erotic potential related to the body, whilst being unencumbered by material form. Nina Danino's own voice performances interplay with the images, giving them an acoustic dimension that creates a unique sensory aesthetic beyond the indexical visual register.

This investigation of sound is pursued through two key notions in Danino's films. Firstly, she uses multiple voices—describing her own experiences and thoughts, and quoting from others—visionaries, poets, writers. At the heart of this there is another paradox. The voice of the female author is present and, like the Marian visionaries of *Temenos*, she has become the articulator of the enunciations of others. Far from being an exercise in fragmentation, this dynamic constructs a mobile but cohesive subject which is not fixed but offers a completeness and with whom the viewer is transfigured into another psychic territory. We may hear the words of the visionaries but we cannot see them. And it doesn't matter that we don't see them, for their appearance has no meaning. The sound, the voice of the disembodied woman, proves the existence of the unseen thing, and therefore permits the belief in the existence of an invisible spiritual world that is inaccessible to sensual experience and only perceivable

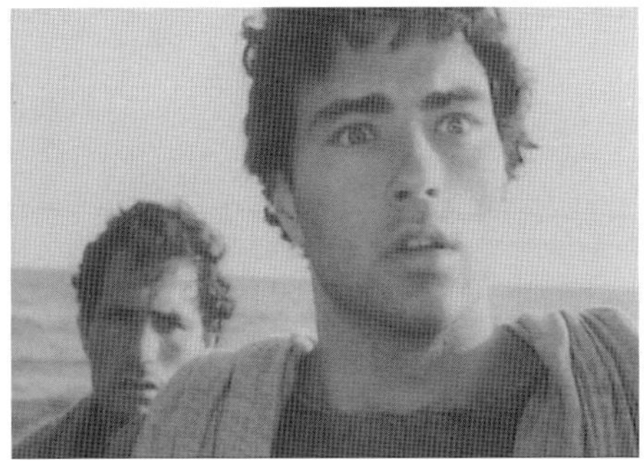
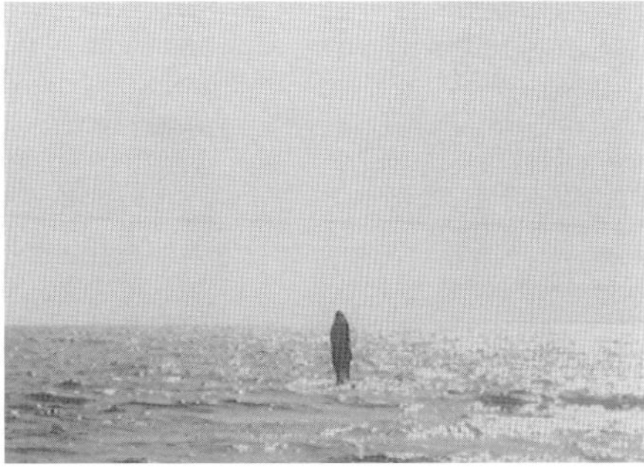

Film stills from Pasolini's *The Gospel According to St Matthew*, 1964, in *Temenos*, 1998

through phenomenological signs. Film sounds, when detached from images, are able to spread unencumbered into space, as sounds in life do.

Secondly, she entirely removes the voice from the cinematic register. The voice is always non-diagetic; it is a performed voice, whether a recitation or a musical rendition. In *Temenos*, Nina Danino combines her own spoken voice with vocal performances by established sound artists and opera singers—her regular collaborator Shelley Hirsch, as well as Catherine Bott, Diamanda Galás and Sainkho Namchylak. These performances are excessive, overflowing from beyond the image—bitter weeping, gentle humming, unearthly sounds, sounds of nature, the scream of dementia and angelic arias creating a heightened sensory experience.

The multiple voices in Nina Danino's films construct an alternative oral history of female experience. Their performed excess refuses to be confined by the rational discourse of the masculine, instead they choose hysterical wailing, the primal scream and silence as appropriate to experiences that cannot be contained or adequately depicted by visual media alone. Unlike mainstream cinema, where sound is often regarded as secondary to the visual image and music is a subliminal signal to the viewer, these are voices that demand to be heard.

Silence, far from being an absence of sound, is also an integral part of the acoustic environment. In *Temenos* there are long periods of silence over images of the haunted landscape. These are equally as intense for the viewer as the performed sound. In this respect, Nina Danino departs from accepted avant-garde film practice, such as that of Stan Brakhage and the London Filmmakers' Co-op Structuralist tradition, who do not use sound so as not to distract from, or lead the film's visuals.[10] Nina Danino's silence is not a lack of sound, but part of the constructed aural expression of the film.

There are moments when the films enter the realm of the real. The filmmaker indicates this by using documentary-style video footage—the Mass in *"Now I am yours"* and the old woman praying at the crucifix in *Temenos*. Here, she emphasises how conventional film language cannot come near to portraying the profundity of spiritual experience or transubstantiation. Even the excerpts from the Spanish feature film of the life of St Teresa

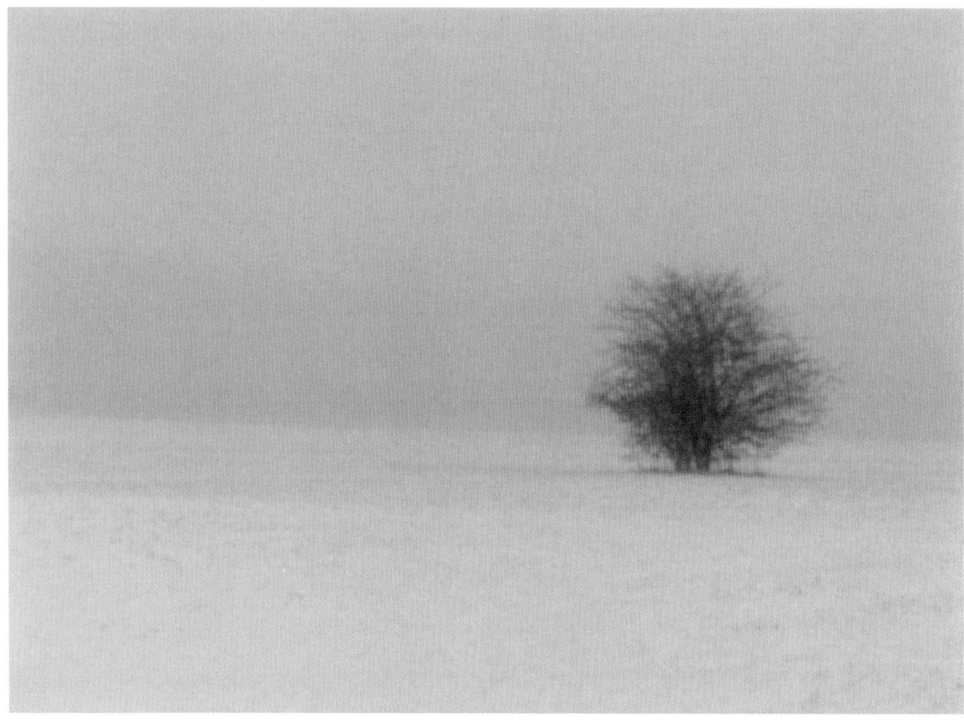

Temenos, 1998

cannot signify. These images are empty of meaning, being a mere record of actual events. Here there is another paradox contained in Nina Danino's work. Film, which has an indexical relationship to its object, is used to convey the transcendental; but the electrical signals of video is used to represent what is most real in a literal sense. The point is key to Nina Danino's practice. As they unfold, her films take signification beyond representation into an altogether different register, beyond the cinematic sight and sound into a realm of pure sensual experience. Again, the adoption of the religious analogy is highly affective. As Durkheim said, "Religious beliefs were responsible for substituting a different world view from the world of perceived senses."[11] Nina Danino employs the religious dynamic as analogous to the transfiguration of the viewer into a more abstract, but nonetheless sensory world of perception.

At the end of *Temenos,* Danino evokes Pasolini, with the final scene from his film *The Gospel According to St Matthew*, 1964, included prior to the Epilogue. After his Resurrection, Christ walks on the Sea of Galilee towards his disciples who occupy a small fishing boat. The disciples are incredulous, but then realise that it is not contradictory that in a world where they need to earn their living fishing, they can also witness the divine. Pasolini, a Marxist filmmaker, imbues Christian belief with a social message of dignity for working people that reveals the transcendental within a secular world. As Deleuze explains:

> And Pasolini adds a valuable comment: the richer a language is in dialectics, the more it allows free indirect discourse to flourish, or rather instead of establishing itself on an 'average level' it is differentiated into 'low language and high language' (sociological condition). For his part, Pasolini called this operation of the two systems of enunciation, or of two languages in free indirect discourse, Mimesis. This word is perhaps unfortunate, since it is not a case of imitation, but of correlation between two asymmetrical proceedings, acting within language. It is like communicating vessels. However, Pasolini clung to the word 'Mimesis' to emphasise the sacred character of this operation.[12]

Nina Danino, like Pasolini, uses the richness of dialectical language to make apparent the sacred tension between the designations of high and low aesthetic experience and between the sacred and profane within religious practice. *Temenos,* the film, is a sparingly beautiful invocation of the persistence of place that has the power to inscribe contemporary political and social circumstances with the memories of the past. A place where the profane does become the sacred. She films the landscapes that have witnessed these transcendental appearances, imbuing them with a sense of the sacred. In the first section of the film, and at points throughout, the screen glimmers with a silver glow, as if the viewer is also witnessing an apparition. The viewers' eyes scour the screen for visible evidence of the divine, but what they are given is the magic and holiness of the space itself. The camera pans in circular movements giving a feeling of unworldly weightlessness.

Temenos, 1998

The landscapes of *Temenos* play with notions of appearance. They are sites of apparition but their phenomenological status is uncertain. It is through cinema that images are freed from human discourse and seen in another way. What makes cinema cinematic is the liberation of the sequencing of images from any single observer, so the effect of cinema is the presentation of "any point whatever", taking us away from actualised objects to the very flow of images. Instead of synthesising images into meaningful progressions, cinema can present images in their purely optical form.[13] A cinema of singularities would present colours, movements, sounds, textures and lights that are not connected into recognisable wholes, that then affects the viewer to see reality in a different way. Nina Danino achieves the freedom of the images from their indexical bondage through the language of cinema. The viewer is not seeing a literal landscape, but a landscape liberated from its geographical physicality through the cinematic. The film has an epic scope with sweeping wide camera movements contrasting with a quiet stillness and an intimate focus on the landscape. The viewer doesn't enter a literal place but one that has been transfigured by the cinematic eye into one that did not, and could not exist without it.

The words of the Marian visionaries are spoken by the filmmaker over the now empty landscapes. Like the land itself, the film embodies the ineffable and the transcendental but persists as material and temporal. Like Pasolini's fishermen, the viewer of *Temenos* has to live in the real world, but only through this film, they can, for an illusionary period, communicate with the temenos and know its frightening and beautiful secrets.

The disruption of dialectical progression is a key to entering Danino's work. She disrupts the image though her structured editing, at once giving it presence and absence through the cut. She interrupts the dominance of the image though the intervention of sound that distracts the viewer from the tyranny of the visual. Her work is about traversing boundaries. Boundaries between present and absent subjects, known and unknowable experiences, defined and undefined spaces, rational and irrational understandings, and, of course, the ultimate boundary, that between life and death. Her work is the inevitable fusion of artistic and narrative forms. It is the transfiguration that springs into beautiful and meaningful existence in and through the audience who gather to participate in it.

Notes

1 *Interior Castle*, 1577, is the title of St Teresa of Avila's most famous volume of mystical theology, detailing her personal visions of Jesus.

2 Deleuze, Gilles, *Cinema 1: The Movement Image*, London: Athlone, 1992, p. 29.

3 Joyce, James, *Ulysses*, Harmondsworth: Penguin, 1980, p. 680.

4 Bruckner, Jutta, in Sandra Frieden et al eds., *Gender and the New German Cinema*, Providence: Berg, 1993, p. 244.

5 Deleuze, Gilles, *The Fold: Leibniz and the Baroque*, London: Athlone, 1993, pp. 121-124.

6 Deleuze, *The Fold*, p. 125.

7 Thornham, Sue, *Passionate Detachments: An Introduction to Feminist Film Theory*, London: Hodder Arnold, 1997, p. 37.

8 Deleuze, *Cinema 1*, p. 1.

9 Kennedy, Barbara M, *Deleuze and Cinema: The Aesthetics of Sensation*, Edinburgh: Edinburgh University Press, 2002, p. 68.

10 Experimental filmmakers have been extremely wary of sound, and not without reason. In talking pictures the spectator's attention is inevitably divided, and the resulting loss of attention serves illusionism of cinema as much as do the master shots and eye-line matches of narrative grammar. See Nicky Hamlyn, *Film Art Phenomena*, London: British Film Institute, London, 2003, p. 167.

11 Durkheim, Emile, *The Elementary Forms of Religious Life*, quoted in S Brent Plate, *Representing Religion in World Cinema*, New York: Palgrave, 2003, p. 140.

12 Deleuze, *Cinema 1*, p. 73.

13 Deleuze, Gilles, *Cinema 2: The Time-Image*, London: Athlone, London, 1989, p. 2.

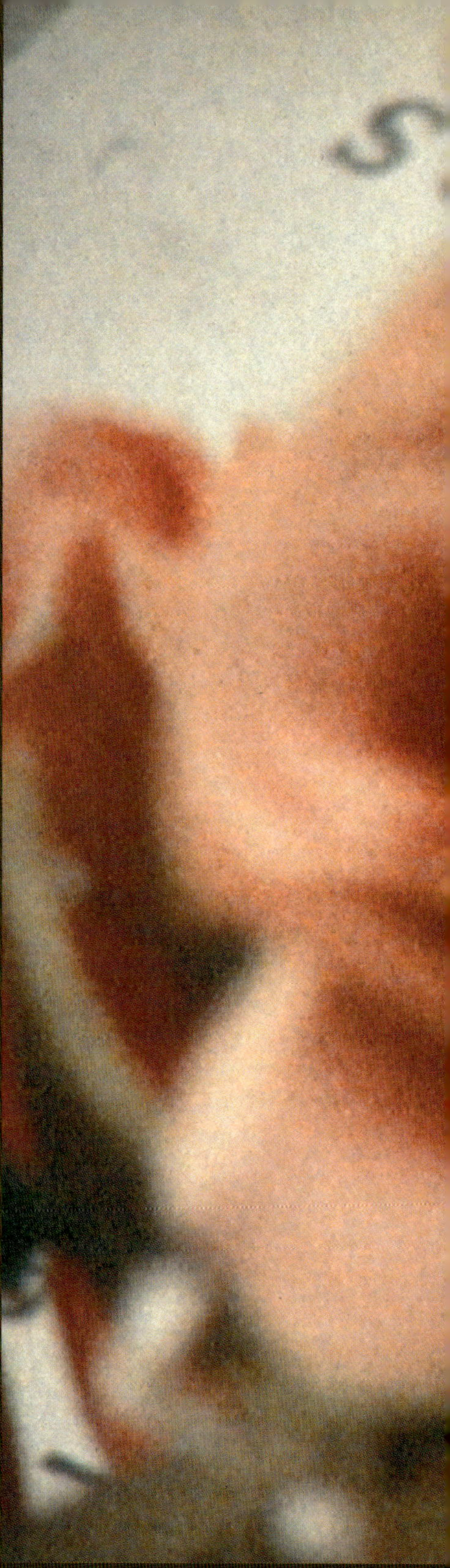

“Now I am yours”
1992

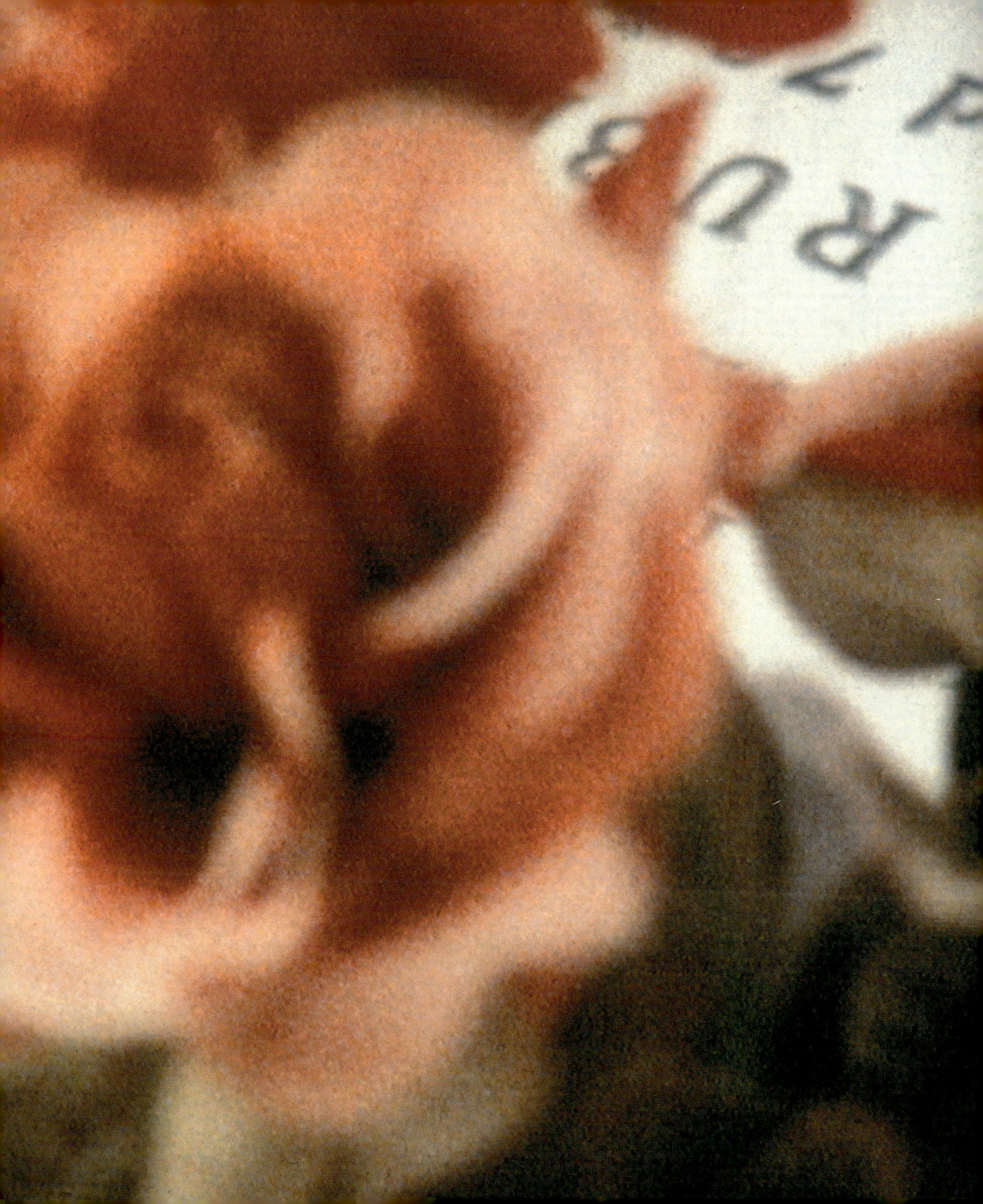

Vision, Mirage, Dream

Nina Danino

"Now I am yours" contains readings from the works of the sixteenth century writer and mystic Teresa of Jesus. The central images are from the famous sculpture by Bernini, *The Ecstasy of St Teresa*, in Rome.

> You have only to go and look at Bernini's statue in Rome to understand immediately that she's coming, there is no doubt about it. And what is her *jouissance*, her *coming* from?[1]

Teresa's image is depicted in a religious, sexual ecstasy which surfaces on the body as a kind of death—the body is in a corpse-like state. Unseeing, her vision is of a masculine, eroticised figure of Christ. The garden—metaphor for exalted and extreme states—is also the meeting place of lovers; the theatre of the erotic but also of pain and loss; a burial place, a pestilential spot. This garden is a place of opposites—the drive to death and the pull to life—a push and pull—a borderline territory in which Teresa is petrified in stone but whom the film attempts to 'resurrect' to life. The crisis of the film is the desire to bring back to life, to ward off death: this warding off is a snap of the fingers or the sign of the cross, but the corpse is also the beloved. Christ is dead on the cross, but in Teresa's vision his body is not corrupted but glorified. The voice cuts through the mortal, carnal body in its lament, in its cry, its scream, its utterance, calling forth everything that is beneath the surface, the dæmonic suppressed, the unsayable, passing over, breaking through the body/tongue.

> The mystical is not everything that is not political. It is something serious, which a few people teach us about and most often women or highly gifted people like St John of the Cross.... There are men who are just as good as women. It does happen. And who therefore feel just as good... they get the idea, they sense that there must be a *jouissance* which goes beyond. That is what we call a mystic.[2]

With voice performances and electronic compositions by New York improvisational vocalist and composer Shelley Hirsch.

1 Lacan, Jaques, "God and the Jouissance of ~~The~~ Woman", in *Feminine Sexuality*, Juliet Mitchell and Jacqueline Rose, ed., Jacqueline Rose trans., London: Macmillan 1982, p. 147. Originally published in French in *Le séminare XX: Encore, 1972-3*, Paris: Seuil, 1975.

2 Lacan, "God and the Jouissance of ~~The~~ Woman", pp. 146-147.

Pages 58-65: Film stills accompanied by their sequence inter-titles

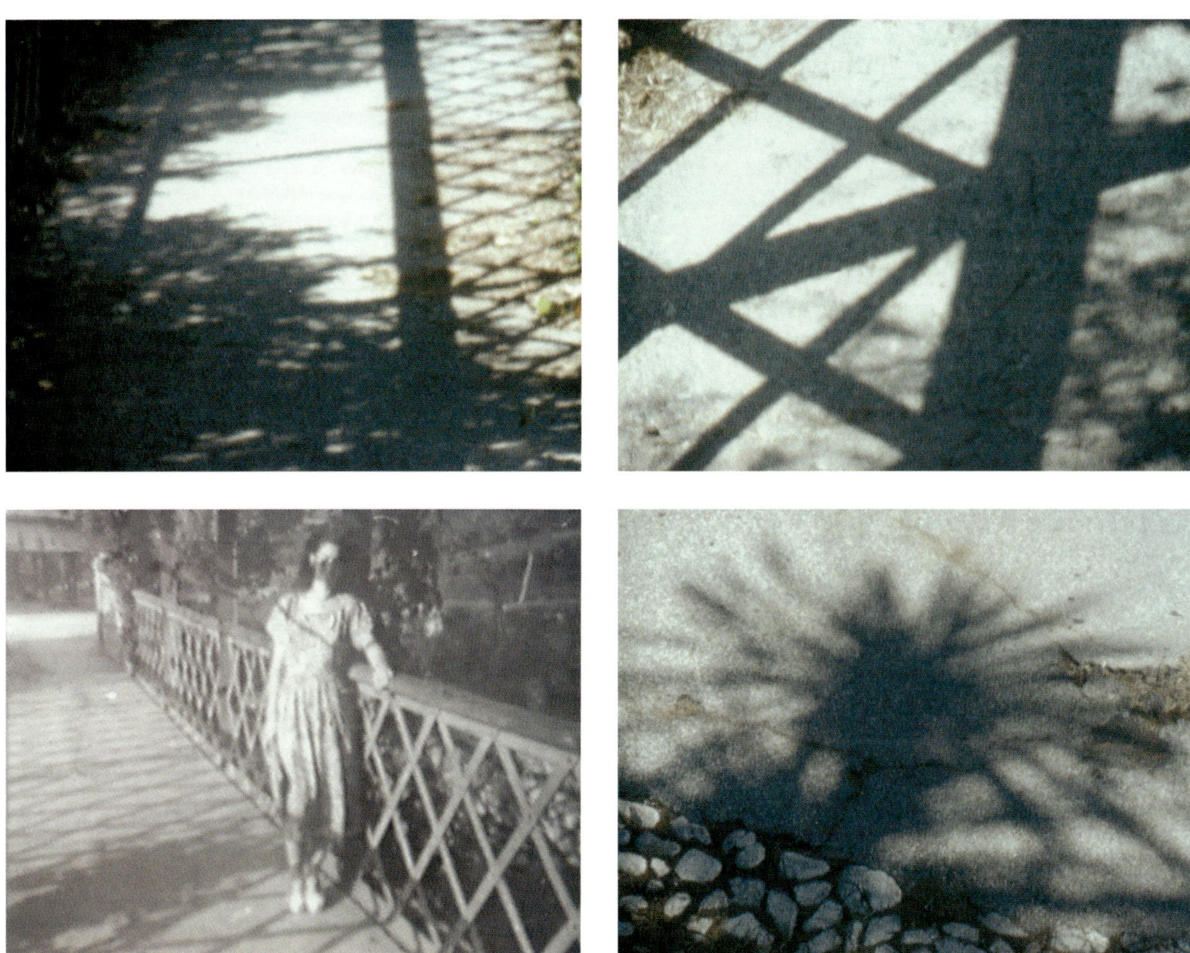

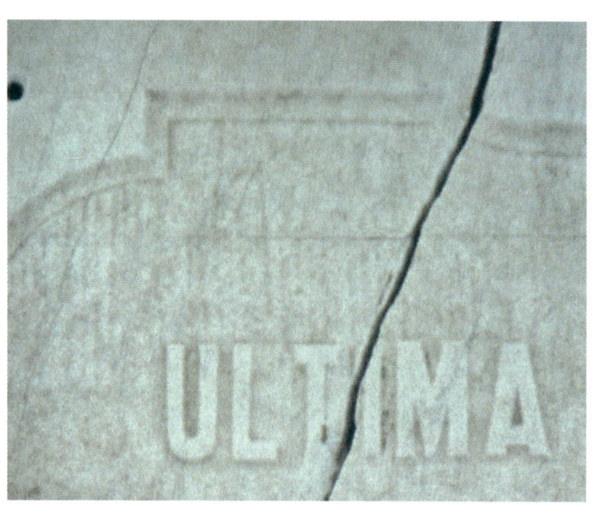

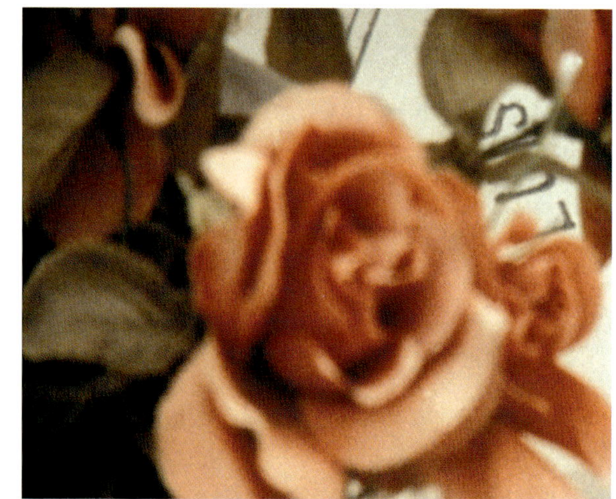

At the point of Death: mors ultima linea rerum

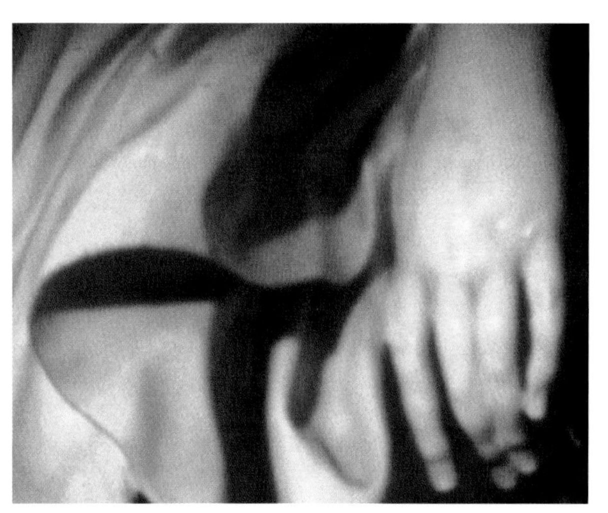

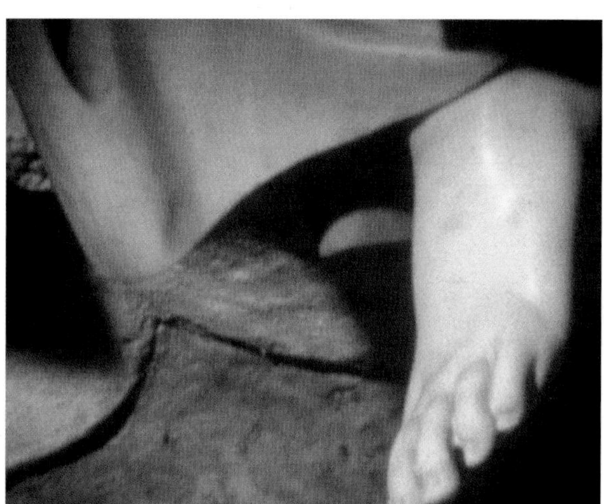

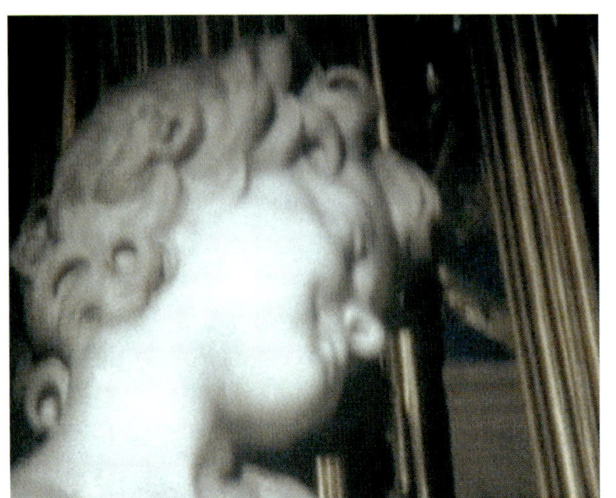

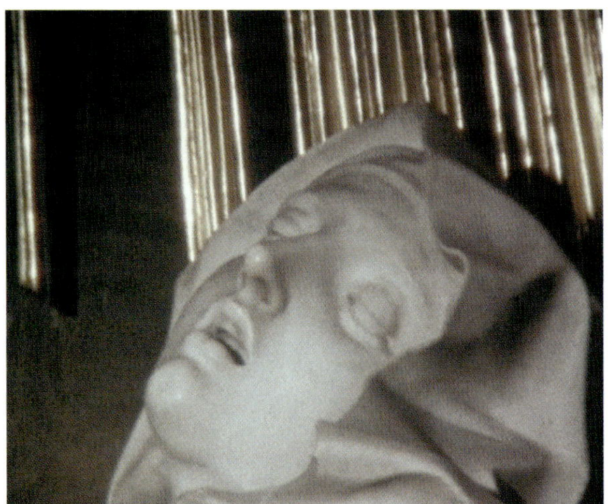

The Devil, the Devil!: delusion, perdition, prohibition, governance, reverance, errance...

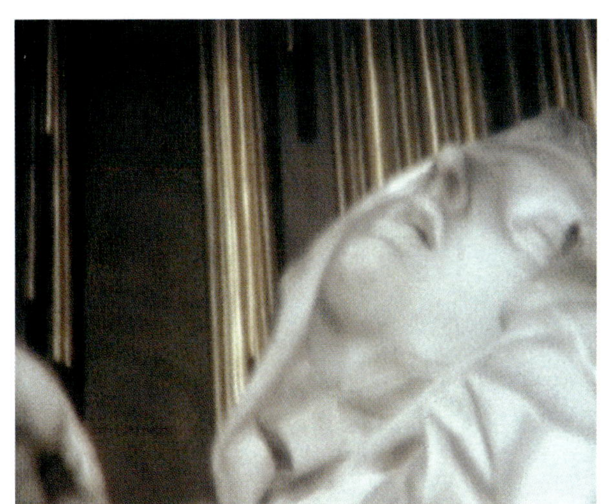
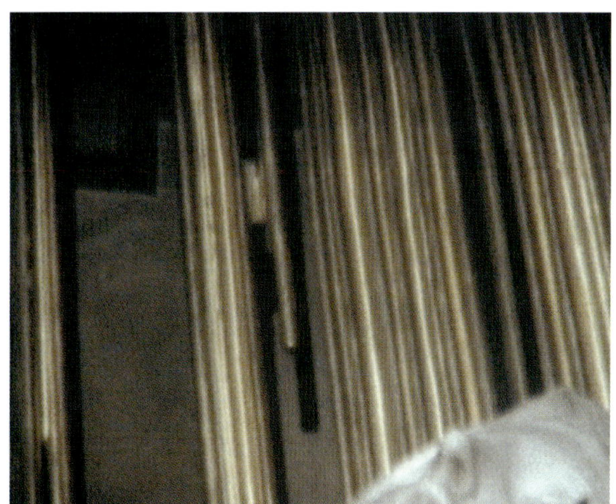

obedience, rhetoric, fear

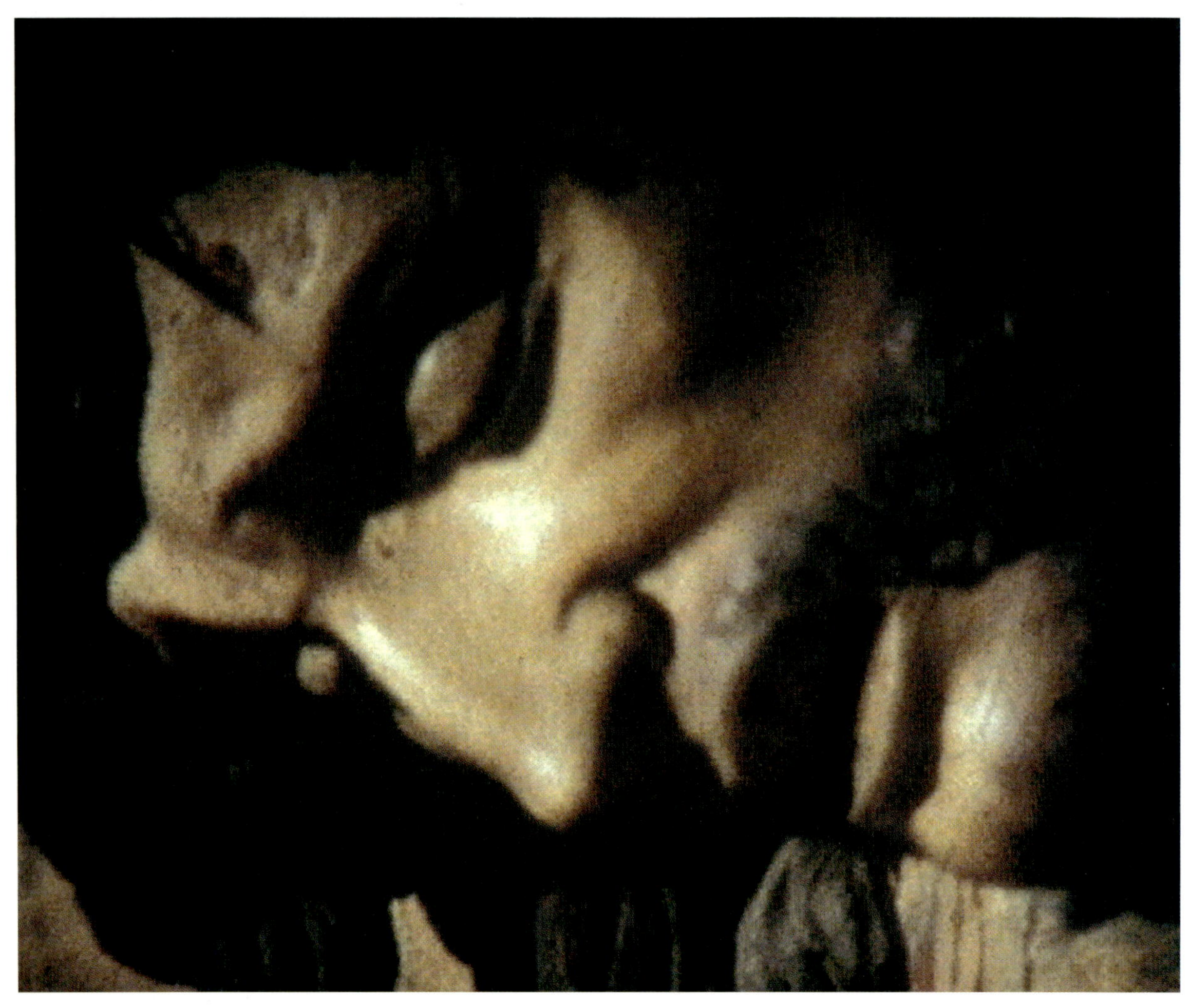

Face to Face: imaginary vision — pictures, portraits, shadows, traces —

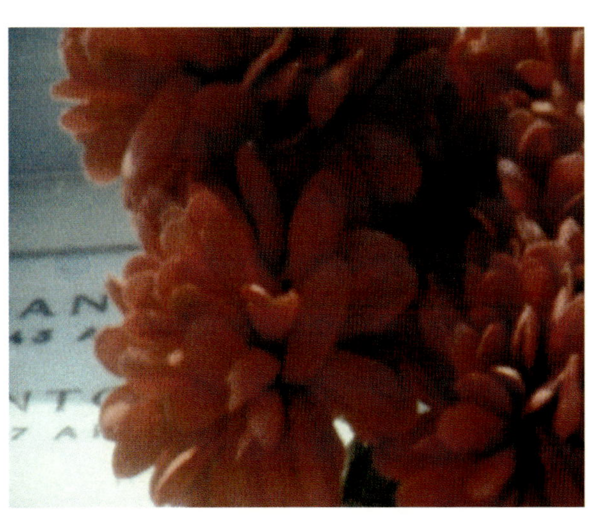

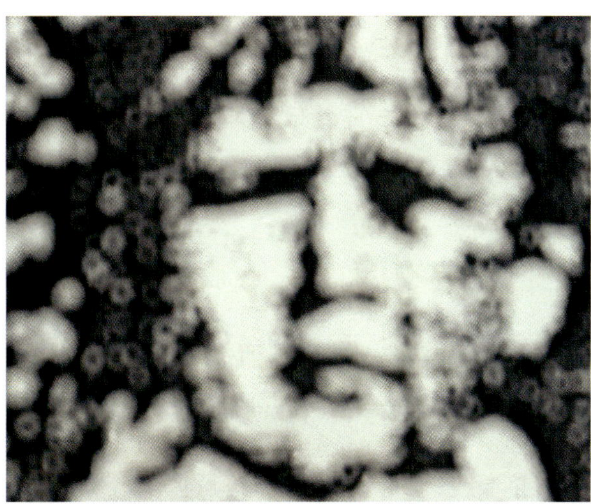

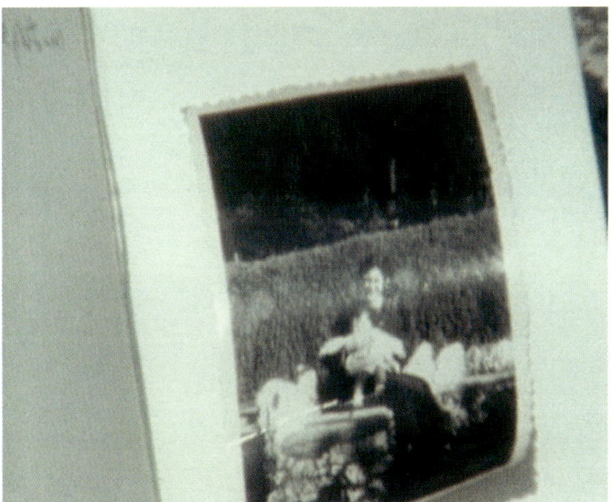

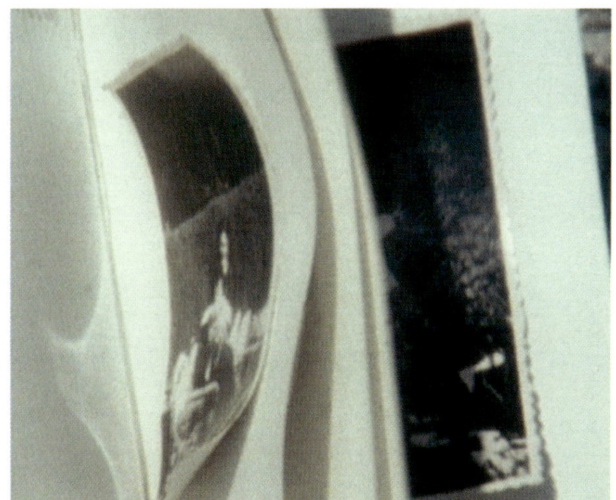

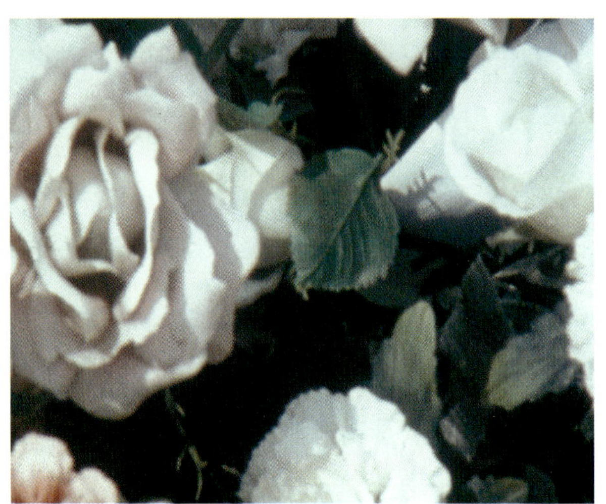

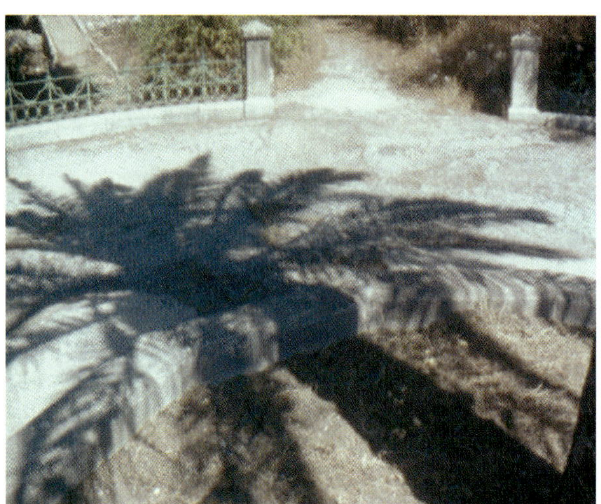

A Stone, a Tree, a Flower: imperfection and loss

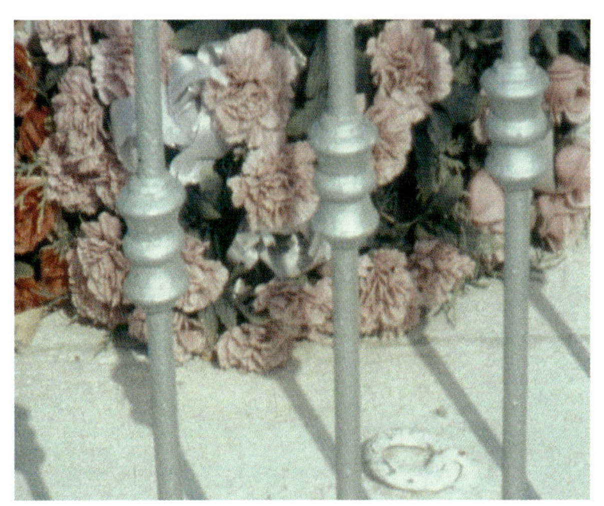

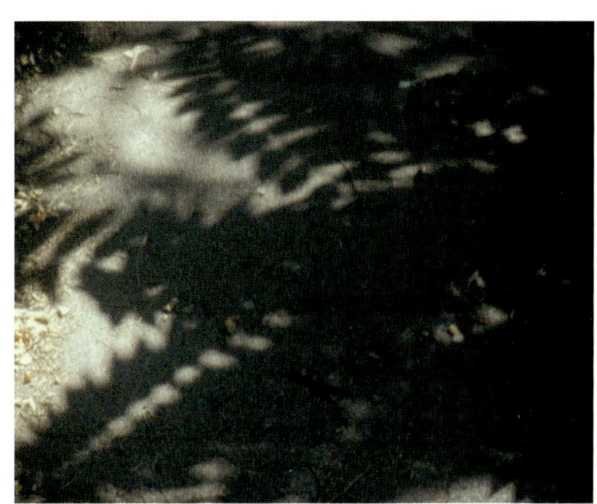

Speaking in the Dark
Film, the Voice and Teresa of Jesus' 'speaking texts'

Nina Danino

Church of Santa Maria della Vittoria, Rome

We are in Rome for the location recce of the film.... Here is the Church of Santa Maria della Vittoria on the corner of a busy and noisy junction.[1] We enter into the semi-dark interior, the traffic noise fades out as the door shuts slowly behind us.

> We returned to Santa Maria della Vittoria to see the St Teresa of Bernini. She is adorable, in a swoon of ecstatic happiness lies the saint with pendant hands, naked feet and half-closed eyes.... Her features are emaciated but how noble? Even the folds of the drapery, even to the languor of her drooping hands, even to the sigh that dies on her half-closed lips. Words cannot render the sentiment of this affecting rapturous attitude. Fallen back in a swoon her whole being dissolves; the moment has come, and she gasps, this is her last sigh—the emotion is too powerful....[2]

Inside it is quiet. No sooner have our eyes become accustomed to the penumbral dark than we immediately come face to face with her! Here she is! Her eyes stare out at us directly, in her arms the abundant roses which are the mark of a dead body which does not decay but which on exhumation gives off the smell of roses—olfactory sign of sanctity.

Shan Short compares the light that falls on the statue of St Teresa through the occuli—the eye-like opening in the dome of her niche—to the literary fragments which "'illuminate' the sculpture for the author's and the reader's pleasure".[3]

She quotes from the illustrious pens of Stendhal, Taine, Zola and Lacan, whom, among many others she suggests write through "the practice of ekphrasis" where, through rhetorical ploys, the authors re-imagine the figure of Teresa and project their own desires on to the pictorial rapture in front of their (or the narrator who stands in for the author's) mesmerised eyes and "give voice to the mute sculpture".[4]

Inside it is quiet. Only the echoing footsteps of a few tourists like ourselves reverberate on the cold stone floor of the cavernous space and the occasional coughs and shuffles of supplicants at prayer dotted around in the pews. We approach the vast picture set over the altar of the chapel. No, this upstanding woman, with her constant gaze which meets ours, is not the subject of so many descriptions, the object of that famous encounter of which we are in search. We move on.

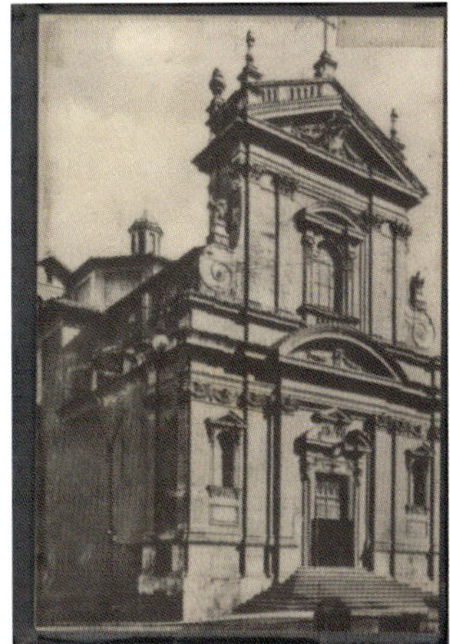

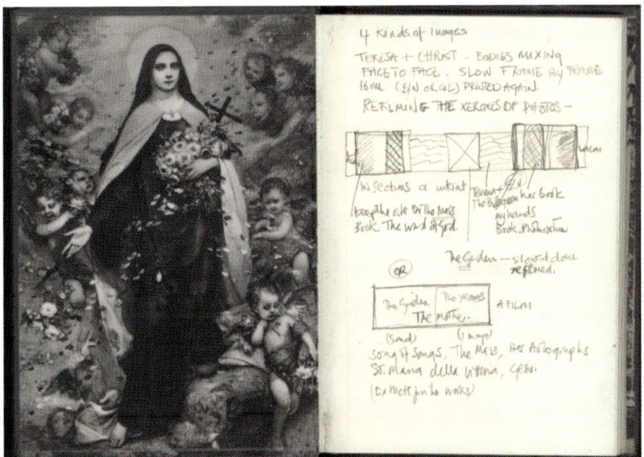

Notebook with location postcards and diagram of film structure for *"Now I am yours"*, 1992

> Just go... in particular see his statue of St Teresa In Ecstasy.... Ah! That Santa Teresa! It is like heaven opening, with the quiver that only a purely divine enjoyment can set in a woman's flesh, the rapture of faith carried to the point of spasm, the creature losing breath and dying of pleasure in the arms of the divinity![5]

You make your way down into the shadowy pit of the Church. Your steps resound on stone. Rising ahead of you the main altar is, the guidebook tells you, "decorated in the extravagant and highly ornate sculptural artifice of the high baroque". Multi-coloured marbles, gilts, gilded stucco, glimmer in the gloomy darkness. Above a semi-circular cornice and frieze which, from this position below can be partly read—"O Maria Magnificata Est."

You arrive, at the cross of the transept and nave. You turn and suddenly.... Yes, you see her! In the brown and gilded light of the chapel on the left transept. Here she is! You catch your breath, Ah! Santa Teresa!

> What divine art! What voluptuousness. Our good Monk believing that we did not understand it, explained this group to us: 'e un gran peccato'.... Bernini has known how to translate in this statue the most passionate writings of the young Spanish woman.[6]

What exclamations, what exclamation marks, what a spectacle!

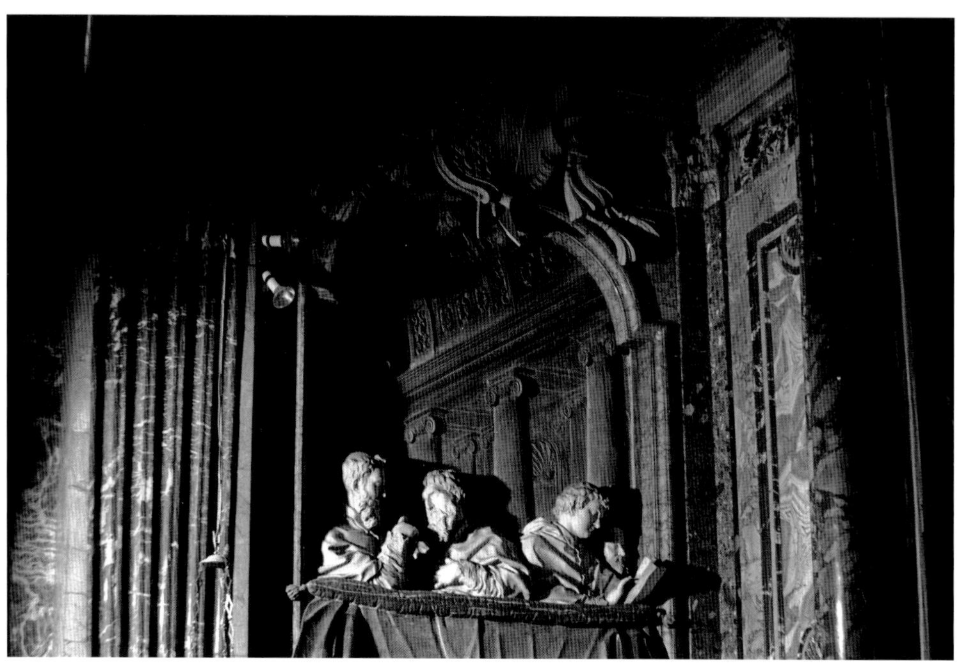

Location photograph for *"Now I am yours"*, 1992

Sonic Chamber

The composition of the Cornaro Chapel is organised on the frontal relationship of an audience to a stage. It is only from a prime place directly in front of this stage that we are in command of all the complex elements of architecture, sculpture and painting deployed by its maker. The stage is the niche which contains the main sculpture, of St Teresa of Jesus depicted at the moment of one of her visionary experiences—the famous Transverberation.[7] To the sides of this stage are theatre boxes or balconies—in fact they are prayer stalls, from which the various members of the Cornaro family look out. Except that, as we know, because the perspectival depth of the balconies is illusory—being high relief—and because of the position of the balconies to the central niche, which are set back, it is not possible from their perspective for the Cornaro Witnesses to have a view of the scene that is being enacted (for them?) below. The organisation of the chapel conspires through the dynamic of a silent network of looks to offer up the image of the female figure (in the niche) to us as privileged viewers, and through us, to the Cornaro Witnesses in the balconies. From our position in front of the niche we are as if at an audition, the sole spectators to an unfolding private show. A theatre with lights dimmed and centre-stage is the star in mid-trance, in mid-performance, in freeze-frame, her own eyes closed, self-absorbed, her head tilted back, her throat stretched out, as if in the mid-cry of a mute. A muteness which has become the excess of the voice in operatic high drama, for there is no doubt, her open mouth, her throat stretched out, is nothing if not the passage for song, "It is the Traviata in the third act! Wouldn't one say that she is singing.... Look at her open mouth! Why would she open her mouth except to sing?"[8]

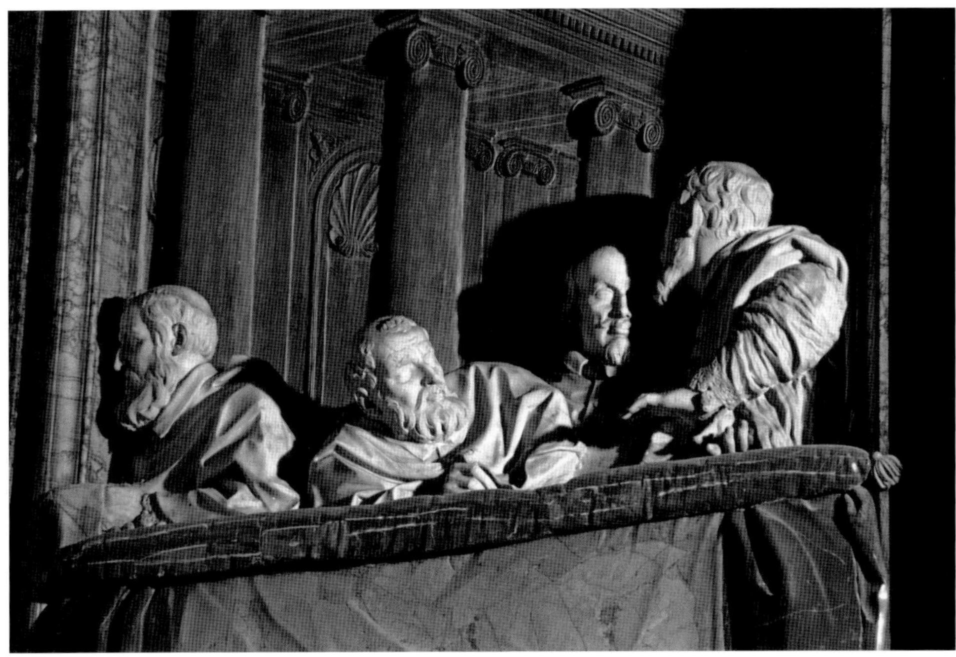

This page and overleaf: location photograph for *"Now I am yours"*, 1992

Ekphrasic spectatorship—without which there can be no show. A view from where the whole, can come together, for him who reads, listens, speculates, desires—a line of vision at the vanishing point of which is the woman in the niche.

Silence of rebounding vision, illuminative texts, transports of prose, the clamour of voices, discursive abandonment, soaring pitches of excess—which in so much writing, in so many descriptions, reverberate, and resound in this little theatre as if in a hollow grotto—a sonic chamber.

Epitaph

Standing in front of this little theatre, I can only hear the silence of the sepulchre. Only the reverberation of stone steps. Here is her entombment, for the Cornaro Chapel is dedicated to death. Death many times over. It is a monument built on the illusion of a temporal present built over a sepulchral chapel dedicated to the memory of the dead. Wordsworth says that monuments and epitaphs exist because of the "consciousness of a principle of immortality".[9] Lest we forget about mortality, the floor on which we walk are graves. Here are the wildly gesticulating skeletons to despair and hope inlaid in the stone, inside the shallow space of the chapel, under which lie the remains of the Cornaro Donor inhumed. A maverick space, which draws us in to join in this play of death. The portrait busts of the Donor and his family of

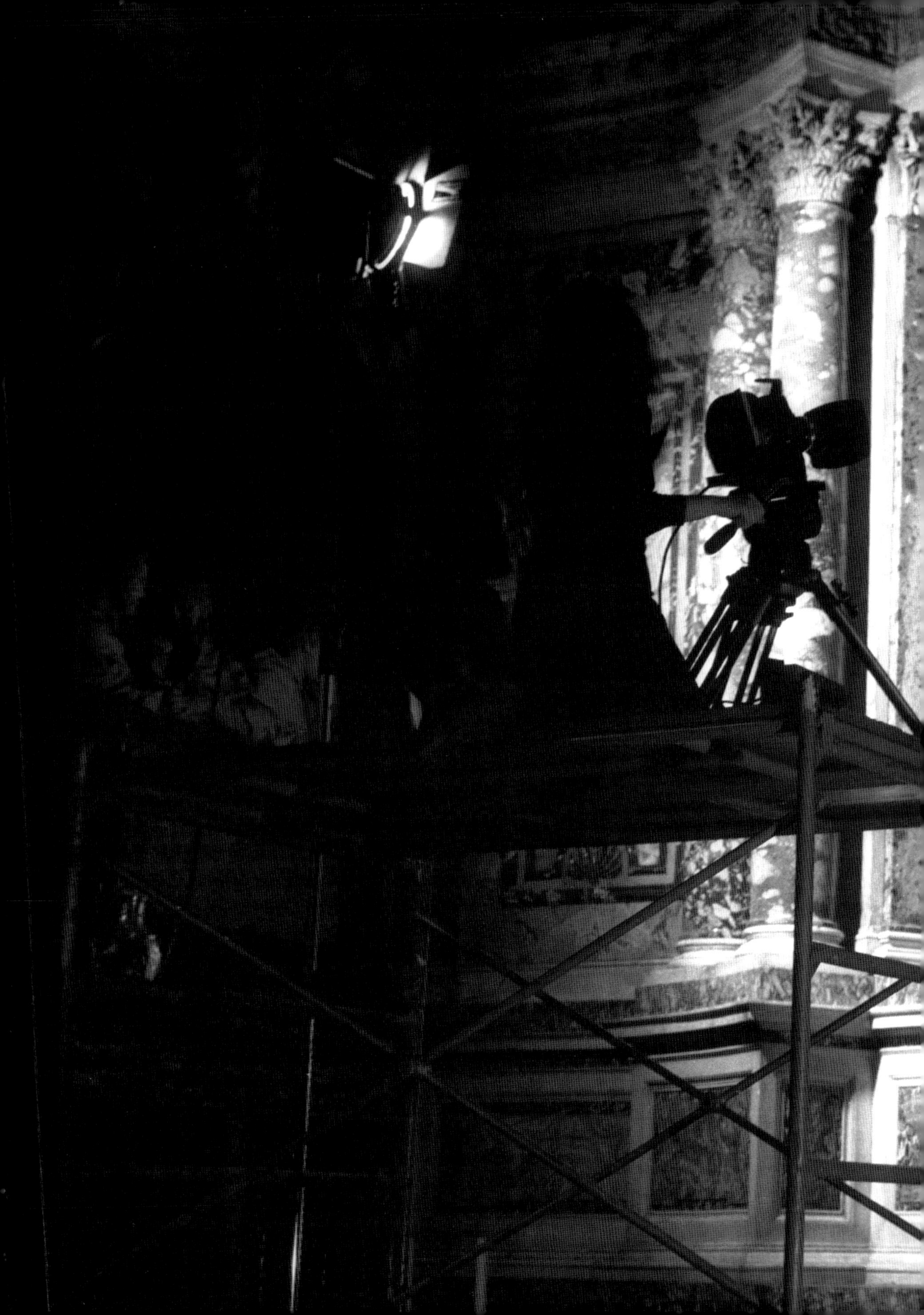

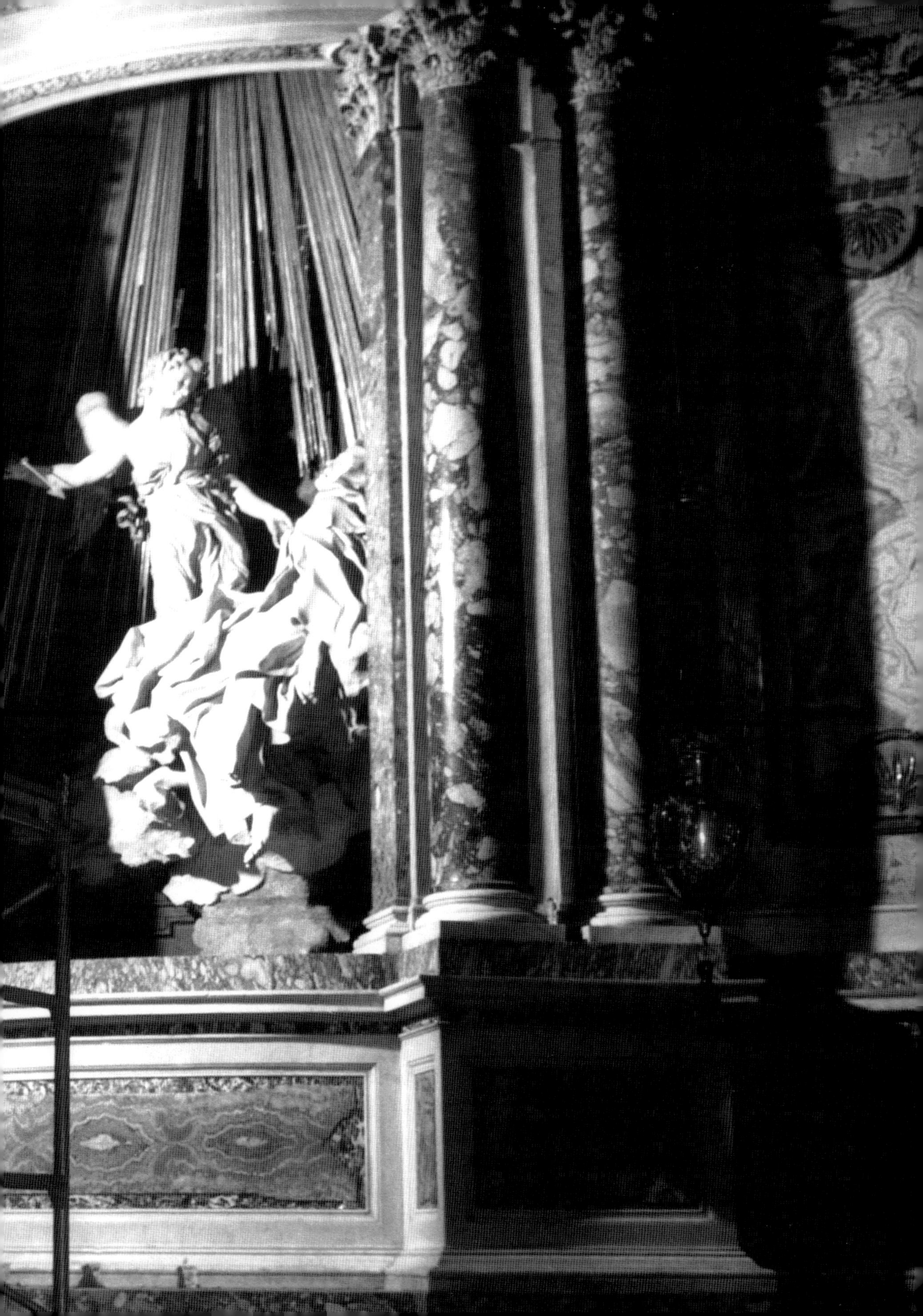

Cornaro Cardinals, in animated postures—engaged in lively conversation or concentrated on the act of reading, praying or in silent meditation—are the posthumously sculpted figures of the long-dead, whose memory is summoned from another temporality. They are invited to join the Donor in his vault of spectacles, but since they cannot see or hear a thing, we are their witnesses and upon our absence, they also die anew and conversely, we are co-opted to this death scene, that through our sight they may relive.

Many many dyings—a spectacle of death.

In the centre of this show is the death-defying figure in the niche. Between corporeality and transcendence. Like the epitaph, she is a shadowy interposition between the world of the living and the dead. "The wall opens up to reveal an unnatural space framed by pairs of columns set ajar as if some gigantic force had heaved open the curtain of wall and bent it towards us."[10] Hibbard's description situates the niche in another layer of temporality. In an apocalyptic future tense, an end-of-time scenario where the tomb/niche opens at the moment of the final judgment day, to reveal the sepulchral figure—offered up to the eye of God in whose place we stand. An exhumation which gives off the smell of roses neither in nor out, pliable yet petrified, petrified but not corrupted—funerary statue, walled up, encrypted within the disclosure of the opening tomb, frozen in the moment of her own description. Caught as a subject in her own writing. From the balcony, one of the Witnesses reads from her/the petrified book in his hands. His blind eyes look at the open page. A stony text. In this spatial conundrum, her image is impervious to his blindness, his eyes impervious to her textual voice, this is their communication. Nothing circulates here, except silence. Her muteness, out of her open mouth, pours forth words we cannot hear. The occuli atop her niche lets in the gilded shafts of light, the backdrop to her performance. Imaginary being, figment of the dead 'segnieurs' hallucination, like a film show in which they are blind edits—like a shot without a reverse shot in the fictional space of editing. The niche is her entrapment, her screen, the stone is her encryptment, at the vanishing point of our gaze and in the ekphrasis of dying acoustic reverberations. A cry from the other side, a most eloquent/silent epitaph.

El Escorial, Madrid

We find in the Cornaro Chapel a trapped silent object, yet her voice from beyond this stony representation is there for us to read in what she appositely calls a "living book" from where she gives us her own descriptions of her visionary experiences in the form of her own writing.

We go to Madrid to see if it is possible to read, to touch, to film, her book. In the film sequence titled "Algarabía" the camera scans the pages of Teresa's original autograph of *La Vida* which is kept in the library of El Escorial. I could no more read its indecipherable hand than understand what she was communicating so urgently. To see, in her hand, without self-corrections or revisions, page after page set down. So caught up was I in impregnable illegibility yet visual display of virtuosity, and so overwhelmed at handling an object beyond

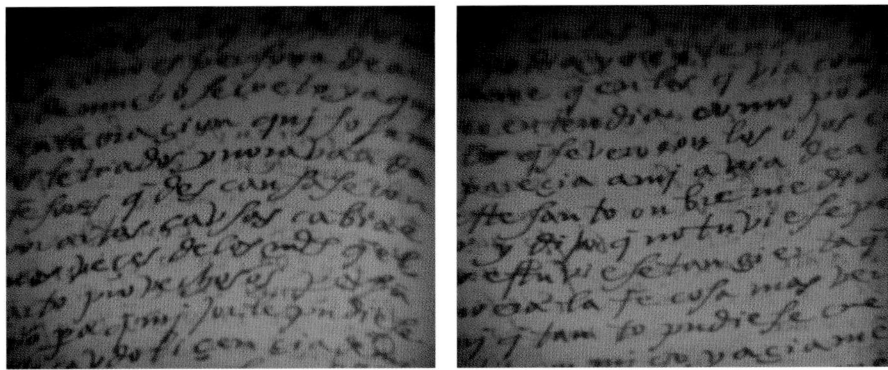

Film stills from *"Now I am yours"* showing the original pages of *La Vida* by St Teresa

value that I had to be reminded that the library would be closing soon and would I get on with what I had come to do.

Returning to the pages of her book in front of me, I see the strikings out, alterations and revisions (contemporaneous and posthumous), set in the margins or over her writing in the differing hands of her various editors and scribes. Through these markings she writes that she has no control over what is coming out, a driven writing/speaking, like the 'gift of tongues', "I am writing this as if it were not myself that speaks."[11]

A writing which she describes as "the pen in flight", "a vuela pluma"—a free, automatic writing, set down quickly, at first hand, with very few revisions. A chaos of algarabía (Arabic: gabble, din, clamour, uproar (Cassell's Spanish Dictionary)) which, in setting out to describe abstract experiences and elusive states 'reproduces' and 'constructs' in the act of reading, a mirror or perhaps a shadow, of the unrepresentable and unnameable.

In this performance, she is a vocal passage through which language and words pass, herself becoming the amanuensis for a divine voice—a literary mediatrix. Her text conflates the hand of writing with the act of speaking into a single act of hand and tongue—speaking and writing are one.

Is this 'sweet disorder' a rhetorical strategy to circumvent the strictures of being a woman with a pen? Her writing, far from being improvised, has been analysed as deploying complex rhetorical figures such as questions to the reader, 'colloquialness', misspellings as mispronounciations.[12] So that "disorder, digression and imprecision—are the tactics that disguise a charismatic text as women's chatter".[13]

An excitable and uncontrollable vocality is a writing style, developed to enable her to express herself freely in writings which reach their apotheosis as 'speaking texts'; "Teresa speaks in writing".[14]

The anxiety of transgression surfaces as unmediated orality, as the voice of the woman who checks her speech, claims to be ignorant, is anxious to not be thought of as displaying linguistic virtuosity, disavows and self-abases as the mark of her gendered site. Her text is troubled by this and she repeats her willingness to submit to correction, guidance and supervision. What she knows is that to have control of the word is to be in excess of her designation as a woman, what she senses is that the act of writing, puts her in danger. The rhetoric of orality is a subterfuge and shield. Following the uncovering of the circulation of her private writings in *La Vida*, the book is censored, silenced and inhumed.

The speaking voice is an attempt to break out of that control. Yet, she cannot break out, her text is always bounded by the very rhetoric of a woman's voice, which is also its defence from the authority to which she must submit, which bears pressure on her tongue, which—like her mute image in Rome, petrified in a restricted economy of supervision—is also constantly invigilated.

The circulation of the voice

In the dark of cinema the voice circulates in a limitless territory outside of the boundaries of framing, it installs an unseen presence which cannot be controlled by vision. The voice unattached to the image, transcends the body whilst creating a body because it springs from it so directly. In acoustic close-up, it creates an intimacy which summons up the eroticism of the body, particularly the throat and mouth, sites of pleasure. It brings with it the threat of absence because it resides in a realm which is inaccessible—beyond vision. Kaja Silverman suggests that in psychoanalytic terms, it is the maternal voice with its early associations with storytelling, spatiality, aural comfort and threat of both absence and presence that is the original banished prototype for the disembodied voice of cinema which has been cast out and replaced in mainstream film by the male voice.[15]

Very rarely does the voice of the woman resonate in cinema except in the scream or cry or else "it is forced again and again into diegetic 'closets' and 'crevices'".[16] Even when it is heard as voice off, it is often eventually to be coupled with the image which is a kind of death. "Synchronisation marks the final moment in any such localisation, the point of full and complete 'embodiment' which stops this free circulation."[17]

The woman's voice, free from her image, becomes a mobile element by refusing easy identification with a unified and localised subject in representation. Yet it enables the creation of a mobile subject through the charge of eroticism and other relations to the body as well as the dissolution of boundaries. It challenges the conventions of mainstream cinema as well as avant-garde and experimental film forms from which the woman's voice has been doubly banished, both from the possibility of narrative and from presence through the aural, since both elements have either been absent or taken second place to the visual.

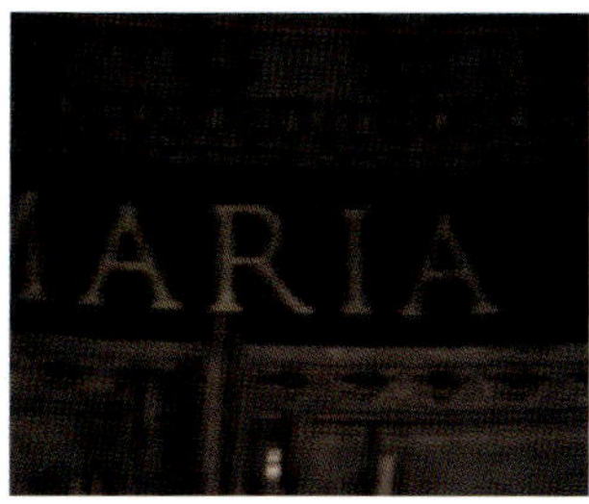

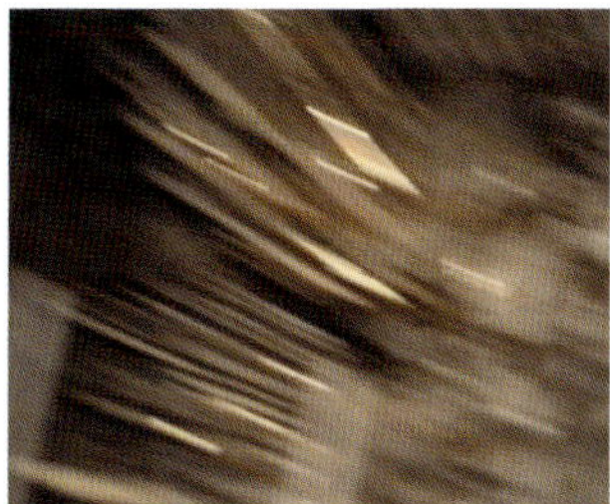

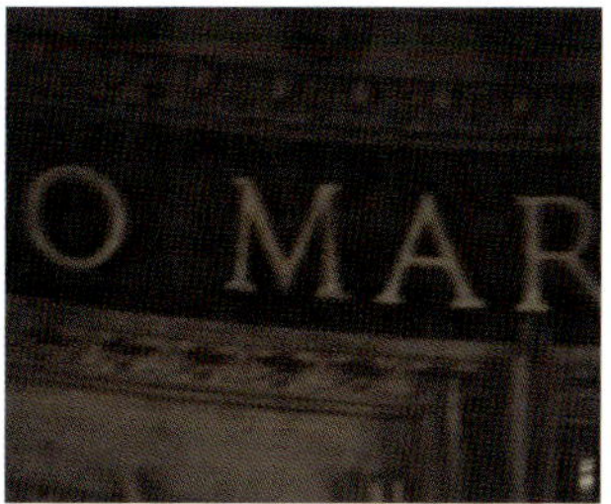

Film stills from the sequence "Tomb: vision, mirage, dream" in *"Now I am yours"*, 1992

The single voice with long pauses of silence and flat, close-up delivery, is balanced on the edge between speaking and reading and delivers a speech, without personal inflection or characterisation, yet the body and a subject is at the centre. The voice becames faster and faster so that holding back and silence is taken into a torrent of words, reading voice into song, verbal language mixed in with non-verbal sounds, fractured language, ravings, vocal music as performed elements of the act of speech are taken to a limit. An acoustic territory is produced through multiple tracks: single voices, reading, song, incantation, speaking, non verbal sounds, stray words and phrases, wild sound from location, electronically processed sounds from the voice and silence as a sound. This is the voice of the film. This voice is not the cut-off voice over which always resides on the same plane over the image, nor the out of frame voice off, waiting to be coupled with the image in a narrative logic since there are no characters or narrative codes of this type, but it is a more ambivalent presence.

In *"Now I am yours"* two weaving voices, a single reading/speaking/pronouncing voice and a performing, singing, non-verbal voice interweave with other sounds to cohere as a fragmented yet always potential subject which is marking itself out as an entity or becomes like a force which is breaking out of its borders. It is set in a tension with its potential for emanating from the image and in another plane beyond the image. The voice (in the multiple sense described) performs a kind of ekphrasis; an illuminative speaking falling an the image, as the light that falls from the occuli on Teresa. A fast, breathless locution. A vocality beginning to deteriorate into the unintelligible—babble, gibberish, the inexpressible—but also a trajectory which directs the film and its soundtrack through a series of transitions. The voice touches the image, works against the image, with it, hovers over it, but resists the total embodiment of sync or the stable relation of voice over. The film attempts an audio/visual experience or rhetoric of the feminine. The lack of her image as subject is a refusal of the representation of acting or characterisation or narrativisation or the coupling of sound and image as a refusal to be mastered and contained.

The voice of the film is a composition of tracks gathered around voice, pace, rhythm as the 'heartbeat' and site of the absent feminine subject arranged like a form of music.

It is a voice made for the cinematic space, outside the control and in excess of vision, in the darkness beyond, above, outside the luminosity of the frame.

In the sequence "Tomb: vision, mirage, dream" the camera glides along the frieze inside the cupola as if suspended in space. On the soundtrack the whispered words become more breathless and harsh, echoing around the cavernous hollow of the dome. Intimate, it is the female voice at the point of emptying, suspended in mid-air or entombed in the self, out of which it cannot break, the enveloping womb or uterine nightmare, the sound reverberating in the niche /tomb. A sonic chamber where the woman is petrified in stone and under constant surveillance. The niche and the words from which she tears herself away—a cinematic entrapment? *"Now I am yours"* releases a voice from the pressure which suppresses it and the muteness of the stone.

This paper was first written a year after *"Now I am yours"* was finished and was presented with an extract from *"Now I am yours"* at the conference *Woman/Image/Text* on the relationship between women's writing and visual art practice, Sheffield Hallam University, 13 November 1993.

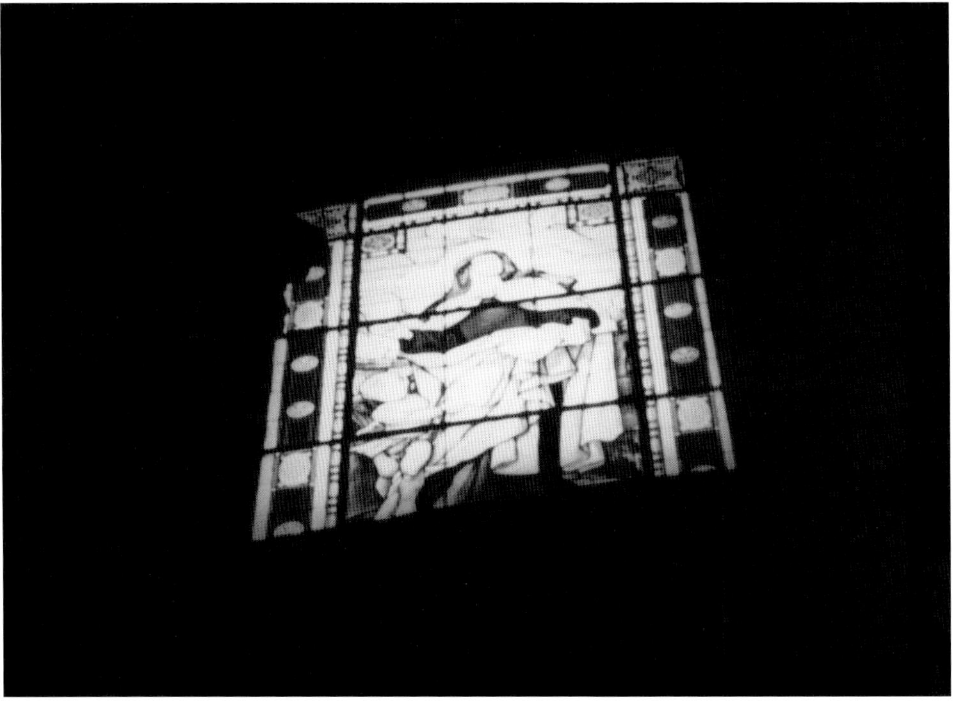

"Now I am yours", 1992

Notes

1 *Recce* is abreviated from reconnaissance and in film production refers to a preliminary visit to the location prior to the main filming and production.

2 Taine, Hipolyte, *Italy, Rome, Naples*, J Durand trans., New York: Holt and Williams, 1872, quoted in Shan Short, "Come again? Bernini's St Teresa as a Site/Sight for the Writing of Male Desire", *Australian Journal of Art*, vol. viii, 1989/1990, p. 86.

3 Short, "Come again?", p. 84.

4 Short, "Come again?", p. 84. Short describes the correspondence between interpretation of vision and textual description in terms of "the practice of ekphrasis where the rhetorical ploys of the authors describe and give voice to the mute sculpture"—and of course to their desire—which she suggests is a re-formation of male re-investment and narcissism mediated by the object.

5 Zola, Emile, *Rome*, Ernest Alfred trans., London: Vizetelly, Chatto and Windus, 1896, quoted in Short, "Come again?", p. 84

6 Stendhal in "The Representation of Ecstasy" by Walther Weibal in *Bernini in Perspective*, George C Bauer ed., New Jersey: Prentice Hall, 1976, as quoted in Short, "Come again?", p. 86.

7 The Transverberation is the moment depicted in Bernini's sculpture, in which St Teresa in a vision experiences her heart being pierced by a cherub's arrow.

8 Fernandez, Dominique, "La Bouche Ouverte", *Le Banquet des Anges*, Paris: Plon, 1984, p. 24. Quote translated by Nina Danino.

9 Wordsworth, William, "Essay upon Epitaphs, I" in *The Prose Works of William Wordsworth*, WJB Owen and Jane Worthington Sawyer eds., Oxford: Oxford University Press, 1974, vol. 1, p. 50.

10 Hibbard, Howard, *Bernini*, Harmondsworth: Penguin, 1965, p. 70.

11 *The Life of Saint Teresa by Herself*, J M Cohen trans., Harmondsworth: Penguin, 1957, p. 290.

12 Webber, Alison, *Teresa of Avila and the Rhetoric of Femininity*, Princeton: Princeton University Press, 1990. Webber analyses Teresa's rhetoric of femininity through her use of a deliberate strategy of orality rather than as some of her translators have proposed as a result of unconscious 'habit'. Thus her text sounds like direct unaffected speech with "the lifelike reproduction of the inflections of her voice" and the use of complex "rhetorical figures as alliteration, antithesis, catalogue or etymological repetition", p. 7.

13 Webber, *Teresa of Avila*, p. 109.

14 Webber, *Teresa of Avila*, referring to Ramón Menéndez Pidal's phrase "Teresa habla por escrito" ("Teresa speaks in writing"), p. 6.

15 Silverman, Kaja, *The Acoustic Mirror*, Bloomington and Indianapolis: Indiana University Press, 1988. Silverman in *The Acoustic Mirror* argues that "the maternal voice would (thus) seem to be the original prototype for the disembodied voice over in cinema", p. 76. She refers to the two opposing concepts of the voice: Chion's "dystopic version of the maternal voice" and "Rosolato's 'operatic' version of the maternal voice fantasy", p. 73.
For further reference see Michel Chion, *La voix au cinema*, Paris: Editions de L'Etoile, 1982; Guy Rosolato, "La voix: entre corps et langage", *Revue francaise de psychoanalyse*, 37, no. 1, 1974.

16 Silverman *The Acoustic Mirror*, p. 76.

17 Silverman *The Acoustic Mirror*, p. 49.

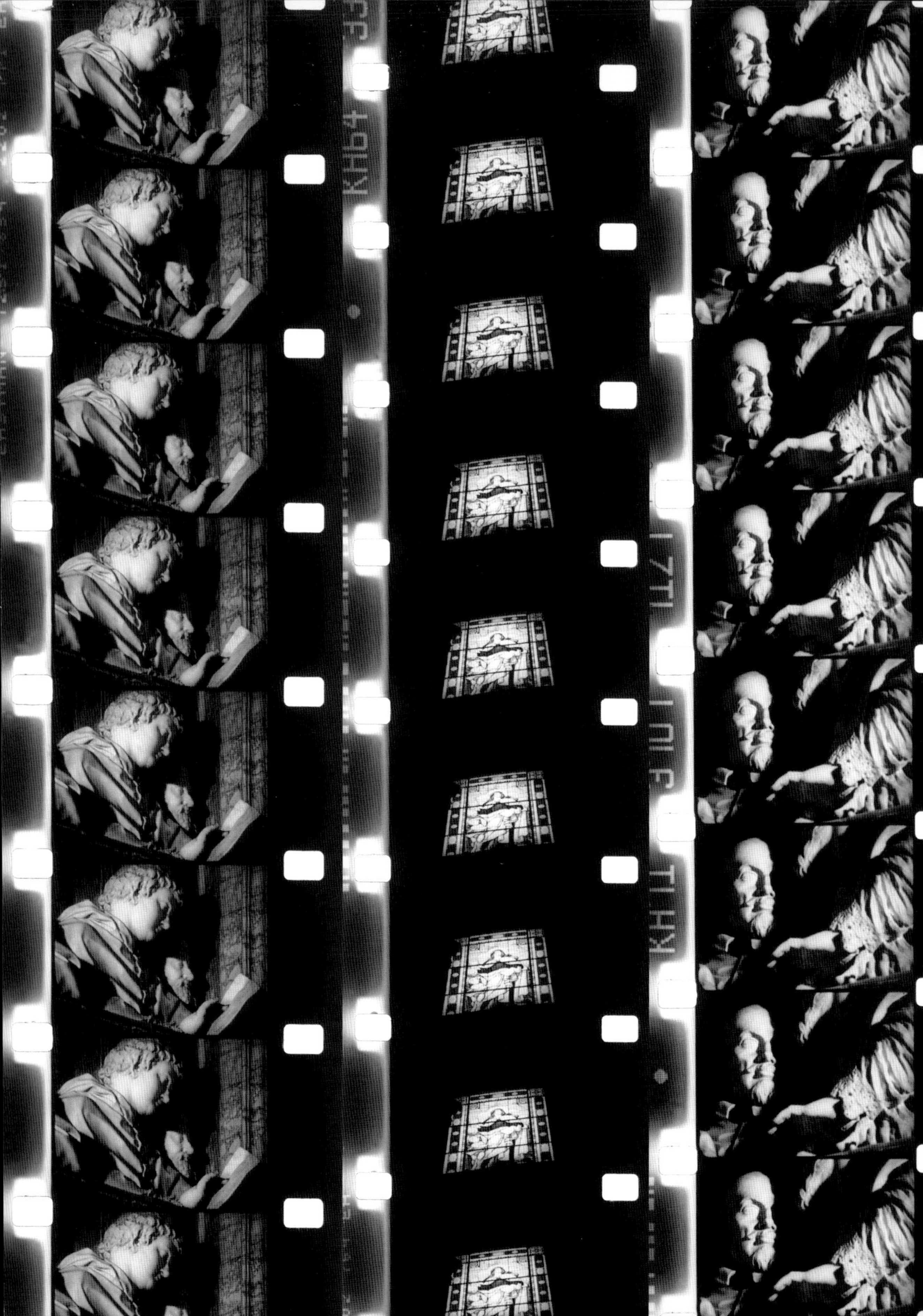

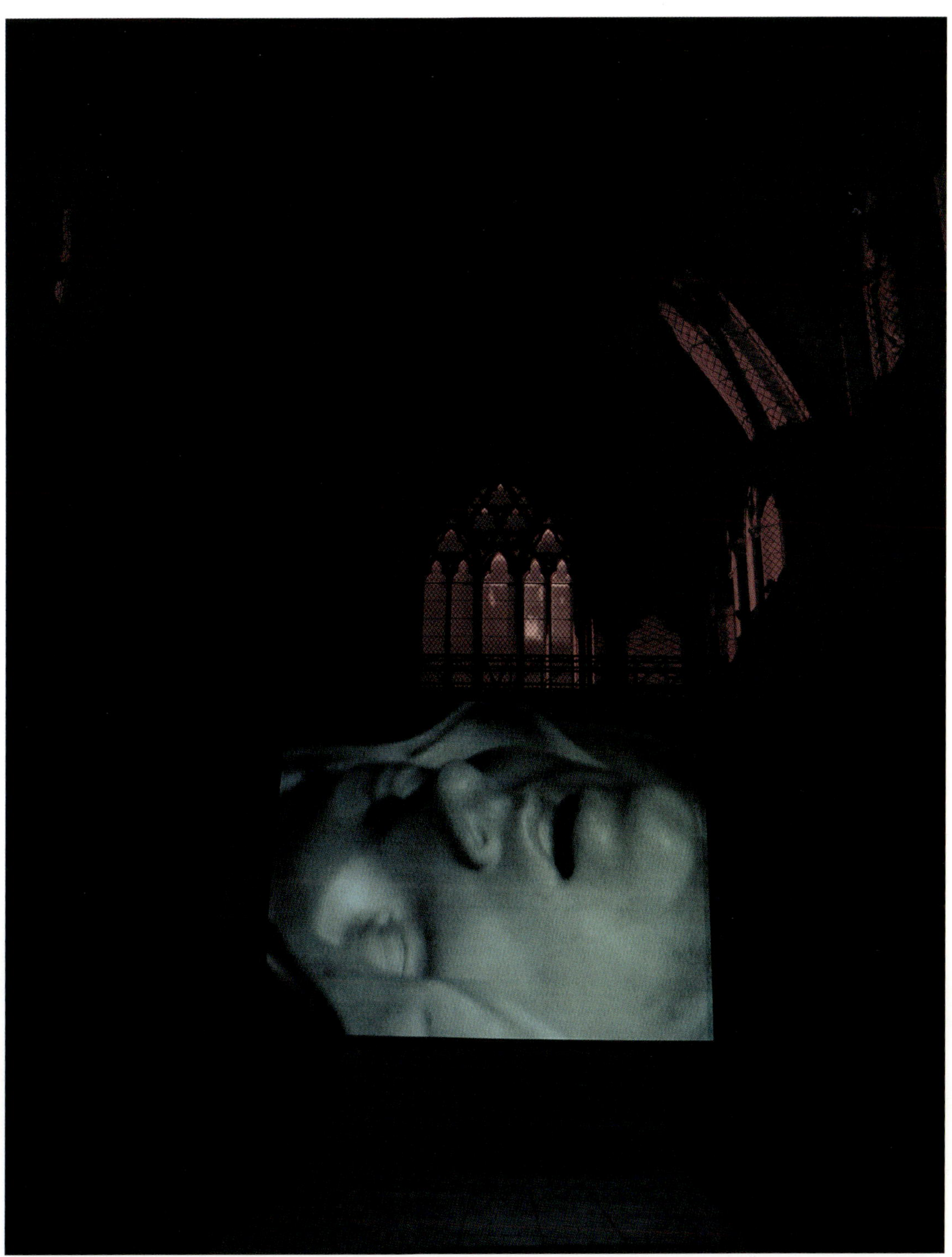

"Now I am yours", 1992

Above: site-specifc projection at the 291 Gallery, London
Opposite: film strips

The Silence is Baroque 1997

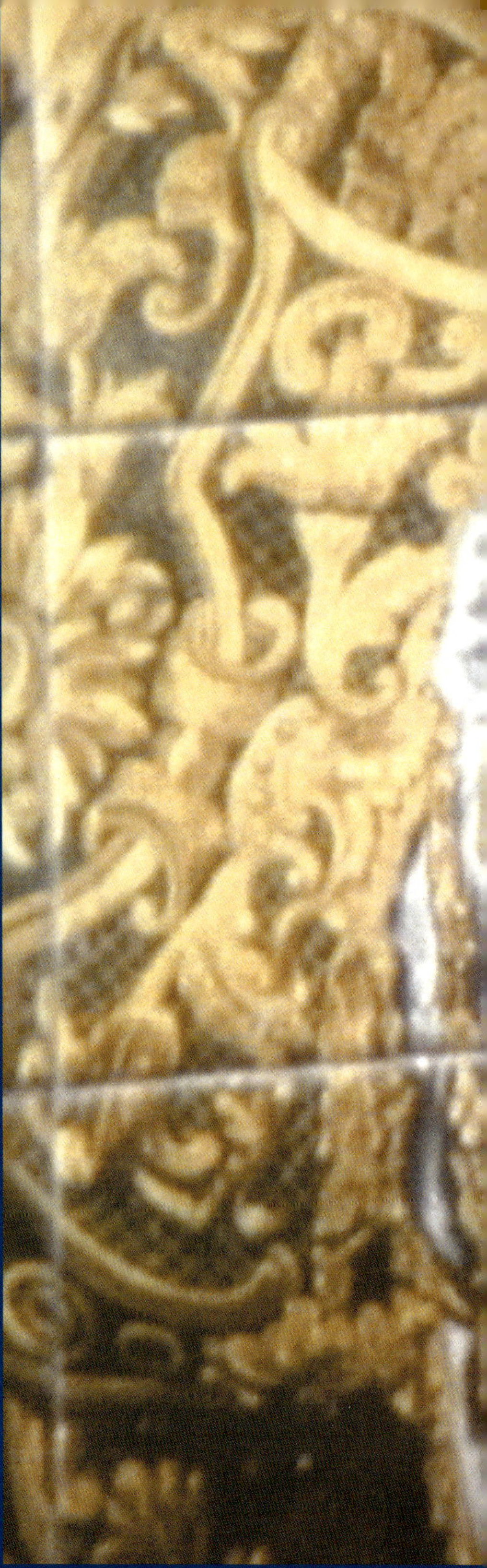

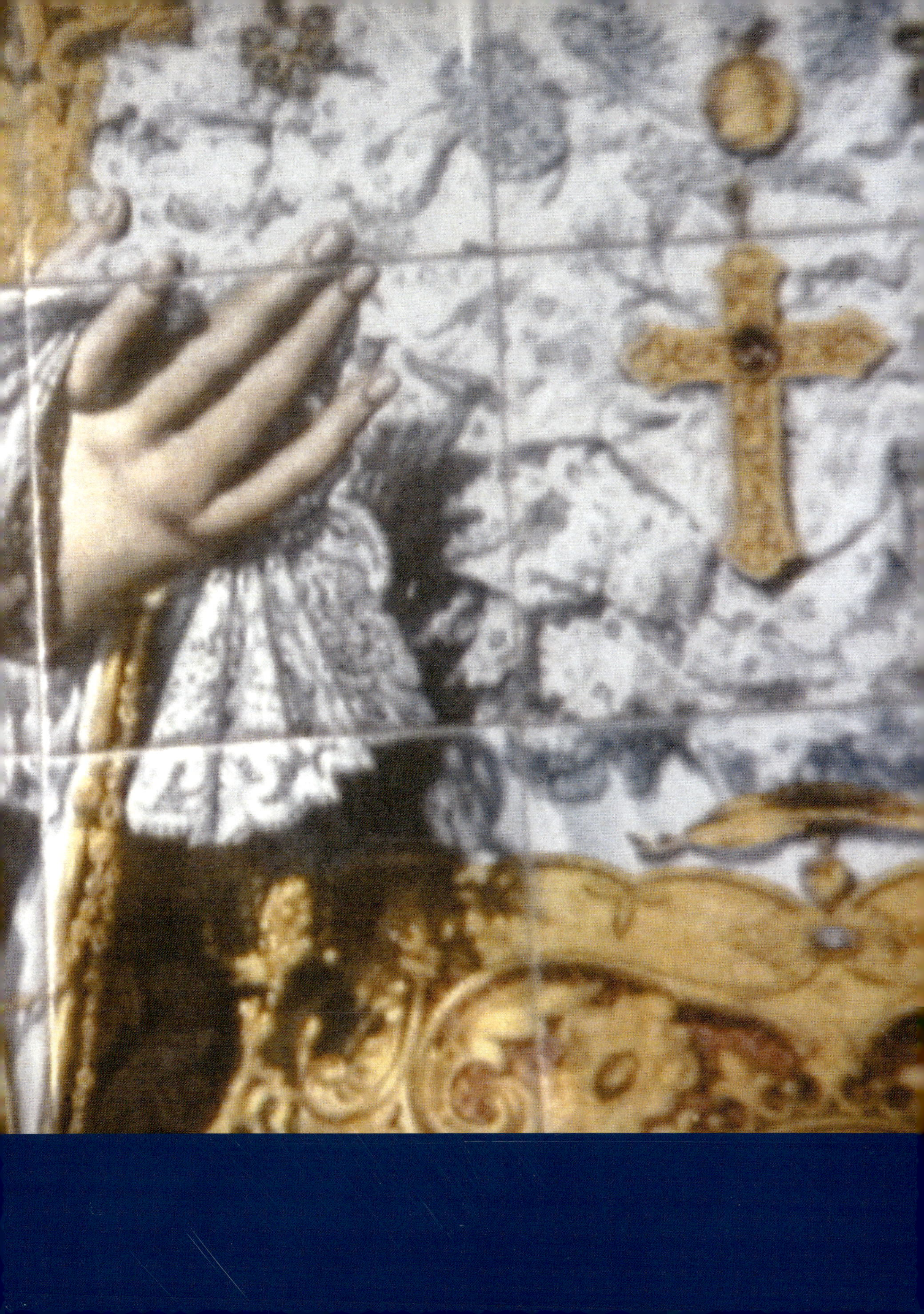

Documenting The Silence on Location in Granada and Seville

Nina Danino

This film was shot in Granada and Seville during Holy Week of 1995. The rough voices of men open the film soundtrack, they call out to one another in Spanish, "Primo!" From Pasolini's *Accattone*, two other voices banter in Italian about taking flowers to *Divino Amore* (Divine Love), a working class neighbourhood and the name of a cemetery in Rome: "You're always joking. I've always been in the mud, I want to be amidst flowers" retorts one to the other. There is an aerial view of a city; it could be Rome or Seville, with roads lined with palm trees, a roundabout, houses, but we realise that it is not a city of lively people but a cemetery. The images of its artificial flowers and stone Madonna are in *"Now I am yours"* and *Stabat Mater*. Like the noisy processions that commemorate the Passion of Christ, in the middle of life there is death. In the film we are in a city square, noisy trumpets and the cacophony of people can be heard in the nearby streets. In these processions, the images of the local Virgins and Christs come out of their parish churches in all their finery, jewels and flowers, and are processed around the neighbourhood. The descriptions of vibrant colours, textiles, crafted objects and music resound off the pages of the itinerary brochures and are in the spoken film soundtrack. Some of the sculptures and the decorative objects in precious metals date back to the artisan workshops of sixteenth and seventeenth century master craftsmen and Baroque sculptors. The most life-like of the faces of Christ in agony are attributed to being death-masks of the murdered or the dead found on the banks of the Quadalquivir river. There may be many such processions taking place at the same time around the streets of a city, all competing with each other for audiences and in the spectacle that they put on. The heavy floats are carried from underneath by as many as 100 carriers. The procession may take as many as 12 hours to return to the parish church from which it first exited, travelling all night to return at daybreak. Taking part in the procession becomes an act of endurance and sacrifice for both participants and bystanders. The movement of so many sweating carriers and the heavy *palios* and *pasos* (floats) have to be rhythmically syncopated so as to keep the structures moving to the music but not to topple on to the bystanders (who sometimes wait for many hours to reserve the best spots) around the narrow streets. The music keeps the movement jerking and swaying, inching forward until the float stops for another break on the route.

The sound in the film was recorded live on location. Some parts of the soundtrack are built up of various sounds, with for example, one track of people talking, one track of clapping, and a track of band music, coming together to create the atmosphere of the street. The quality of the live music varies greatly, some bands sound amateur and out of tune. The grand bands and the highly orchestrated music is in Seville. In the sound recorded in Granada you can hear a strident high-pitched bugle or trumpet-like sound that doesn't hold its notes well. These trembling horns are echoes of an earlier archaic sound in the midst of modern life. They can be heard in the film soundtracks of Pasolini, in which the ancient fate of Medea or Oedipus is sealed by the clamour of these horns.

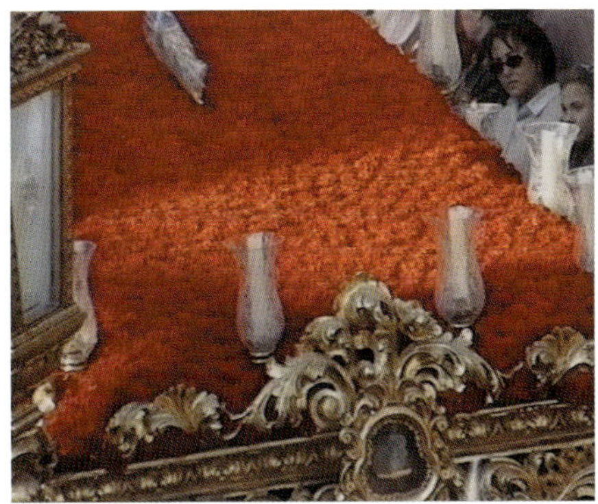

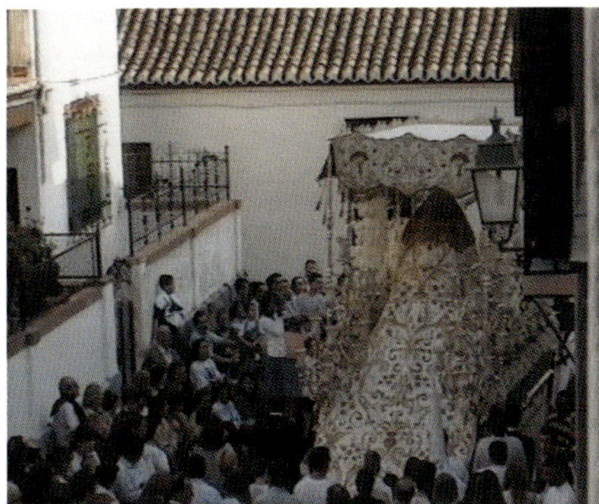

The Silence is Baroque, 1997, location photographs

The sound records people in the urgency of life. In the midst of the procession a man calls out "Ceda el paso!" (Clear the way!), a mother pulls the girls out of the way "Agarra las niñas!" (Grab the girls out of the way!). Amidst the amazing music freely available on the streets performed by the bands and orchestras, also recorded was the *saeta*, a 'song without a guitar'. This is a short, improvised, vernacular form sung by an anonymous voice in the crowd without musical accompaniment, it is a form of lament, delivered in a virtuoso performance sung to the figure of the Virgin or Christ as they are carried in the procession. A *saeta* is sung at the end of the film; we hear it in the distance with the sound of the crowd in the foreground. The tumult dies down and people hush each other to listen. A mother scolds her child for talking over the singing: "Cállate ya la boca chiquilla!" (Be quiet!). Nowadays *saetas* are tightly scheduled and highly paid performances by professional singers, who appear at their balconies at appointed breaks in the procession to perform.

The procession of *El Silencio* filmed in Granada appears out of the black screen. It processes at midnight accompanied only by the totemic sound of one solitary drum and the chains dragged by the penitents who follow the heavy crucifix. Because of the quiet observed by the crowds, the sound of swallows can be heard all the more distinctly on the soundtrack as they swoop around the *Rio Darro* that flows by the Alhambra behind us.

The film goes to the familiar-alien world of processions that as Juan José Tellez says "pass in front of the ice cream cafés and the Baroque silence of Spain". Under Franco the processions were tainted. Later, in the *democracia* the processions became associated with *retraso*; a backward, obscurantist and dark Spain. Fervour, belief, exuberant spectacle, music, art and drama are all part of a solemn, celebratory event which is not just entertainment but is full of religious, historical and cultural popular knowledge—an ordinary event which comes round every year. A chance for people to throng about in the streets and sit in the cafés and enjoy life. The film is a noisy, lively musical piece around this theatre, realism and poetry of the street, not high but low art—the applause for life pitted against the celebration of the passion and death in the defiant energy of the Baroque.

The Silence is Baroque was commissioned by the Dutch production company Studio één as one of a cycle of nine episodes in the artists' portmanteau feature film *Rainbow Stories*.

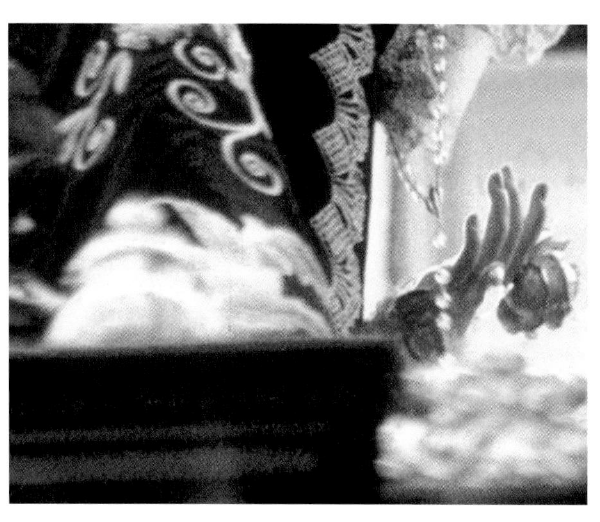
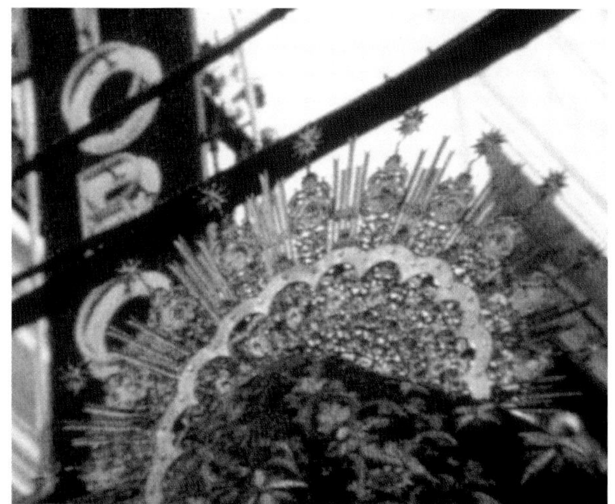

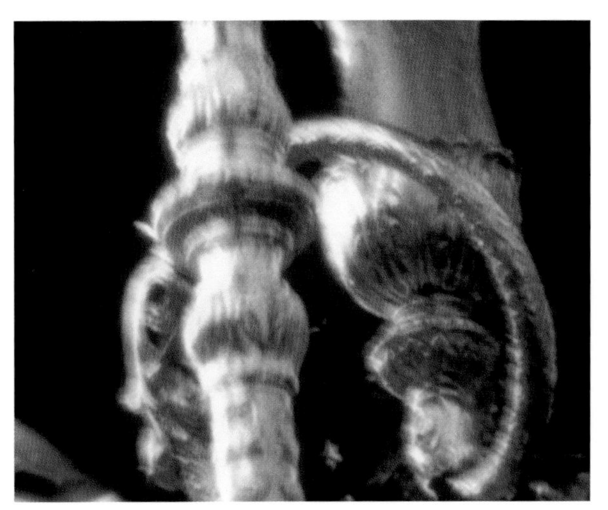

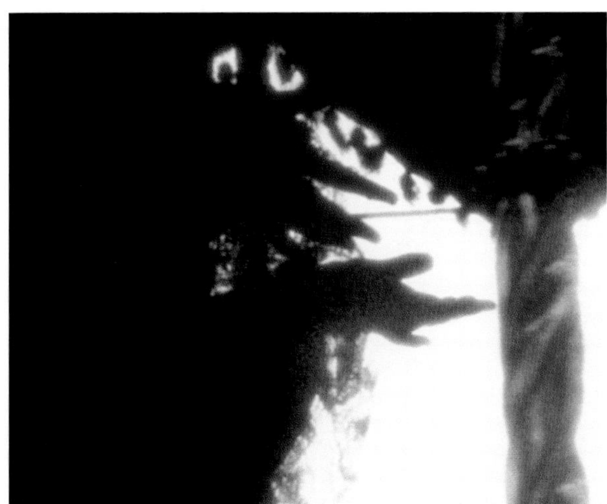

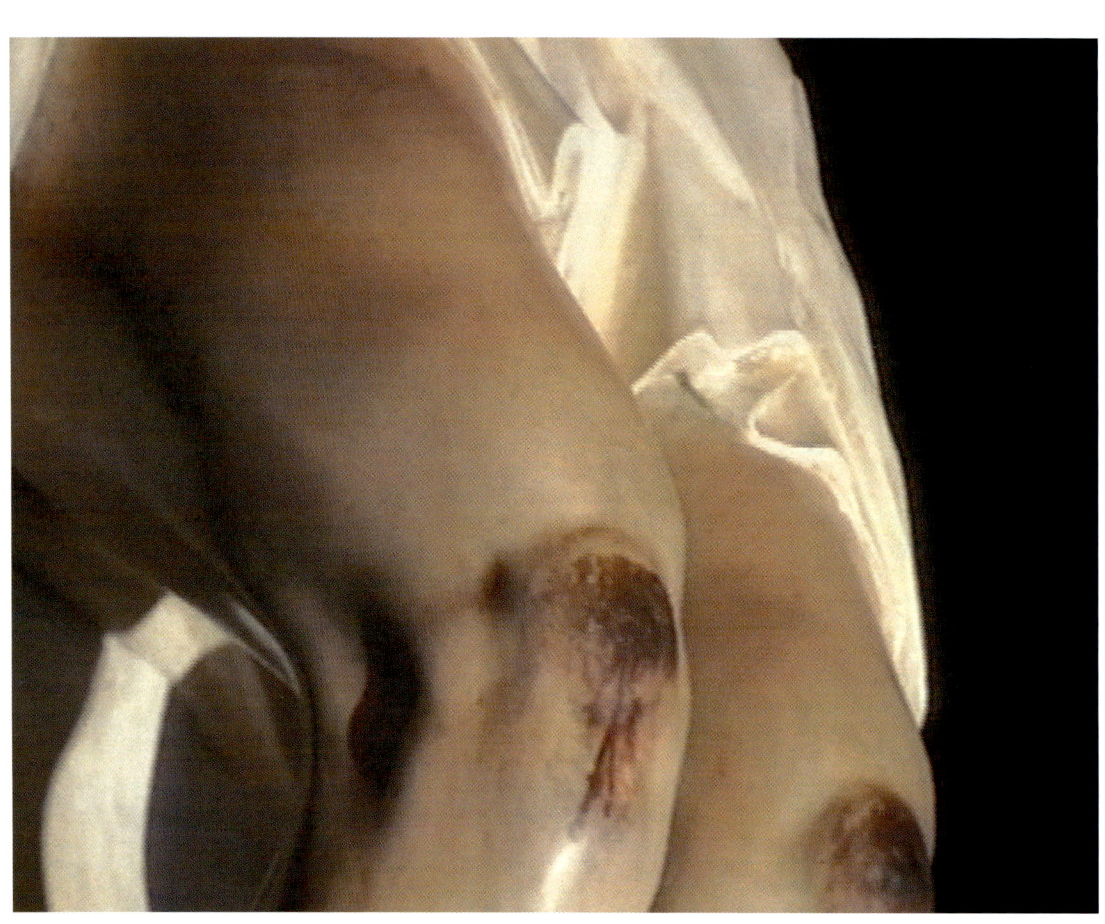

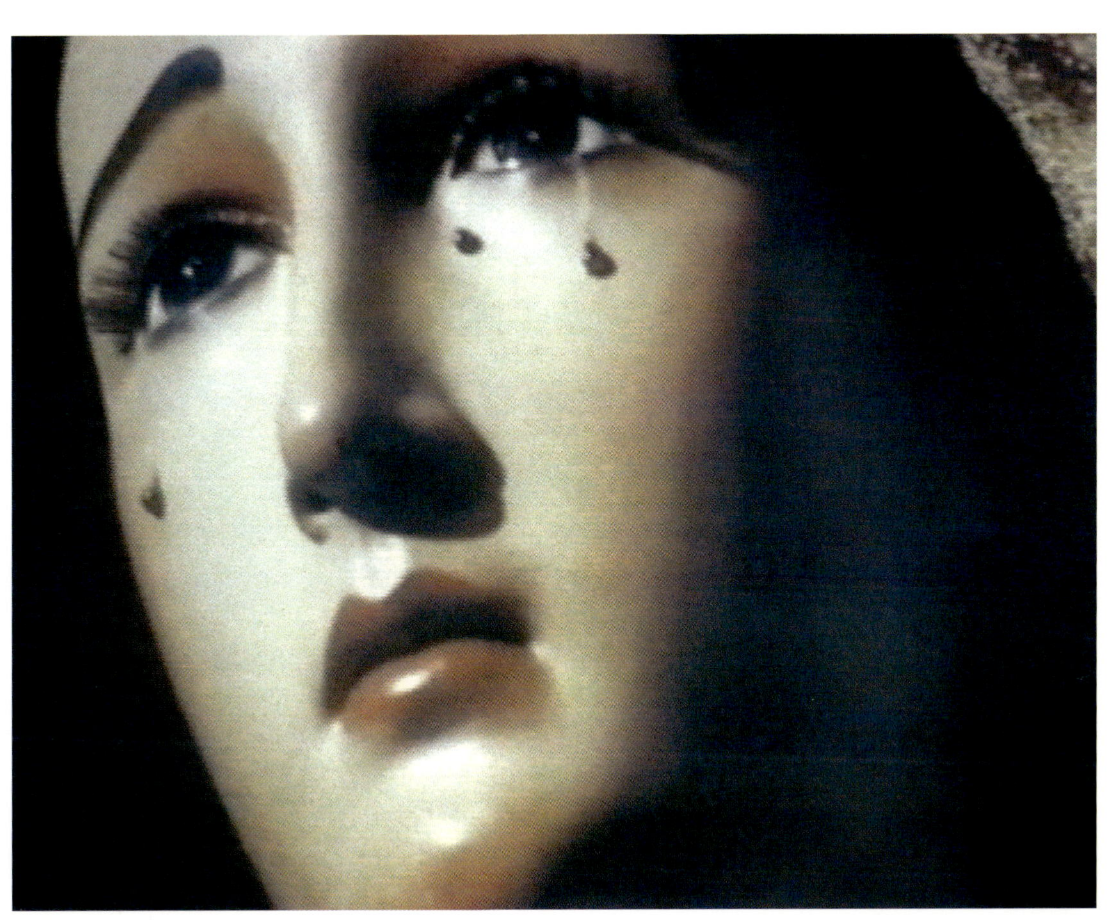

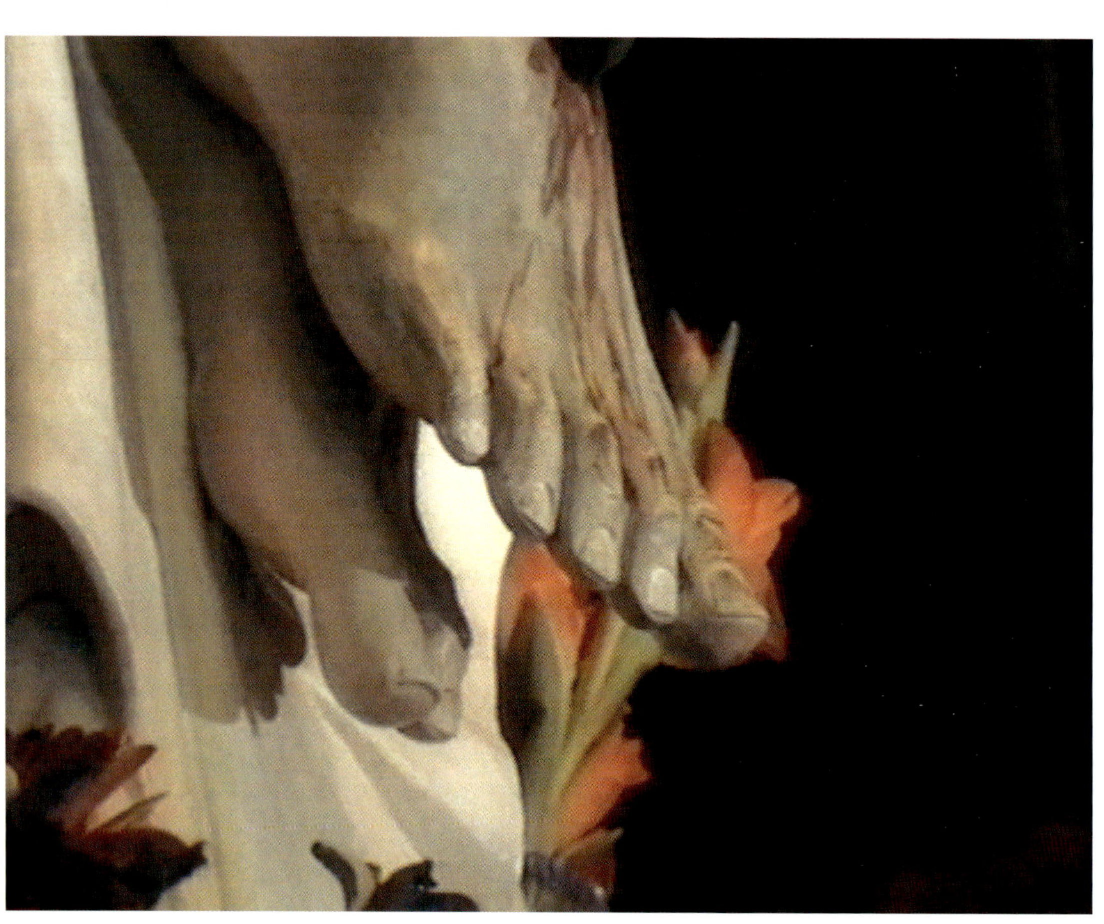

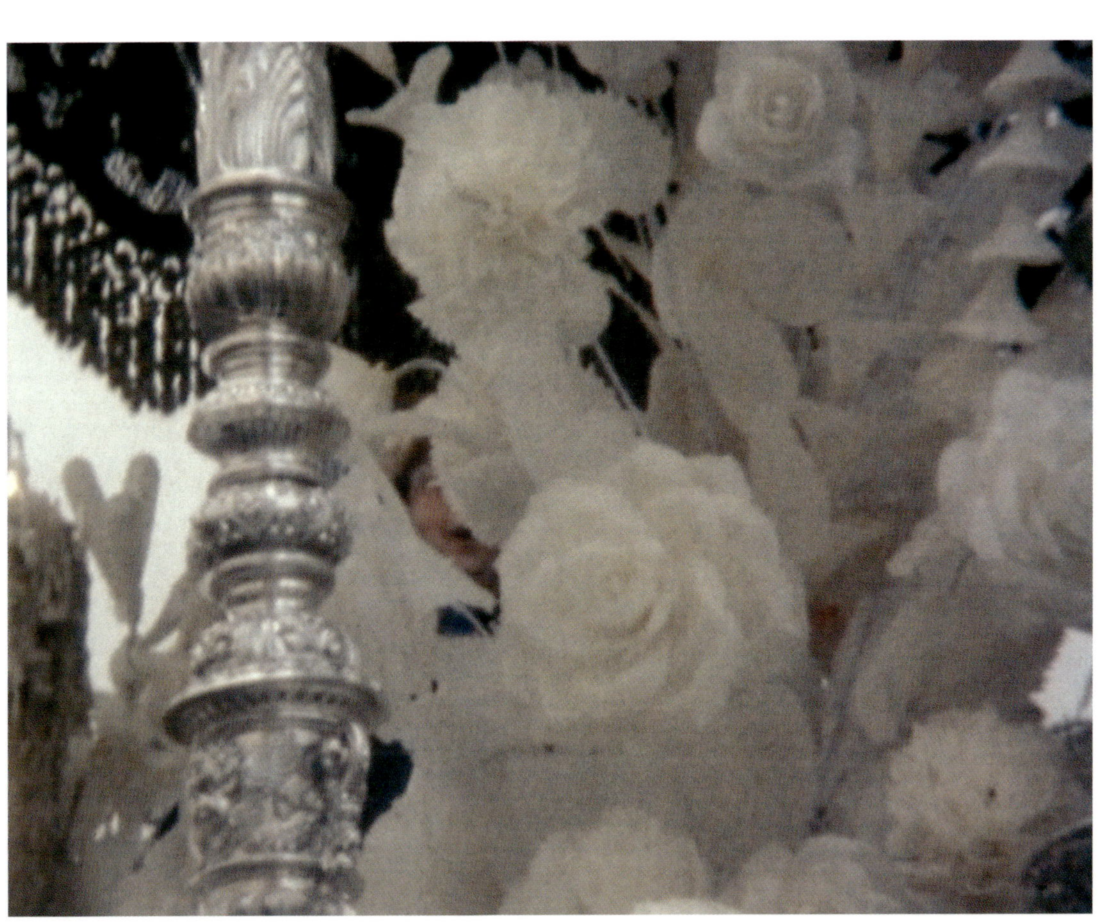

Ways of Hearing

Louise Gray

> In a frail thin voice with piercing tones, which she must have used to terrible effect in wailing lamentations at the time of the death, she sang some verses in shortlined rhyming sextets. The melody was pitched very high—it made me think of ice—and composed of a few notes, a statement of such anguish so naked as to seem impersonal. I had the feeling … of hearing something unconnected with the singer. It was as though these words, this music, were always drifting on air, a cry from afflicted humanity, but inaudible to common beings, and the singer, possessed of a finer receptivity, had the grave privilege of apprehending and transmitting them.[1]

Towards the end of *Temenos*, 1998, viewers are transported to a rough pile of stones, very much off the beaten track, in Bosnia's Medjugorje. The rocks mark the site of an apparition of the Virgin Mary. Other than the rocks, there is nothing to mark the spot as any way out of the ordinary—unless, of course, one considers the intermittent sound of bombs exploding in the far distance of Mostar. While the appearance of this makeshift monument in itself is not exceptional in a body of work where religious ritual is often used to indicate the existence of other, less discernible ritual behaviours, our sudden transportation there is, like many edits in Danino's work, unheralded.

Temenos is, among many other things, a film that institutes a poetic exploration of the nature of these sites, and Danino's editorial shifts are those of a deliberate strategy. Rather like some tectonic shift, it is a sudden transition designed to jolt and here, its significance is marked out most obviously by an accompanying change from the previous monochrome and colour film footage to video. A few moments before, we had been listening to storm noises against a background of women chanting. The filmmaker's movement into video underlines the importance of, for the spectator, a heightened way of considering the scene

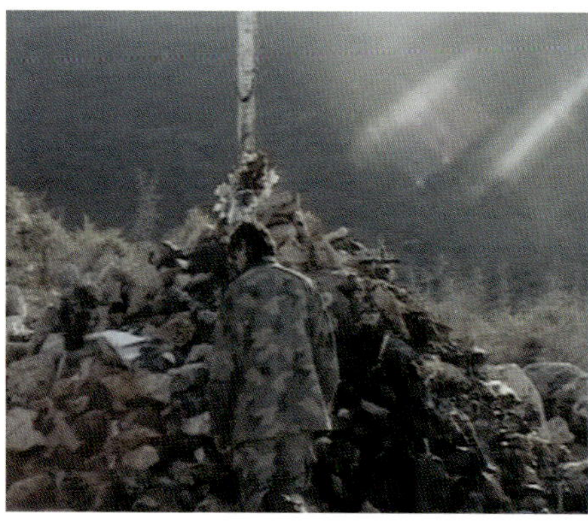

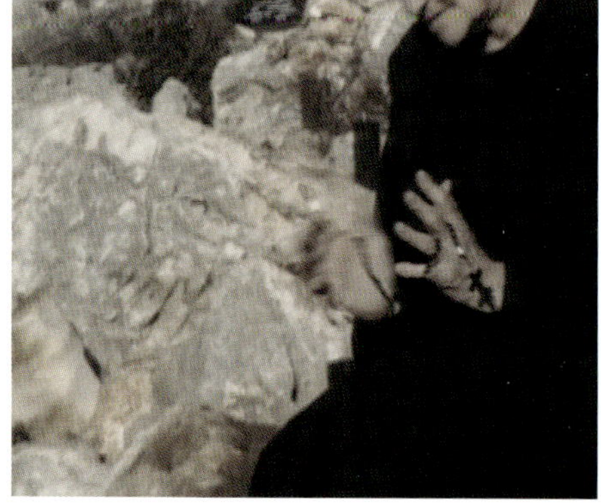

Temenos, 1998

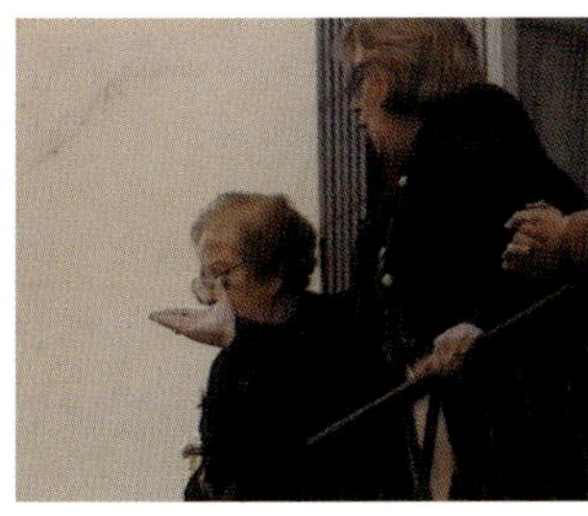
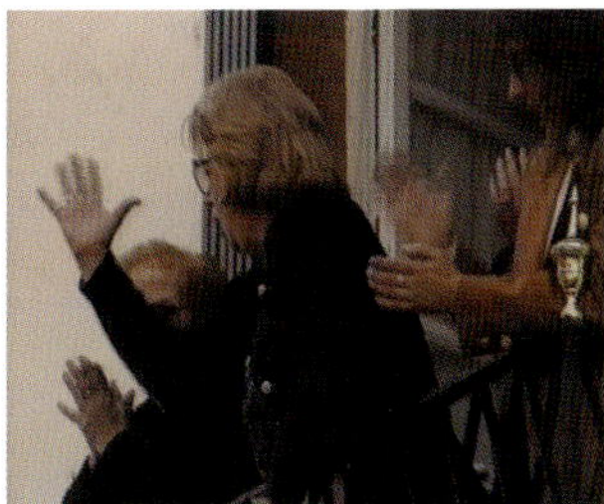
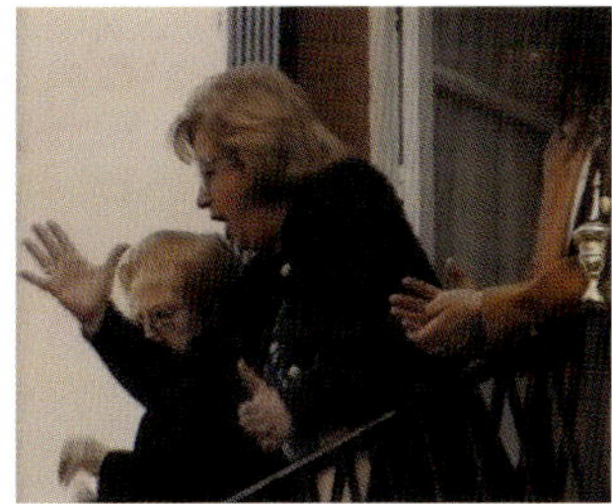

Video rushes showing the singer featured in the film soundtrack of *The Silence is Baroque*, 1997

presented. But what is it that we are seeing? The unidentified landscape is arid, and there is a stony path leading up to the site, which is stark in its simplicity: a life-sized crucifix planted in the centre of the stone pile. There is a wide shot of a standing woman and later a close-up of the same woman, sitting on a rock, clad in the black traditional for widows and matrons, whose hands move her rosary beads in slow revolutions. Close by kneels a man in combat fatigues. The accompanying soundtrack concentrates on an *a cappella* woman's song, the singer's voice operating at the limits of its capacities. Even though the song contains no discernible words, the singer's brief sobs suggest that it is a lament.

The way that the archaic underlines the contemporary is a consistent focus in Nina Danino's work. Her method—indeed, one may say it is a hallmark of her work—is to do this by means of song. She employs improvisational singers, often from the most experimental reaches of contemporary music, to access a realm of women's song, which occupies, through social structures, ritual or power, a space apart from that of men and formal control. We hear it in the improvised laments of *Stabat Mater*, 1990 and *The Silence is Baroque*, 1997. Such improvised laments, a staple of oral traditions across the Mediterranean, have always had a number of functions: that they offer a site for virtuosity, wit and a musicianship is obvious enough; that, in different circumstances (for example, that of a murder or some action of dishonour) they may urge listeners to take revenge, less so. What is most interesting is that female song has often had a supernatural link. The old woman—or voceratrice—described so thrillingly by Dorothy Carrington in her account of her travels in postwar Corsica, belongs to a similar Mediterranean tradition. Even the transmission of this power is wreathed in mystery. A few years later, Carrington relates meeting another elderly woman, a widow who had lived in Paris for forty years, and only returned home to Corsica in later life. She had no history of delivering the voceru or laments until the death of her sons and husband. "It was death herself who unleashed the gift", the widow tells Carrington. She used this gift regularly. "I speak for the dead", she continues, adding, "The priest disapproves.... He says it's a pagan custom".

The trope of the singer who has an access of sorts to other worlds, who exists, by virtue of her gift, in an unstable, changing position between established power structures, is used fully in the films of Nina Danino. Throughout her career, Danino has used vision, and its close corollary, sound, as ways of inviting us to look—and listen—beneath whatever surface imagery

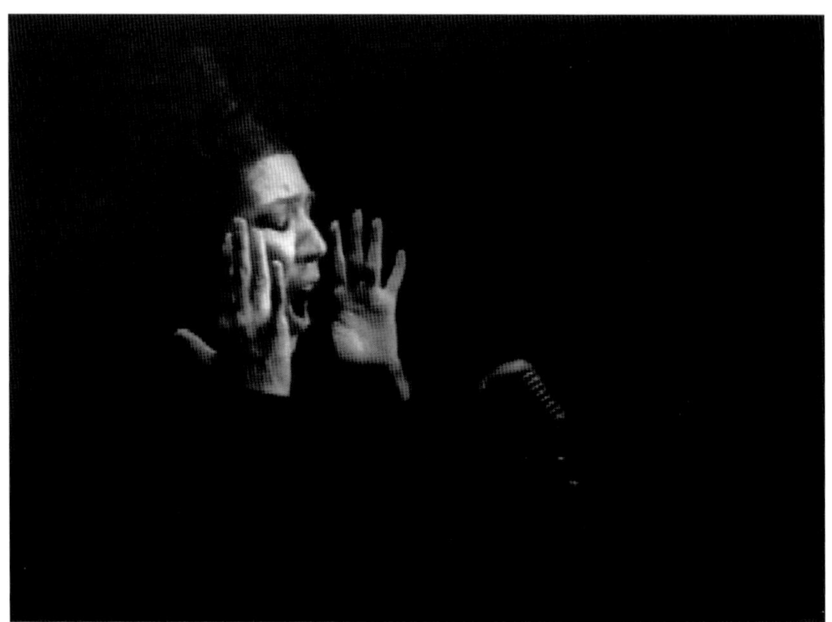

Shirin Neshat, *Turbulent*, 1998, film still

we are given. The impulse on watching *Temenos*, an elegiac film, shot in the landscapes associated with appearances of the Virgin, is to do so obliquely in order to approach the material hidden beneath the manifest content. How central this process is to Danino's work is made clear by a few lines spoken against a near-black screen in *The Silence is Baroque*, a film shot on the streets of Granada and Seville during the Easter processions in 1995. "Listen! Shhhh! Listen to the sound of the Silence that is coming," exhorts one voice, referring not only to the procession, where a heavy crucifix is processed in a silence broken only by the rhythmic thud of a solitary drum and the jangling of chains worn by penitents, but also anticipating the ritual death of Christ the next morning.

The use of sound—as dialogue, as music, and various ambient noises—has become a highly developed and coded component of filmmaking in general. In the realm of artists' films, the richness and diversity that sound offers has often been neglected in favour of the image. In this respect, Danino's work is rare. For her, sound and music can become an object in itself, but it is also used to explicitly convey that for which no image is—or ever will be—available. A point of comparison can be found in the collaborative work of two Iranians, filmmaker Shirin Neshat and composer/performer Sussan Deyhim, particularly *Turbulent*, 1998. Powerlessness and the operation of language are broad themes addressed by the use of sound. In this double-screen film installation where the two screens face each other, Neshat pitches two singers, male and female, and two distinct songs against each other. Both take place in the same auditorium, although at different times. The male singer, actor Shoja Youssefi Azari (voiced by popular singer Sharam Nazeri) is onstage before a packed audience.

He sings light, romantic songs in Farsi; his all-male audience enjoy themselves. It is a very different case with an enrobed Deyhim. Looming on the screen opposite, she is quite alone and her song—from its first gut-level growlings to its ululating arpeggios—is wordless, sensual and terrifying. Is it an incantation or a love song? Neither Neshat or Deyhim tell us, and that refusal certainly informs much of the film's power.

Danino's films explore similar emotional and social disjunctures through the subtle use of multi-layered soundtracks and voice overs. There are the disorganised cadences of the elemental and the accidental echoing through the live street sounds of *The Silence is Baroque* or the far-off bombs heard in *Temenos*. In *"Now I am yours"*, the New York composer and performer Shelley Hirsch uses her voice and various electronic processes to produce wailing, speaking in tongues, incantations, death rattles, hissing sounds, the feeling of extreme heat and spoken fragments. Hirsch has a substantial role in *Temenos*, where she is joined by the Tuvan-born, Vienna-based performer and composer Sainkho Namchylak. Practising throat, or overtone singing, in which a single singer can produce two or three voices simultaneously, Namchylak brings a traditional method to contemporary ends. Both singers put improvisation at the heart of their composition, both in their own projects and those with Danino. While Hirsch's techniques of vocal production differ from Namchylak in as much as she is based firmly within a Western experimental tradition, the result are similar in an important respect: an access to palates of colour, microtonal ranges and timbres unreachable to most singers. These are the sounds of the human voice at the limits of its production. In a more

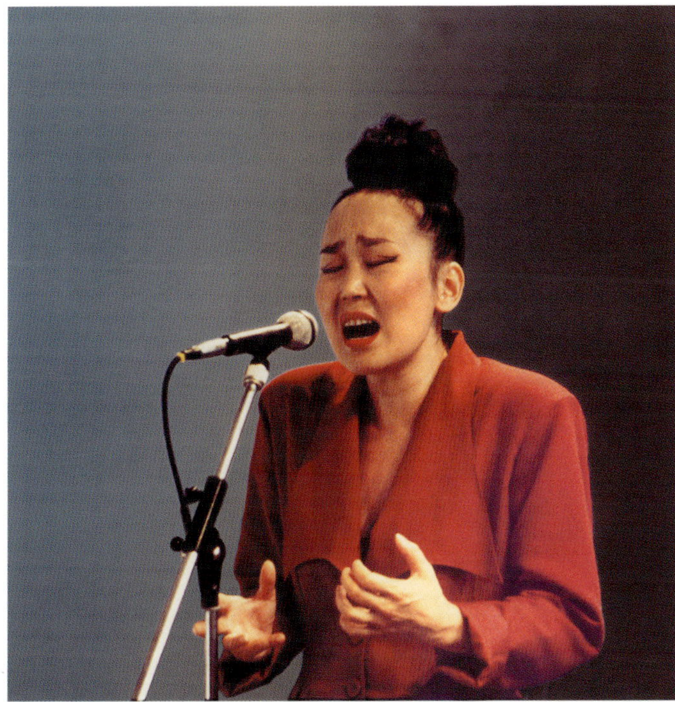

Sainkho Namchylak

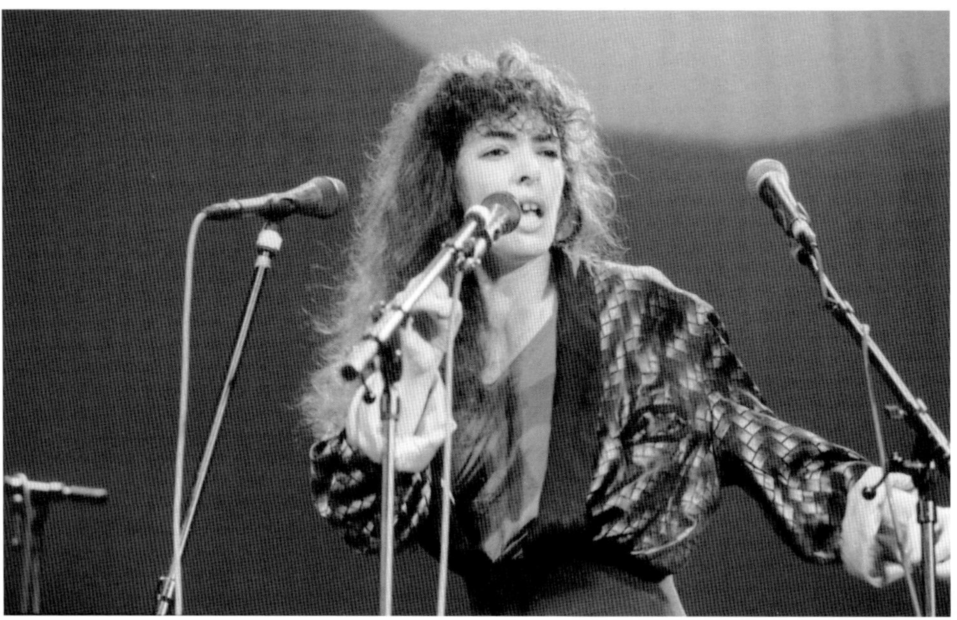

Shelley Hirsch

formal area, there are also spoken voice overs, folkloric song and other music. The combination of these elements means that we are often not sure what it is that we are hearing.

Danino has set up an extraordinary dynamic that can—as it very much does in *Temenos*—carry the viewer/listener through. The difference between recognition and its counterpart is not an absolute one, it is rather part of an overarching scheme to draw our eyes and ears to which can neither be seen nor heard. By way of a series of subtle undercurrents, her works set up a continual tension between multiple sets of oppositions: the sacred against the profane; the masculine and the feminine; the ritual text against the spontaneous babble, organisation against its counterpart. Yet it is a further opposition—the one suggested in the root of the Greek noun 'temenos' itself—that provides a means to consider Danino's wider interest. Glossed in the film's promotional material as a "ritual precinct, a sacred place, a place apart", *Temenos* is indeed all these things, but—to continue a linguistic analogy—Danino consistently focuses not only on the thing-that-is-set-apart, but the repetitive, continuing act of the setting apart. (In fact, temnein, the infinitive of the verb that provides us with the noun, refers to severance, to cutting off.) For Danino, it is a fundamental separation whose resonance, ritualised in both sound and vision, draws attention to the unseen and unheard, the submerged themes of her works.

The soundtracks to Danino's films can be experienced as the performance of separation: one type of music separated from another; one type of vocalising from another.[2] In the first instance, musical performance may be located in the distance between the formality of sacred liturgical music and that of the popular devotional song. With particular reference to *Stabat Mater, "Now I am yours"* and *The Silence is Baroque,* these two musics—existing in tandem as almost a conceptual conflict—form a rich vein of reference. It is in these films that we are introduced to music (and its accompanying sounds) drawn from the filmmaker's own childhood and cultural influences from the south of Spain; the unmitigatingly amateur brass bands accompanying the religious processions; the street noises and their complex ambient noises; fragments of untranslated languages; the background voices of the crowd; and the archaic forms of the improvised and unaccompanied saeta which is a religious song of lament sung by men and women. In *Stabat Mater,* it is sung by a woman's voice, Elena Danino, the filmmaker's mother.

If Danino's use of music (and it is nearly always vocal music; instruments have an infinitesimal presence) is to construct associative pathways in order to appropriate certain ideas, then this process is accentuated by her use of vocals themselves. An important focus for *Temenos,* in particular, is the voices of Shelley Hirsch and Sainkho Namchylak, two singers renowned for the vocal techniques that accentuate the physical capacity of the voice and the body's resonating spaces. Using throat-singing (where the sound is placed far back on the vocal chords) and, in Namchylak's example, overtone singing, theirs are uncanny, powerful voices in which improvisational work is key to their strength. Their experimental vocals are also a marked contrast to the film's other featured voice, that of soprano Catherine Bott, a singer with a well-founded reputation in early music and Baroque repertoire. To this, Danino now adds language, or more precisely, its absence. It is a marked severance.

Throughout the history of the musical voice, wordless singing has been a common theme. Vocalisation—singing on a vowel—is a standard exercise in the training of classical singers, and also a feature of pre-eighteenth century choral music; it has a near-counterpart in solfège, where the voice alights on the eight notes of the tonic sol-fa. Operatic singers limbering up to perform will warm up using an array of sounds (sometimes just vowels and diphthongs) that stretch the palate and vocal chords. Outside of the academy, the wordless song is most readily associated with humming or lullabies, in other words, performances made for intimate settings and highly specific audiences. In *Temenos,* voice (and its wordless song) comes into its own precisely because it is unburdened with language. It takes on elemental, sometimes supernatural, qualities. Namchylak is credited as the source for all sounds relating to nature, the Virgin and vocal landscapes. She affords the noises for spring winds and bitter weeping, for bees, winds and forgetting. Hirsch's contribution is no less dramatic. Drawing on her vocal techniques of building up fluid characters, storytelling, collage-like ranges of emotion and using verbal and non-verbal languages, Hirsch is the vocaliser for a panoply of various mystical states and visionaries. It is important to stress that Namchylak is not 'playing' the Virgin in any conventional way, nor is Hirsch assuming the role of a visionary who she is giving expression to. The dynamic of their vocal performances comes from the fact that neither singer represents or presents any one thing. Flux, and the separation between states, is what is highlighted here. One might say that the voices are the expressions of dualities that constitute larger themes in Danino's work. The voices inhabit that space in between.

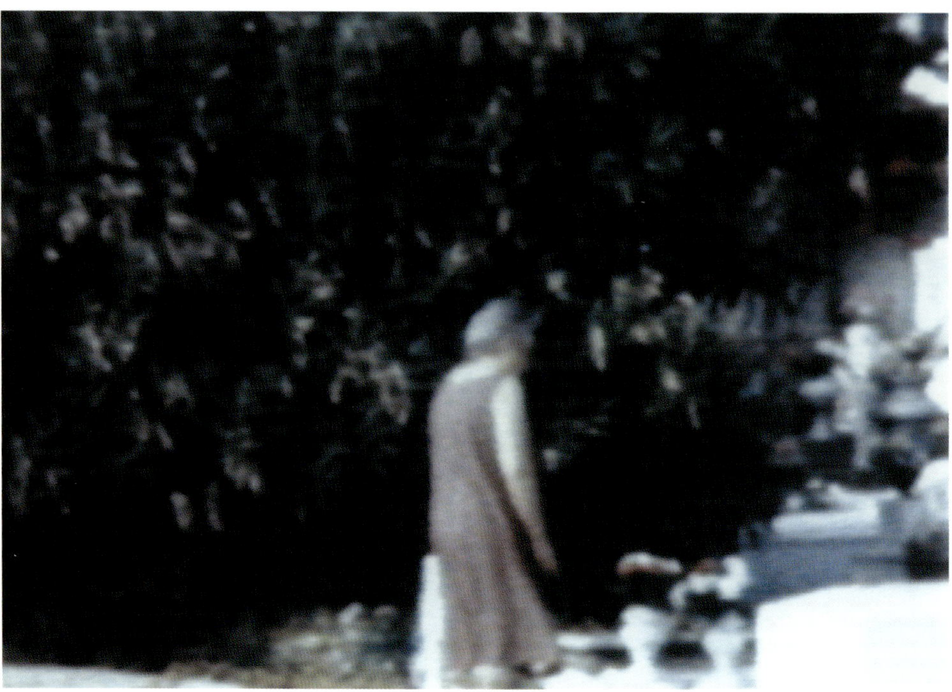

Temenos, 1998

The significance of Danino's use of experimental singers in *Temenos*, whose work is often pitched outside systematic language, is crucial. Performance artist and composer Diamanda Galás, some of whose extant recordings Danino uses in *"Now I am yours"* also falls into this category. Although their vocal work eschews verbal, their vocalisings have a deliberation about them: they do not fall into the categories of glossolalia or the aleatoric where sounds are thrown up by chance operation. On the contrary, the singers have been precisely directed as to the requirements of each scene and mood.

This is important as, shorn of the standard narrative tool of organised language, a precision is needed if the voices are to succeed in conveying atmospheric and emotional mood. In *Temenos*, a film that continually confronts the presence of absence, the central figure—that of the Virgin—is one that significantly never appears, although she is heard via Namchylak's own compositions. Danino imagines the Virgin not as a person, but as an abstract, mobile territory defined by an ambivalence. Sometimes, she is characterised by a comforting acoustic; at other times, there is something altogether more terrifying about her. "Imagine seven places interconnected through image and sound", runs Danino's directions given to Namchylak as a libretto or score to help the singer to compose a palate of sound that could express landscapes, natural phenomena and the suggestion of the Virgin. "Each place is sacred. Each has a different geography."

And also its own sound world. Recording in London, Sainkho Namchylak began to sketch, and then populate, her landscapes. She details a stony place; a cold white landscape; a grotto; a hollow. To this were added insects, animals, winds and, finally, the Virgin herself, the latter generated in a series of houwas or overtone exercises she had learned while studying in Tuva. Listening to the music with or without the visual element, *Temenos* is an intensely concentrated soundtrack. Hyperventilation sounds could be footsteps, laboured breathing, or a presence close by. Does a death rattle generated by Namchylak signify a demonic presence or some social trauma? We are never sure. The film wants us to develop an acuity of listening, but it offers up no answers. In the seventh section, titled "The Virgin's Weeping", a three-and-a-half-minute passage gives us many sounds: sweeping, brushing sounds and some pitch exercises from Namchylak; visionary voices from Hirsch and, tantalisingly, a planctus sung by Catherine Bott. Other grainy voices of visionaries interviewed for the film are heard briefly on an imperfectly tuned radio: the impression is of fast, subtle change and fragility.

Similarly so with Shelley Hirsch, whom Danino had first encountered in 1990 while looking for a possible vocalist for *"Now I am yours"* who was not "constricted within the codes of drama and acting".[3] In the dynamic, unstylised flights of Hirsch's solo work—a combination of raw voice and electronic treatments—she found a perfect collaborator. *"Now I am yours"* required, says Danino, a "re-enactment of the excess of overflowing language into fragmentation and musicality". We hear this surge of emotion on the soundtrack for *"Now I am yours"* where a series of motifs—naturalistic and electronic—bind the film together, and even more so on *Temenos* where Hirsch's voice performs the parts of the visionaries and their states. These parts are imagined much more in terms of characters: some are children, others are on the verge of madness, and the spectrum of relationships veers from extreme gentleness to gut-wrenching rants and sobbings. The effect is to give voice to some unseen drama: there are human histories hidden beneath the surface of each landscape and each sound and yet neither is attached to the other. Gathered together, the improvisations produce a feeling of free-floating emotion. As Gianmarco del Re writes, "the carefully orchestrated soundtrack adds a metaphysical dimension, creating a sense of location which is not purely spatial/physical".[4]

This metaphysical landscape is a place for projections; about memory, about history, about fundamental separations. *Temenos*, like Danino's other works, is not a film seeking some truth about religious experience: the visits to the apparitional sites are, the filmmaker says, a pretext, a surface to develop a narrative. Yet if there is meaning, which is to say, narrative, in the apparent formlessness of Hirsch and Namchylak's songs, what is it, and where is it? There may be a temptation to find in the singers' wordless songs a suggestion of the glossolalia or preverbal utterances of inter alia, babies, hysterics and certain mystical states. (Glossolalia is associated with the phenomenon of speaking in tongues.) Discussing female performance in the world of rock music in their 1995 book, *The Sex Revolts*, authors Simon Reynolds and Joy Press link glossolalia into an expansive (and female) sexuality—an unboundaried "cosmic libido"—based on Hélène Cixous' theories around *l'écriture feminine*.[5] For Cixous, feminine writing (a description of the product itself, not the person who authors it) is a strategy to subvert the strict binary codes of what Jacques Lacan theorised as the

Symbolic order, a heterogeneous realm where language and absence dominates. In the case of Danino's soundtracks, it is perhaps more helpful to think of *l'écriture feminine* as that which produces a rupture from the context that surrounds it, a transformative force that gives voice to something beyond representation. If this is so, then it is a drive that resonates throughout Danino's films, as each film becomes an attempt to speak something that is beyond the grasp or scope of language. So the singers sing and don't sing, they speak and don't speak. Even the voice over to *Temenos*, spoken by Danino, is reported speech. The implication is, once again, of our distance from experience and power. Danino's singers raise the wordless question. What is the thing that cannot be spoken, or, indeed, glimpsed?

As Jean Matthee points out in her essay on Nina Danino's work, "language fails, always fails, must inevitably fail".[6] Danino's films may be too linguistically aware to attempt the folly of evoking some pre-Saussaurian, pre-lapsarian paradise where separation has yet to be made, but the music she chooses makes us painfully aware of what has been lost.

Notes

1 Carrington, Dorothy, *Granite Island: A Portrait of Corsica*, [1971], Harmondsworth: Penguin, 1984.

2 It is important to stress that all Nina Danino's soundtracks are very much integral components of the films in which they feature, and, although a CD of the *Temenos* soundtrack was released by Leo Records in 2000, they are not conceived as stand-alone soundtracks.

3 Danino, Nina, "Sound Journey", notes to the author, 2004.

4 del Re, Gianmarco, "Cinema and the Sublime", *Contemporary Visual Arts*, issue 19, summer 1998, pp. 46-47.

5 Reynolds, Simon and Joy Press, *The Sex Revolts*, London: Serpent's Tail, 1995.

6 Matthee, Jean, "On Wounds, Artificial Flowers, Orifices and the Infinite: A Response to the Films of Nina Danino", reprinted in *The Undercut Reader*, Nina Danino and Michael Mazière eds., London: Wallflower Press, 2003. p. 86.

Opposite: *Temenos*, 1998

Stabat Mater 1990

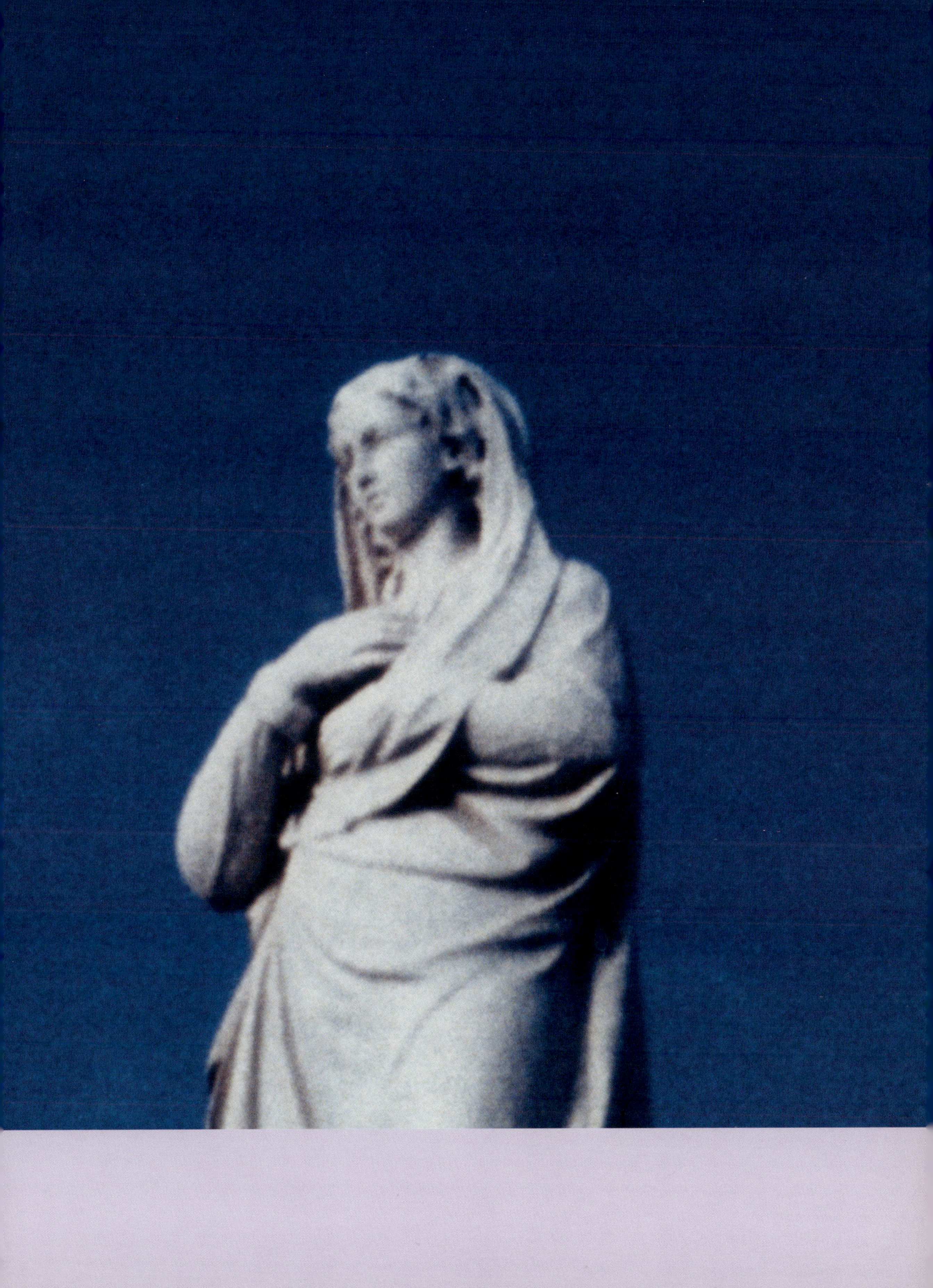

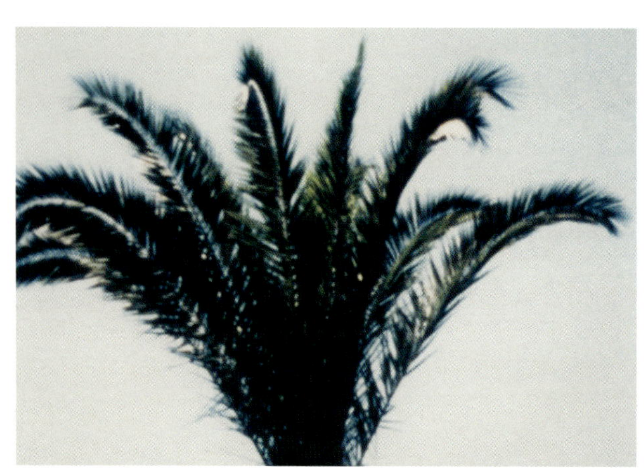

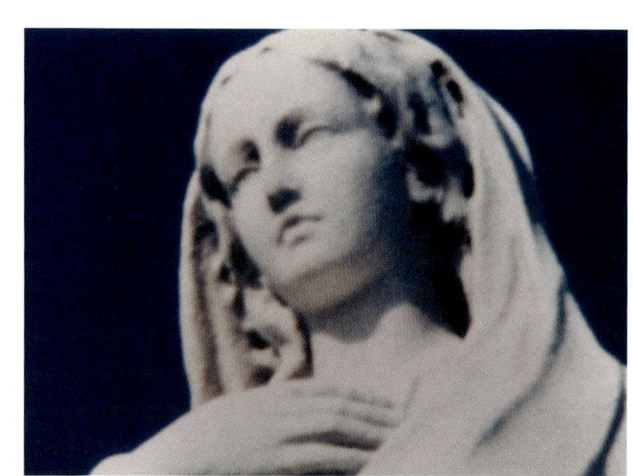

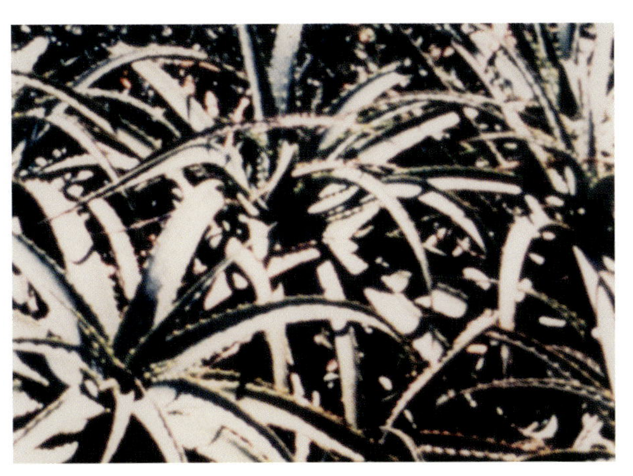

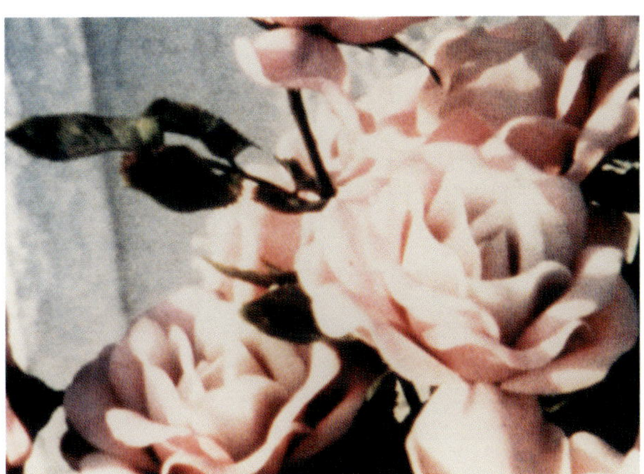

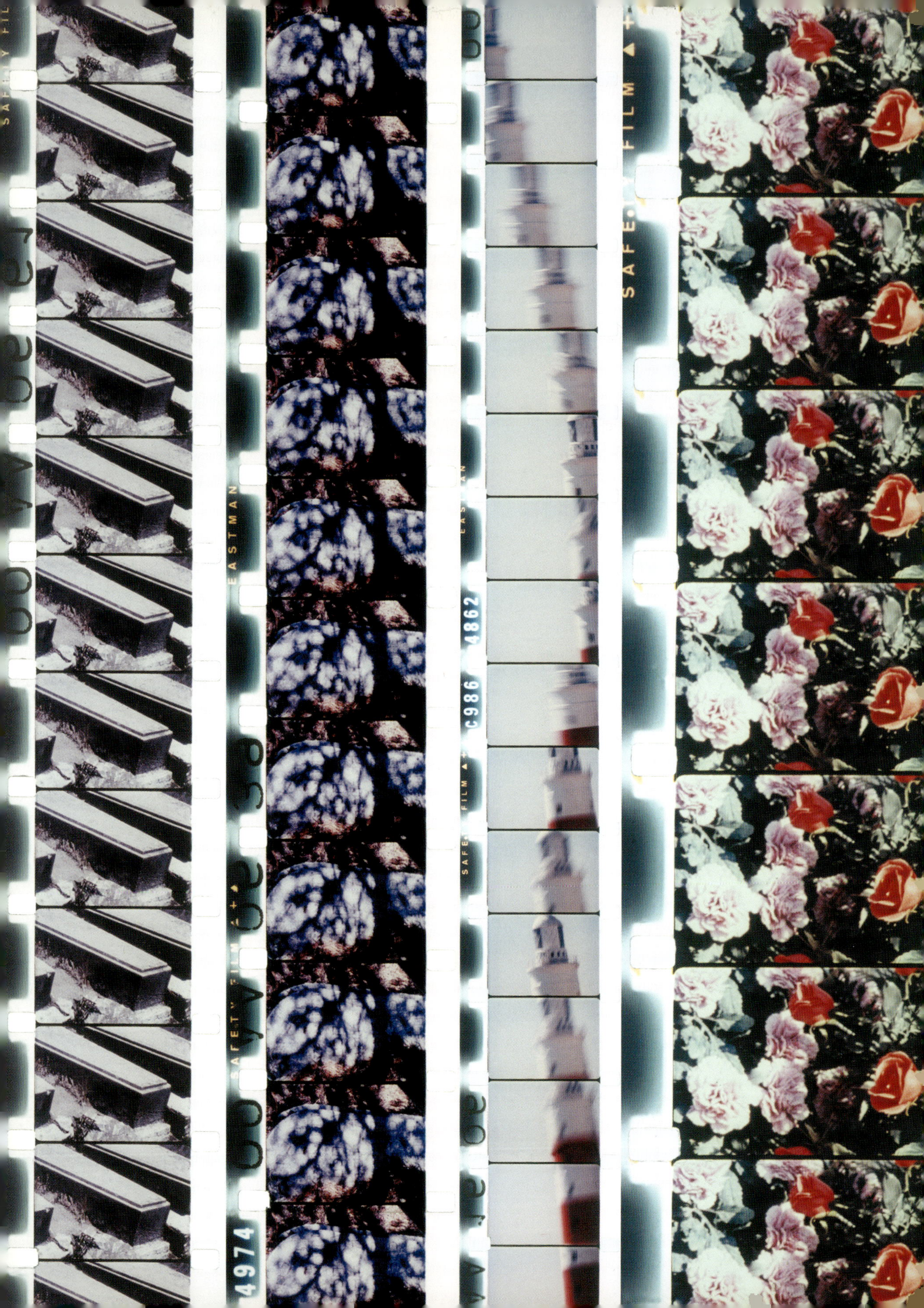
EASTMAN
SAFETY FILM
4974
C986
4862
SAFETY FILM
EASTMAN
SAFE. FILM

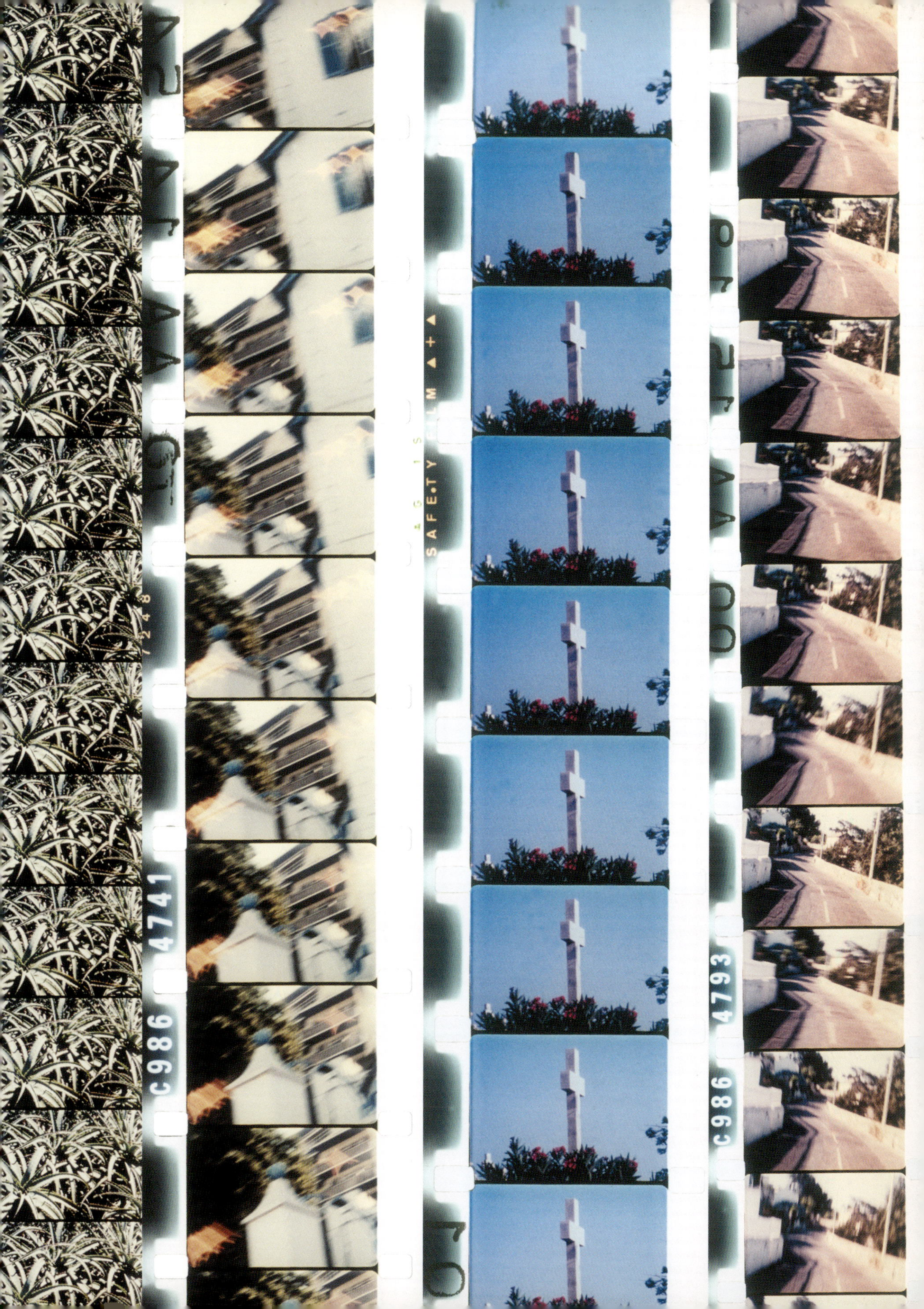

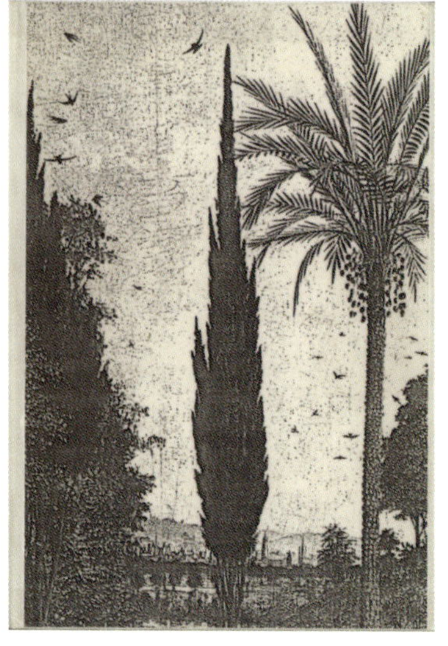

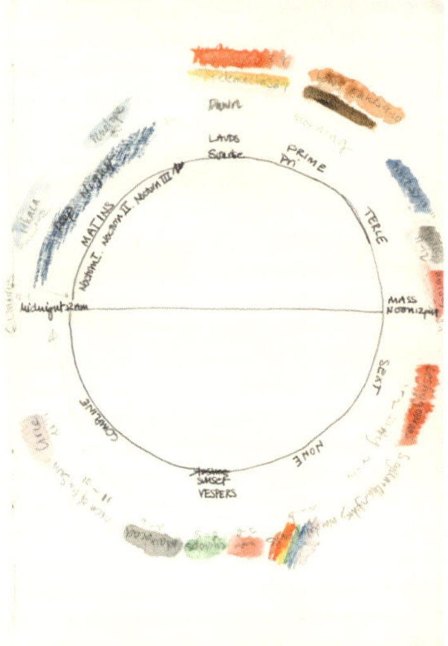

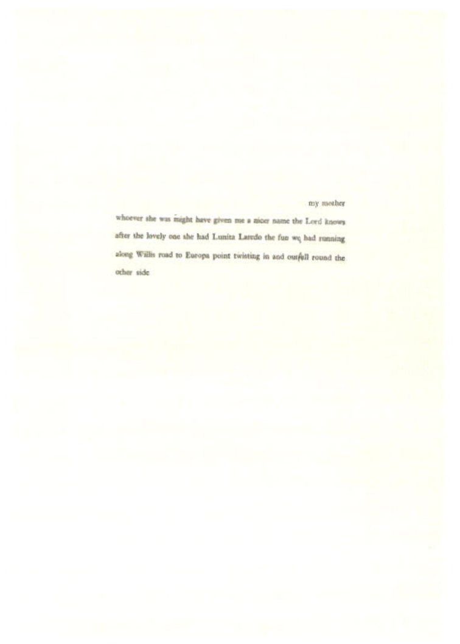

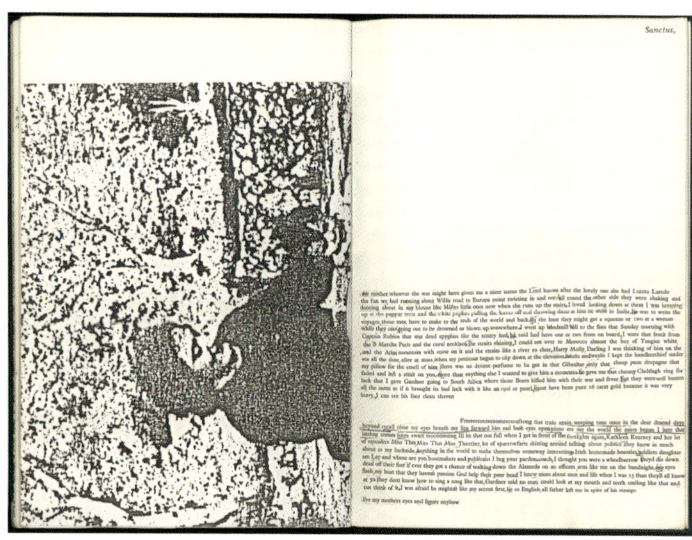

The voice in each woman, moreover, is not only her own, but springs from the deepest layers of her psyche: her own speech becomes the echo of the primeval *song* she once heard, the voice the incarnation of the 'first voice of love which all women preserve alive . . . in each woman sings the first nameless love' (JN, 172).

Stabat Mater Book, 1989

Handmade book containing texts, photocopies of paintings and photographs, as well as a colour diagram combining the prayer cycle of the Office Hours and the cycle of *Ulysses*. The book is a structure, treatment and script for a film in two parts. The second part, represented by the last third of the book, became *Stabat Mater*.

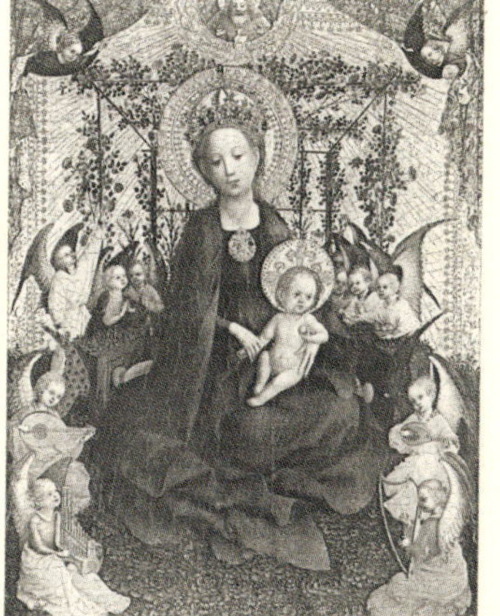

Nocturn III:

light guitar, where poetry is in the air, the blue sea and the moon shining so beautifully coming back on the nightboat from Tarifa, the lighthouse at Europa point the guitar that fellow played was so expressive, will I never go back there again, all new faces, two glancing eyes a lattice hid, Ill sing that for him theyre my eyes, if hes anything of a poet, two eyes as darkly bright as loves own star, arent those beautiful words as loves young star

singing the second verse first the old love is the new, was one of his so sweetly sang, the maiden on the hawthorn bough, he was always on for flirty-fying too when I sang Maritana with him at Freddy Mayers private opera he had a delicious glorious voice Phœbe dearest goodbye sweet- heart he always sang it not like Bartell dArcy sweet tart goodbye, of course he had the gift of the voice so there was no art in it all over you like a warm showerbath, O Maritana wildwood flower we sang splendidly though it was a bit too high for my register even transposed

its a lovely hour, so silent

I used to love coming home after dances

the air of the night

they have friends, they can talk to, weve none

either he wants what he wont get, or its some woman ready to stick her knife

in you.

I hate that in women, no wonder they treat us the way they do

we are a dreadful lot of bitches

I suppose its all the

troubles we have makes us so snappy

Im not like that

he could easy have slept in there on the sofa in the other room.

I suppose he was as shy as a boy, he being so young hardly 20 of me in the next room

hed have heard me on the chamber.

arrah what harm

Dedalus,

I wonder,

its like those names in Gibraltar

Delapaz

Delagracia

they had the devils queer names there

father Vial plana of Santa Maria, that gave me the rosary,

Rosales y OReilly in the Calle las Siete Revueltas,

and Pisimbo and Mrs Opisso in Governor street,

O what a name Id go and drown myself in the first river if I had a name like her

O my and all the bits of streets

Paradise ramp and

Bedlam ramp and

Rodgers ramp and

Crutchetts ramp and

the devils gap steps

well small blame to me if I am a harumscarum, I know I am a bit

Agnus Dei,

a quarter after, what an unearthly hour, I suppose theyre just getting up in China now, well soon have the nuns ringing the angelus theyve nobody coming in to spoil their sleep except an odd priest or two for his night office the alarmclock next door at cockshout clattering the brains out of itself, let me see if I can doze off 1 2 3 4 5 what kind of flowers are those they invented like the stars

a nice plant for the middle of the table, Id get that cheaper in wait wheres this, I saw them not long ago, I love flowers, Id love to have the whole place swimming in roses God of heaven theres nothing like nature the wild mountains then the sea and the waves rushing then the beautiful country with fields of oats and wheat and all kinds of things and all the fine cattle going about that would do your heart good to see rivers and lakes and flowers all sorts of shapes and smells and colours springing up even out of the ditches primroses and violets nature it is as for them saying theres no God I wouldnt give a snap of my two fingers for all their learning why dont they go and create something I often asked him atheists or whatever they call themselves go and wash the cobbles off themselves first then they go howling for the priest and they dying and why why because theyre afraid of hell on account of their bad conscience ah yes I know them well who was the first person in the universe before there was anybody that made it all who ah that they dont know neither do I so there you are they might as well try to stop the sun from rising tomorrow the sun shines for you he said yes he said I was a flower of the mountain yes so we are flowers all a womans body yes that was one true thing he said in his life and the sun shines for you today yes that was why I liked him because I saw he understood or felt what a woman is and I knew I could always get round him and I gave him all the pleasure I could leading him on till he asked me to say yes and I wouldnt answer first only looked out over the sea and the sky I was thinking of so many things he didnt know of

I was thinking of so many things he didnt know of Mulvey and Mr Stanhope and Hester and father and old captain Groves and the sailors playing all birds fly and I say stoop and washing up dishes they called it on the pier and the sentry in front of the governors house with the thing round his white helmet poor devil half roasted and the Spanish girls laughing in their shawls and their tall combs and the auctions in the morning the Greeks and the jews and the Arabs and the devil knows who else from all the ends of Europe and Duke street and the fowl market all clucking outside Larby Sharons and the poor donkeys slipping half asleep and the vague fellows in the cloaks asleep in the shade on the steps and the big wheels of the carts of the bulls and the old castle thousands of years old yes and those handsome Moors all in white and turbans like kings asking you to sit down in their little bit of a shop and Ronda with the old windows of the posadas glancing eyes a lattice hid for her lover to kiss the iron and the wineshops half open at night and the castanets and the night we missed the boat at Algeciras the watchman going about serene with his lamp and O that awful deepdown torrent O and the sea the sea crimson sometimes like fire and the glorious sunsets and the figtrees in the Alameda gardens yes and all the queer little streets and pink and blue and yellow houses and the rosegardens and the jessamine and geraniums and cactuses and Gibraltar as a girl where I was a Flower of the mountain yes when I put the rose in my hair like the Andalusian girls used or shall I wear a red yes and how he kissed me under the Moorish wall and I thought well as well him as another and then I asked him with my eyes to ask again yes and then he asked me would I yes to say yes my mountain flower and first I put my arms around him yes and drew him down to me so he could feel my breasts all perfume yes and his heart was going like mad and yes I said yes I will Yes,

Mulvey and Mr Stanhope and Hester and my mother whoever she was and the sailors playing all birds fly and I say stoop and washing up dishes they called it on the pier and the sentry in front of the governors house with the thing round his white helmet poor devil half roasted and the Spanish girls laughing in their shawls and their tall combs and the auctions in the morning the Greeks and the jews and the Arabs and the devil knows who else from all the ends of Europe and Duke street and the fowl market all clucking outside Larby Sharons and the poor donkeys slipping half asleep and the vague fellows in the cloaks asleep in the shade on the steps and the big wheels of the carts of the bulls and the old castle thousands of years old yes and those handsome Moors all in white and turbans like kings asking you to sit down in their little bit of a shop and Ronda with the old windows of the posadas glancing eyes a lattice hid for her lover to kiss the iron and the wineshops half open at night and the castanets and the night we missed the boat at Algeciras the watchman going about serene with his lamp and O that awful deepdown torrent O and the sea the sea crimson sometimes like fire and the glorious sunsets and the figtrees in the Alameda gardens yes and all the queer little streets and pink and blue and yellow houses and the rosegardens and the jessamine and geraniums and cactuses and Gibraltar as a girl where I was a Flower of the mountain yes when I put the rose in my hair like the Andalusian girls used or shall I wear a red yes and my mother whoever she was yes and the fun we had running to Europa point twisting in and out all round the other side yes and she kissed me would I yes to say her mountain flower and first I put my arms around her yes and drew her to me Yes, and her breasts all perfume yes and my heart was going like mad and yes I said yes I will Yes.

The voice is the mother and the mother's body:

Communion

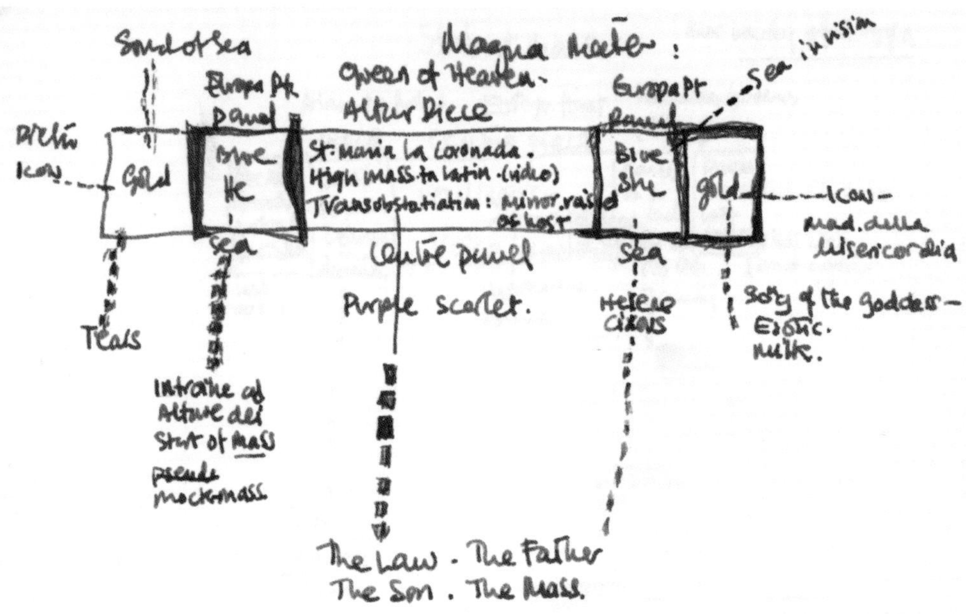

Stabat Mater
Our Lady of Europa.
Alameda Gardens Pillar
Europa Point Centre piece
Alameda Gardens Pillar
voice woman
lost mother
Canto to mute Dolorosa death
nonlinear - disrupted speech
Voice monologue
Woman.
Erotic
Star of the sea.
Beauty.
Poem
voice naked with milk
She has been found again.
deep lament
deep laments

Stabat Mater, 1990

Notebooks with diagrams of film structure

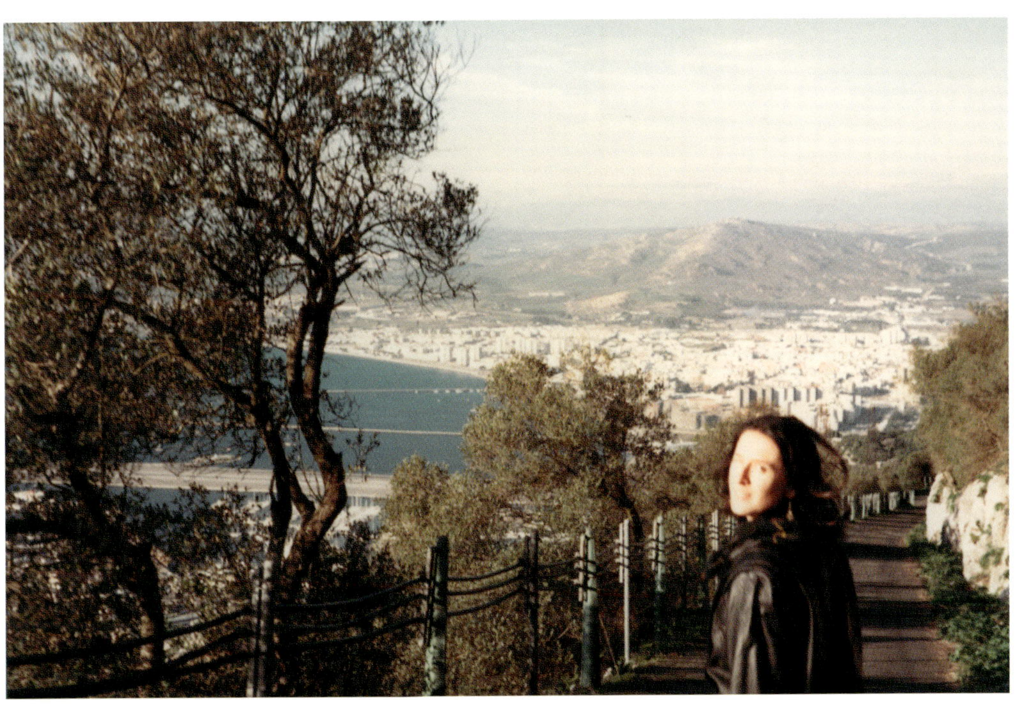

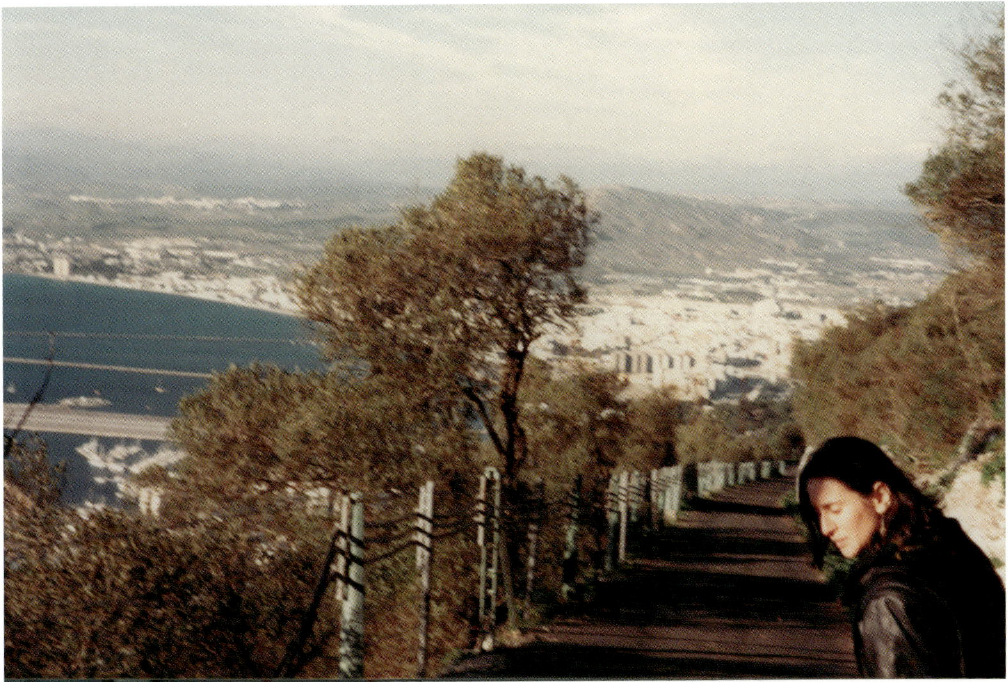

Stabat Mater, 1990

Photographs of the filmmaker on location

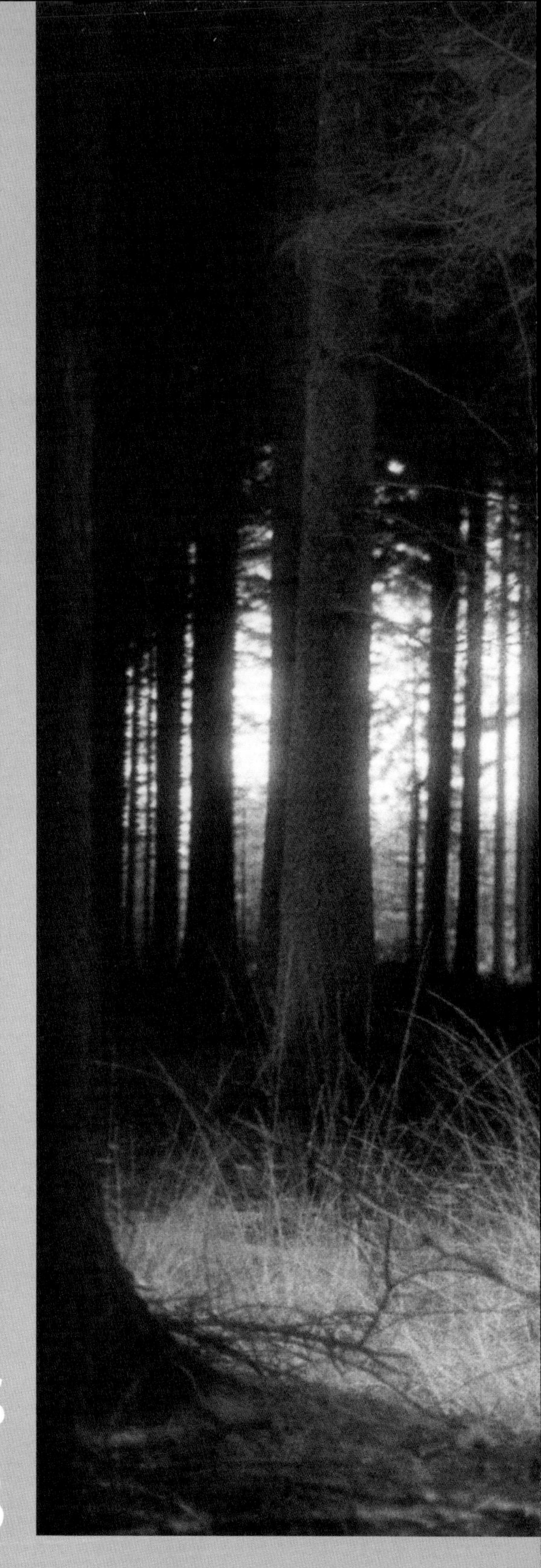

Temenos 1998

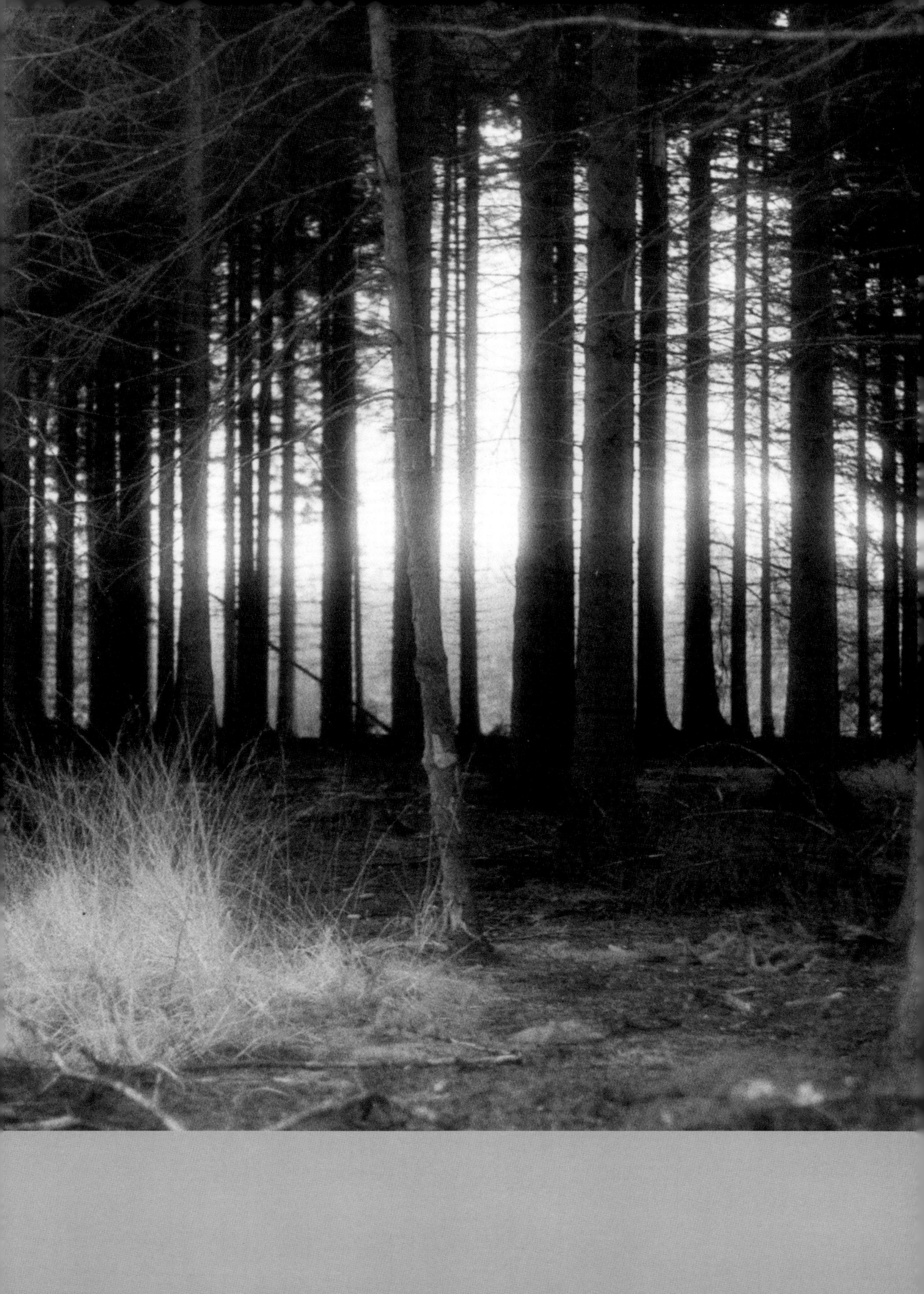

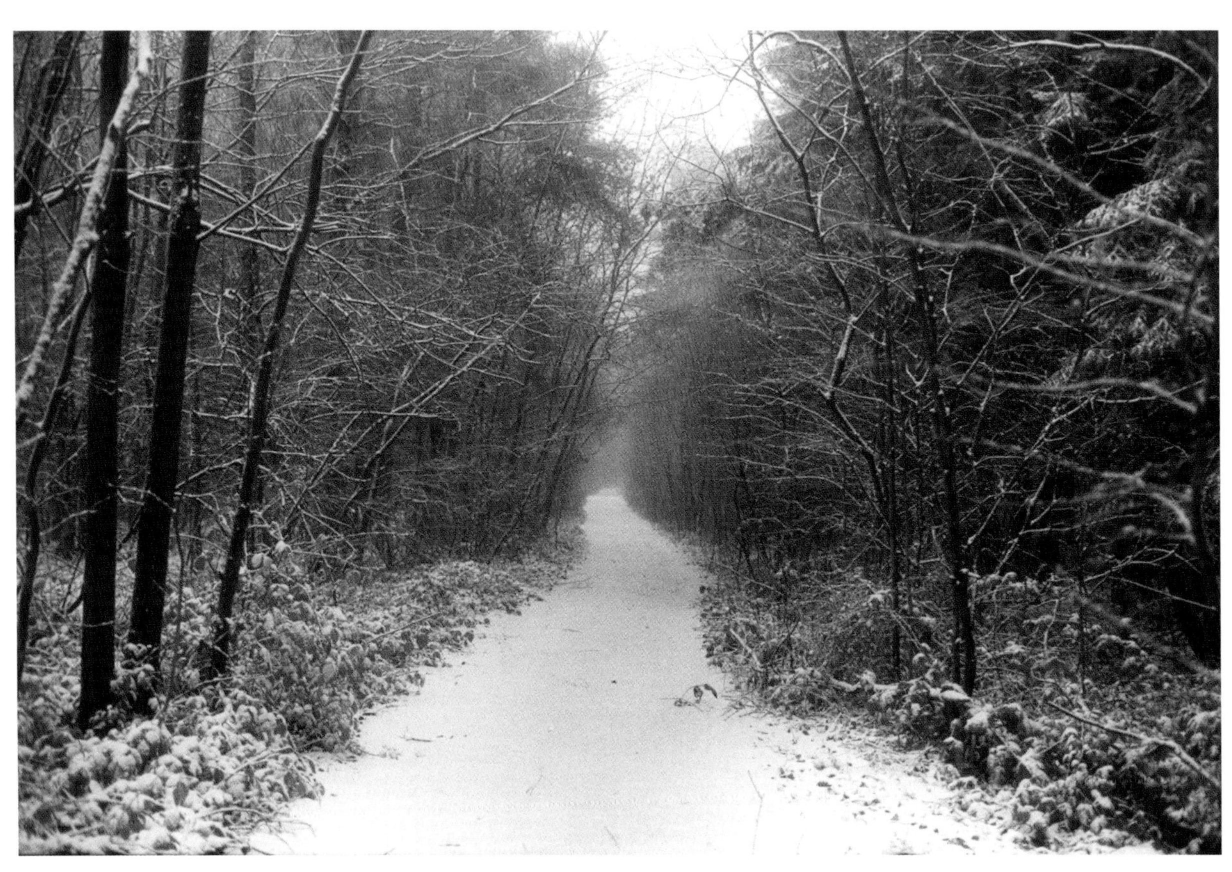

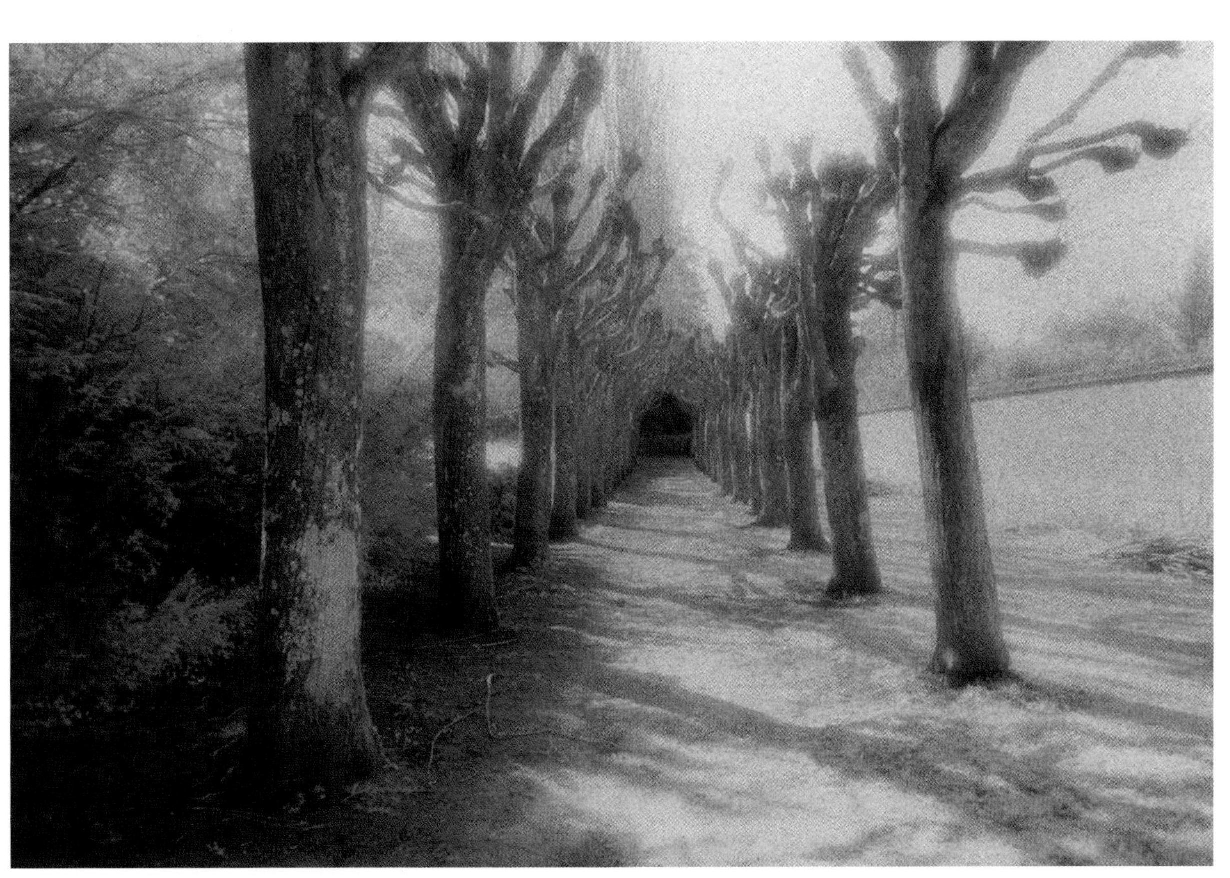

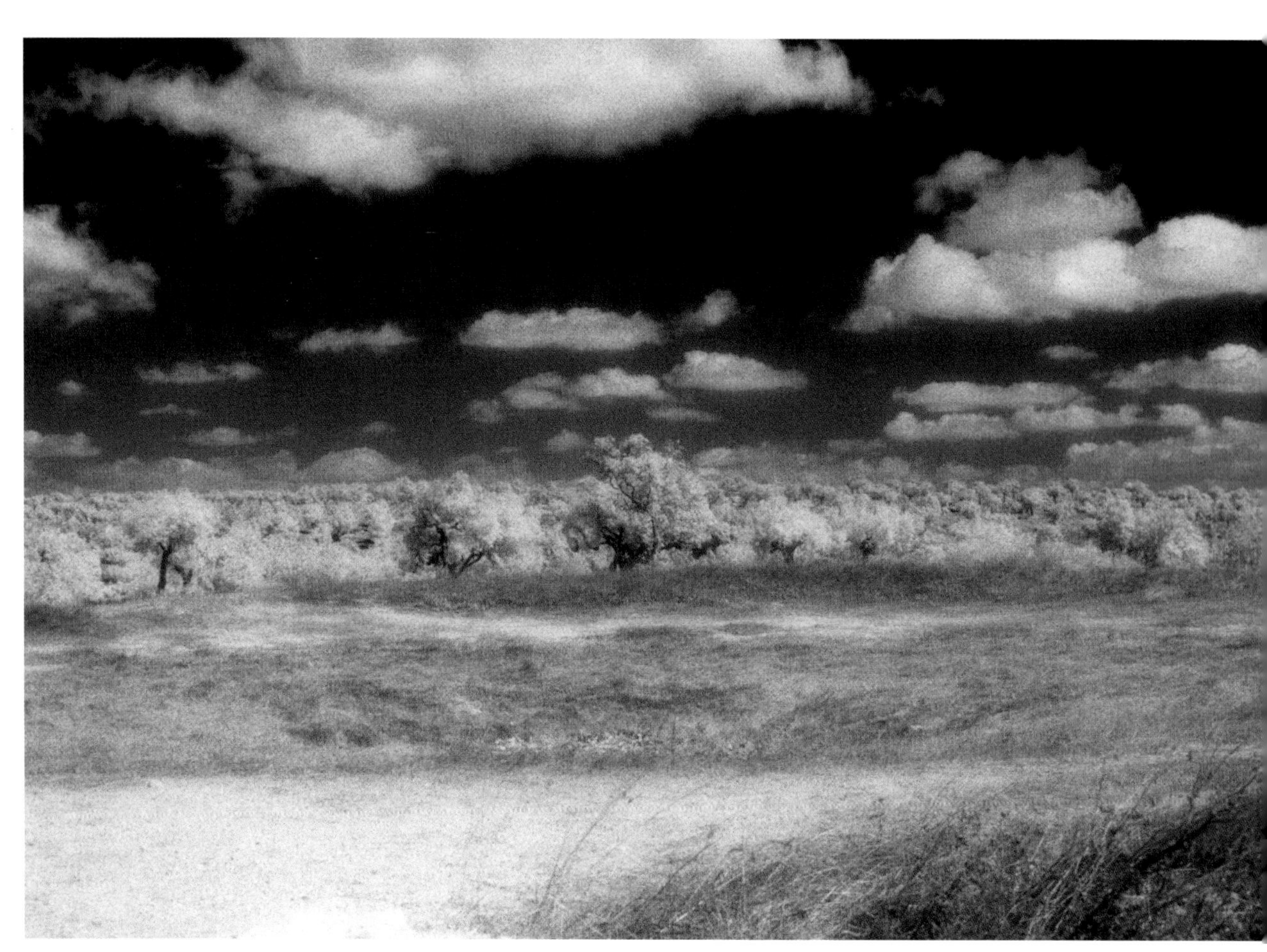

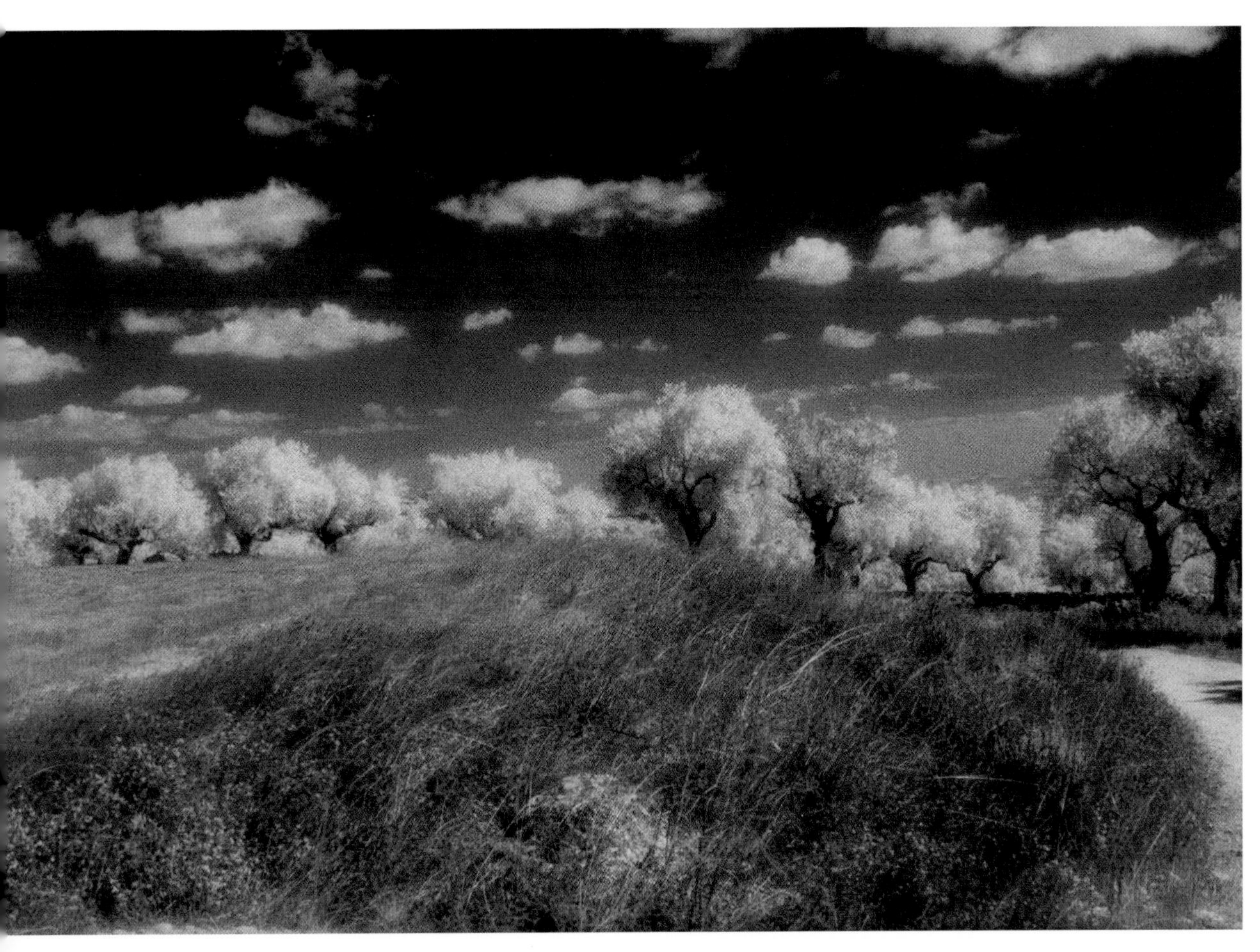

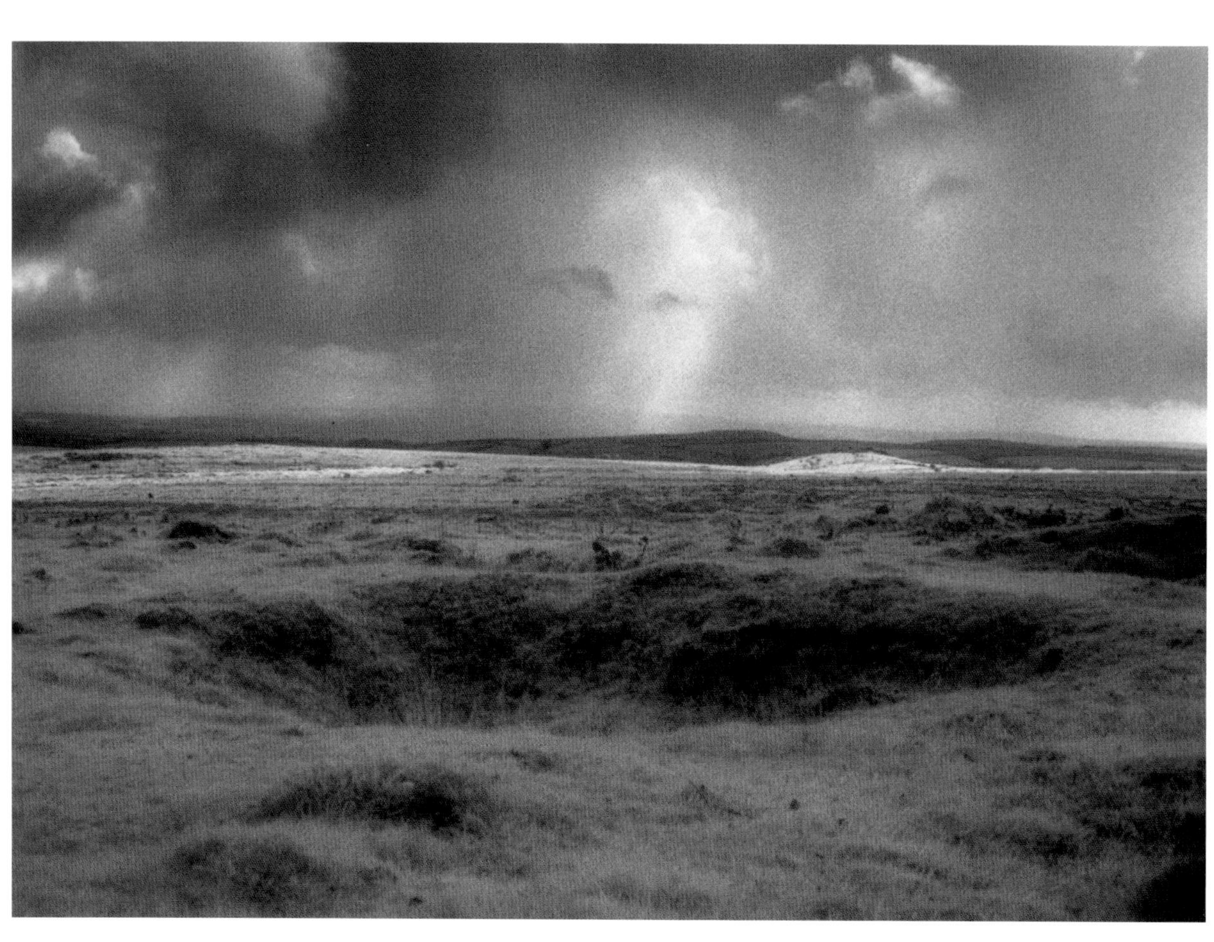

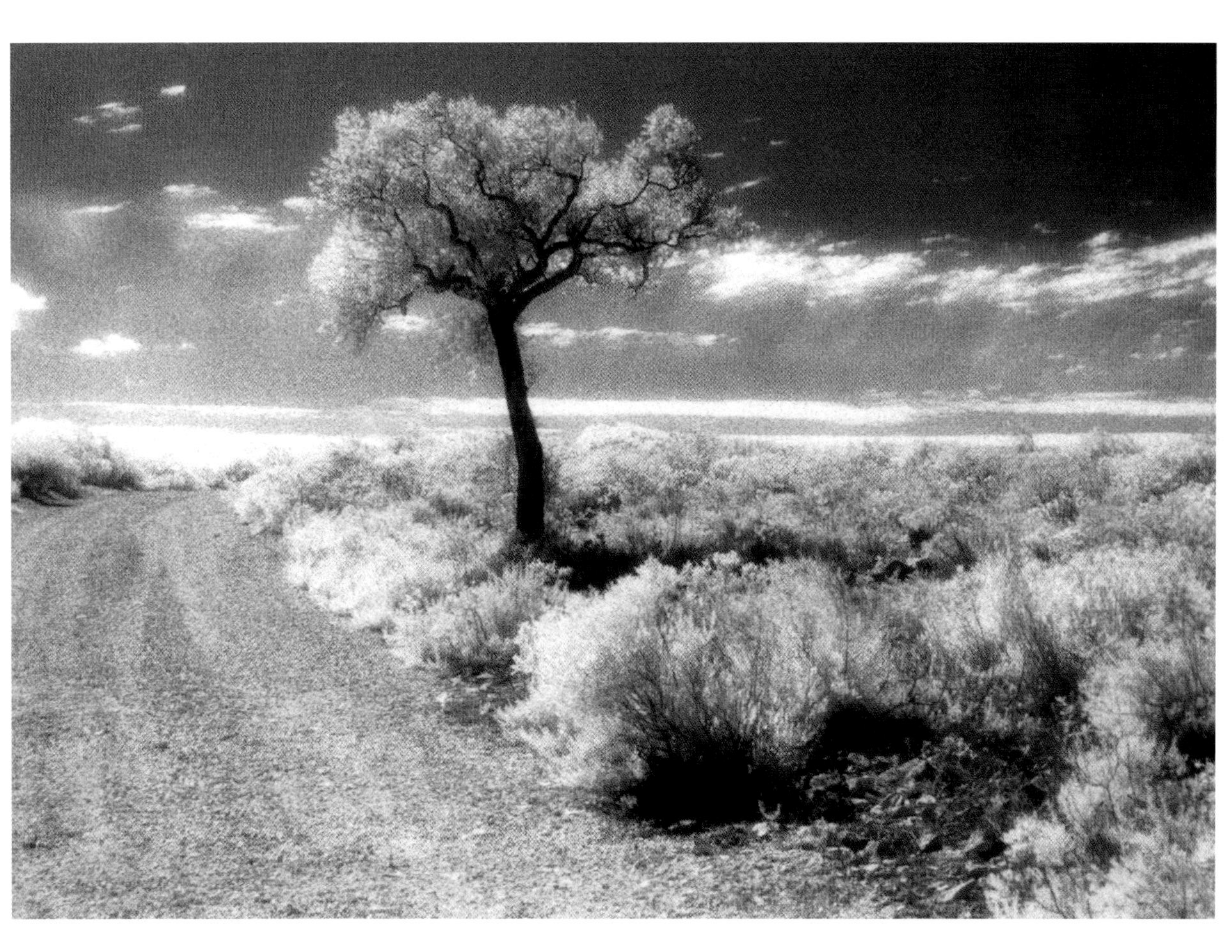

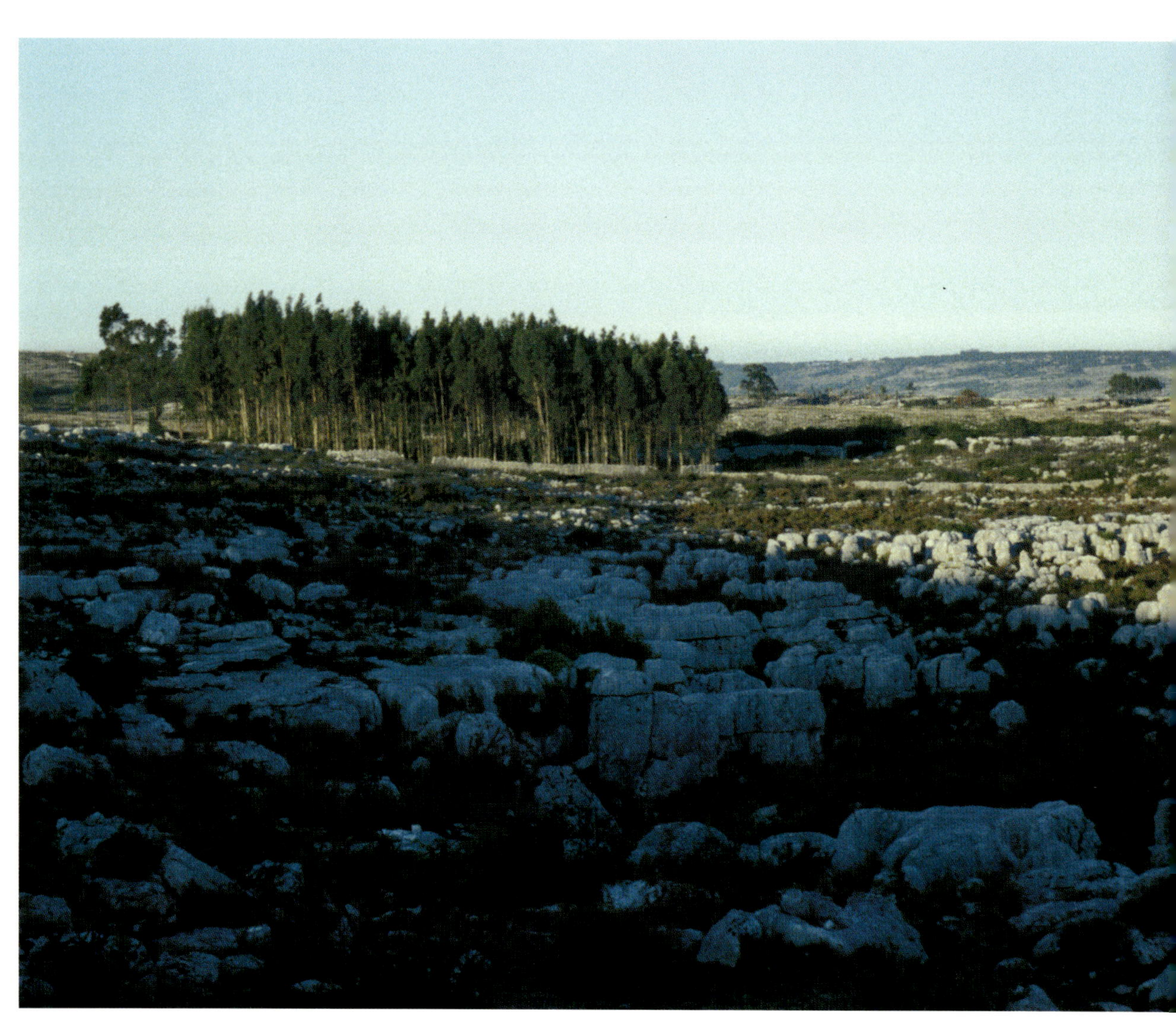

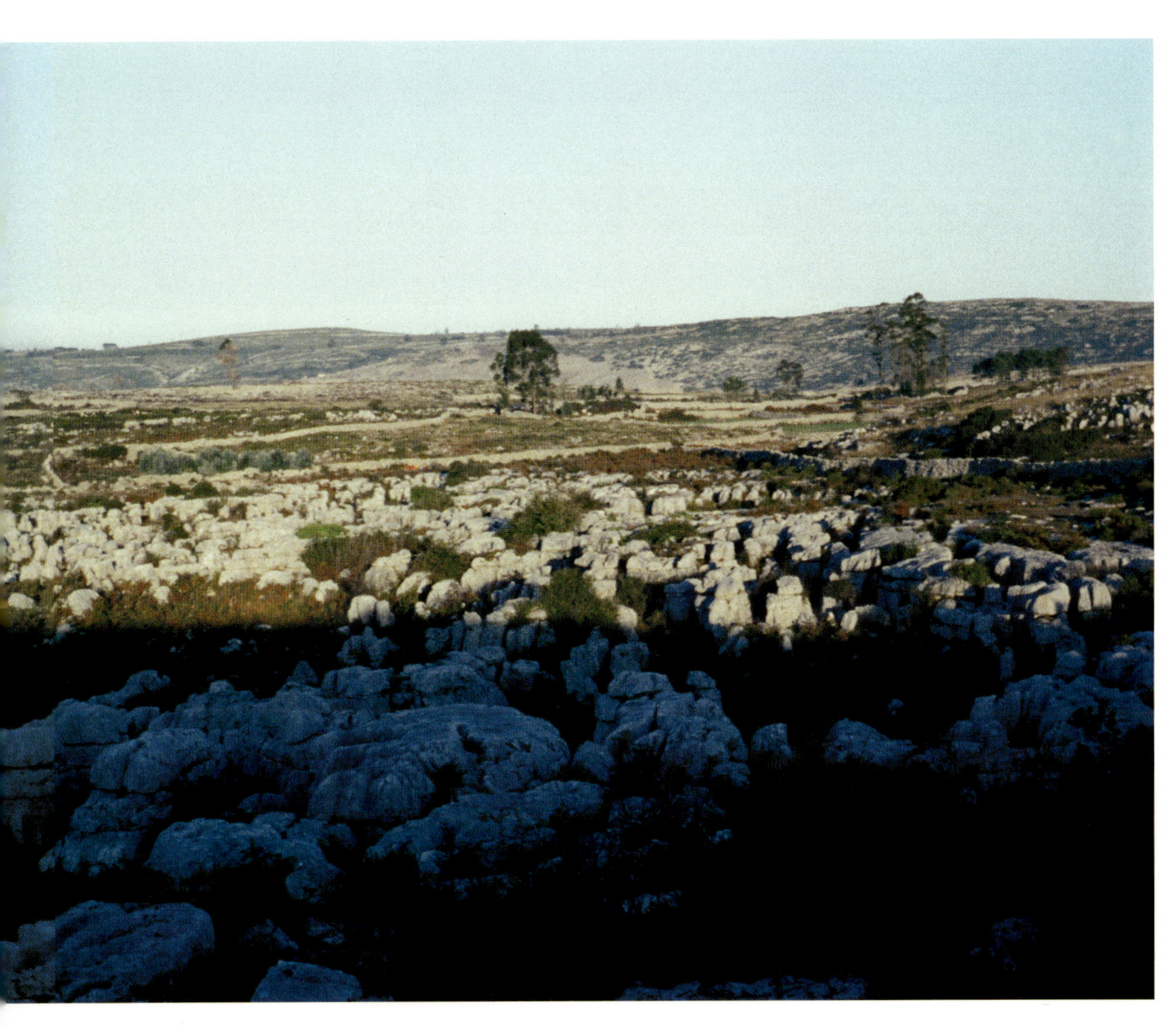

Landscape, Film, Time and the Visionary

Nina Danino

The image of the landscape in *Temenos* appears to be an indexical 24 frames per second photographic imprint of light-time reality. The (chemical) photographic image retains a link with the external world as an original source, a place, a geography which has an irreducible physical dimension which in turn, is transformed through the filmic world in which it appears. The rhetoric is that of cinematic (photographic) realism in which the image is a stable representation of the real world. In this filmic world time slows down, altering our perception of the signficance of things, everything becomes important, insignificant details become crucial. How does film transform the state of the image (and sound) by way of the ordinary (indexical) photographic (not through special effects, metaphor or genre) into an enhanced state? How can film effect a passage of the ordinary into the infra-ordinary?

Barthes identifies something of the exiled nature of all photographic images. However, unlike the sense of loss which we experience when looking at the 'dead' immobility of a photograph which as Barthes says has no future and is cut off in time, a moving image is always moving forward in time in the present of projection.[1] We feel uneasy when watching film images in which there is little movement—they have the potential to reveal the frozen and 'life-less' photographic images which make up film.

The landscapes in *Temenos,* a stony wasteland, the rocks, a view of a city, a snowscape, are not 'dead' but imbued with a sense of quiet. As Barthes points out, the frozen image of a photograph could not be experienced as 'calm' it is always in some sense dead. We can see this in the way in which a still image inserted into a moving image always jumps out as dead. Bellour refers to the interruption or paralysis of movement by "the brutal intrusion of photography".[2]

Calm in a filmic world is experienced as a relative measure, through, for example, the intrusion of slight movement—a breeze might stir a leaf in an otherwise perfectly still tree, a sound suddenly foregrounds the atmosphere of silence as 'alive'. Through these small gestures, stillness and movement are defined against the other. This slight difference lends the image a tranquil quality on the threshold between stasis and movement, i.e. 'life'. In the landscape, evidence of 'life' manifests itself against the background of stillness, something newly visible in the image, movement is perceptible here or there.

"All is calm".

The wind rustles the leaves of a tree, this small event becomes imbued with a sensory quality which seems singular if only because it has been chosen out of innumerable other filmable or edited moments. Virilio calls this the *epieikés,* a moment which is unique and different from the others.[3]

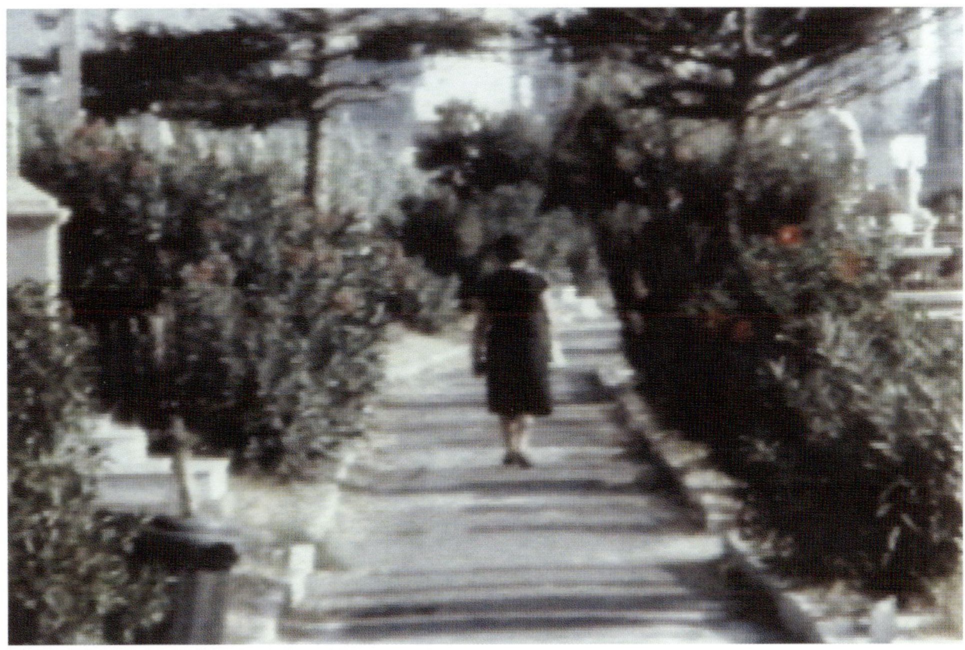

Location photograph for *Temenos*, 1998

Bernadette Soubirous, the young girl who was the visionary of Lourdes, recounts her perception of these ordinary yet singular events:

> I heard a noise like a gust of wind—*coup de vent*—
> I raised my head, I looked,
> I thought that it was the branches of the trees which were on the other side
> I looked but I noticed that they were immobile.
> Soon after, I heard the same noise,
> I turned my eyes (to the Grotto) and it was then that I saw.
> It was the branches which made that noise, they were moving.[4]

The landscape is imbued with a sense of quiet yet at the same time a disquieting dimension manifests itself without apparently disturbing the calm appearance of things—"there's something else of an unfamiliar nature that appears at the same time as familiar things", something which we could call haunting.[5]

A slowing down prepares the landscape as a stage for a manifestation of a different order.

This new designation of meaning appears like the transition in a film dissolve in which an emerging image takes up the foreground against which a previously solid image now becomes a sort of background and fades away. A transition which is a form of shedding of the solidity of the world.

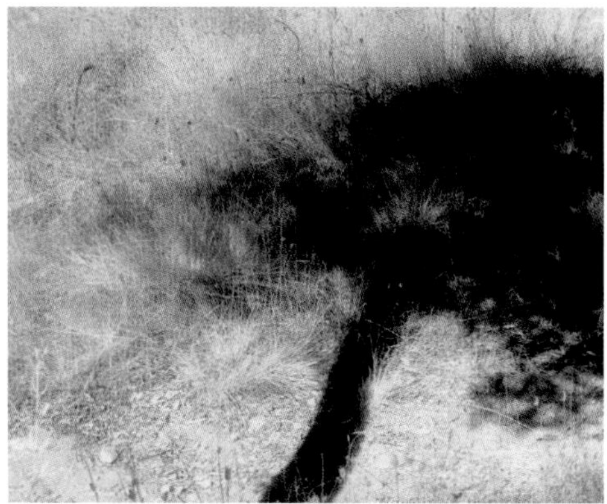
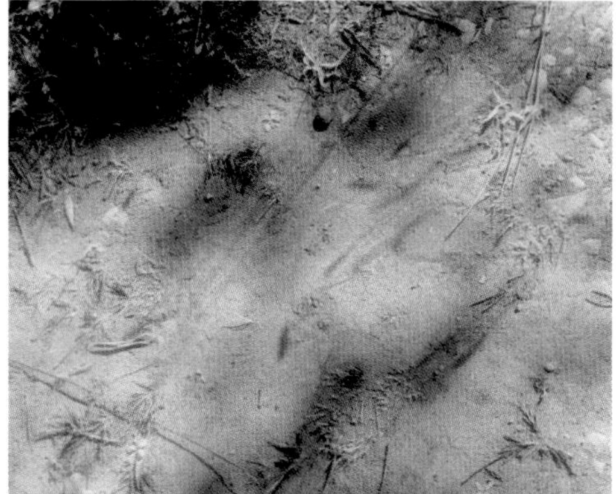

Temenos, 1998

In film, duration is the 1:1 relationship of film time to the viewing time and to the external 'real' time, in which all three are equivalent. But duration does not just have a simple equivalence to 'real time', it is a plastic dimension which alters our experience of 'real' time and our perception of what we are seeing or hearing—the attuning of a sixth sense. "This feeling of duration, lively, perfect, existing on its own, independent of any series of facts."[6] In film, time is a physical as much as a metaphysical dimension. In its physical form, time is a material which can drain an image or fulfil its potential for 'fullness' or 'presence'. Is the filming of a real event in 'real' time a guarantee of 'life'? What is it that ensures or brings out the unique 'life' i.e., the 'presence' of an image?

The ability of video to capture something immediately and in real time does not necessarily deliver a privileged representational experience. In Alexander Sokurov's taped series *Spiritual Voices*, 1998, there is a shot almost an hour in duration of the sun setting on a snowy landscape. It is possible that what we are looking at is only real time passing. This experience eventually drains the image of meaning and makes it fall into a record—something which is too close an analogy of its source and falls into disenchantment. For this reason, as Virilio points out, the early producers of film realised that it was the very realism of "'outdoor subjects' that would quickly have bored audiences".[7] As records of a familiar external reality they could only sustain interest by ensuring the depiction of quick change and movement or the play of the predictable and the unpredictable.[8]

When video and film images register simply as a disinterested record, the image returns from exile, from strangeness into the currency of the too familiar. But these two media inscribe time in different ways. Time behaves differently according to the placement of an image in a cinematic register or in the flat space of video. As Bellour points out, video has almost no time built into its recording process and is almost immediate: "the video image… can appear (both) as a new image that cannot be reduced to the one that precedes it".[9] The distance which exiles the image in the photographic and gives its enigmatic strangeness collapses in the immediacy of video.

Near the end of *Temenos*, there is a scene shot in Bosnia on video. We walk up a stony mountain path to the sacred site in sync sound in a documentary present. The images of video do not have the quality of spectral haunting (unless mediated through the rhetoric of the cinematic). In video the approximation of the image to its source produces an image which is always instant, always present, always new and forecloses the spectral possibilities in which the temporal paradox of the cinematic circulates.

The exiled nature of the photographic image creates a certain estrangement between myself as a viewer and the world represented. A record is devoid of this estrangement. Here, the image returns from exile, into the currency of the present. The image of the landscape in *Temenos* is a metonymic analogue, which has an indexical relationship to an original within the rhetoric of realism, but it is not a disinterested image of that external world. The landscape is empty of human presence and like Bernadette's altered perception of the invisible—'nothing happens' yet something makes itself felt. For Lucia, the girl visionary of Fatima, the ordinary weather and the landscape are experienced as a stage for the emergence of "another designation of meaning".[10] "It was a clear day, there was not the slightest cloud, there was not the slightest breeze, there was a brilliant sun. The atmosphere was still and calm."[11]

In film, stillness opens this space—presents the possibility of staging something. Stillness allows the unseen to become visible. Detail becomes visible through stillness, the snow flake becomes visible and divided from the film grain. In this stillness which is enhanced by duration, insignificant details are transformed. A bird might fly across the frame, a branch moves slightly in the breeze, the landscape is measured by the camera's slow pans. Everything acquires importance. In this world of small things, a particular flower "among others becomes suddenly photogenic".[12] Enhanced perception is also auditory; we hear the cries of a bird circling above the landscape, but could they be the cries of a human voice? Like Bernadette, we give meaning through perception (of the illusion of the world) which is essentially fluid and unstable.

"All is calm."

Time clears a space. The landscape is actually full of small events; a bee buzzes, the wind blows across, a sheep calls.

> To look at what you wouldn't look at, to hear what you wouldn't listen to, to be attentive to the banal, to the ordinary, to the infra-ordinary. To deny the ideal hierarchy of the crucial and the incidental because there is no incidental, only dominant cultures that exile us from ourselves and others.[13]

For Lucia, the stony wilderness in which she carries out her daily chore of tending the goats acquires a new unfamiliar significance one day. The child's senses suddenly attune to altered levels of perception in which, like hearing a pitch which is out of our frequency, a hidden

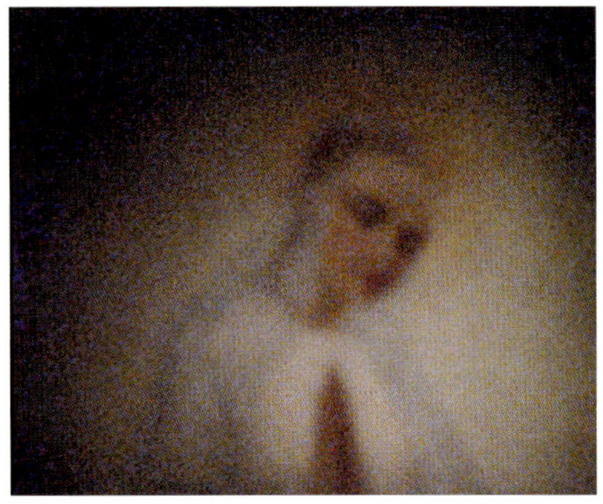
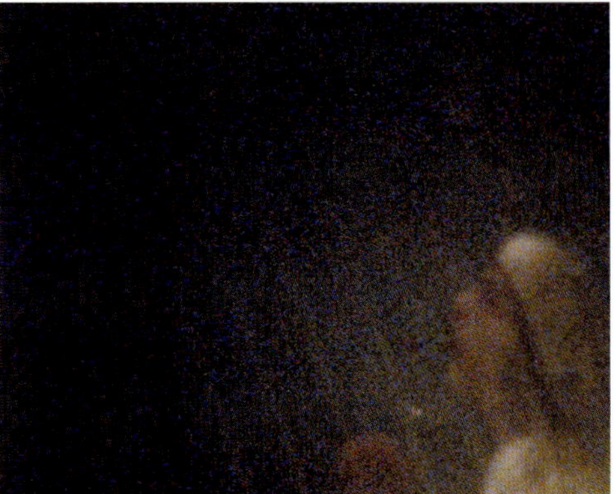

Temenos, 1998

acoustic world is revealed in which the sound of a bee might be heard like a tiny little voice. This is a fleeting perception which quickly passes.

In *Temenos* a sense of an animate nature emerges from the sounds recorded on location: the birds from Fatima, the crows in the snowy landscapes, the dogs from Bosnia: "all techniques meant to unleash unseen forces are techniques of disappearance".[14] The unseen is located by the sentient world of animals, the dogs bark in the far distance and agitate at something which is beyond vision. The viewer strains to listen to cats in the black film spacing, the sound of a bee is accentuated over the others on the soundtrack. The high pitched calls of strange birds over the snowscape are balanced on a vocal threshold between animal nature and an uncanny evocation of a human throat.

In this intense experience of the present, there is a transformation of "true objects into a sort of background against which another designation of meaning suddenly emerges, a background which would be already a kind of dissolving view, reminding us of Paul of Tarsus (but he, also, on the road to Damascus experienced a prolonged absence which effectively altered his notion of reality,) all is calm, and yet: *this world as we see it is passing away*".[15] It is this intense experience of the moment that enables the world to be detached and shed.

How might it be possible to produce a clearing, a place where over-signification is exiled, to bring about filmic presence yet enable the production of meaning (not non–meaning) in conjunction with the tracks of sound and time?

The experience of looking at something for a long time, or the measurement of continuous time by an image enables the opening of distance between the viewer and the image (this was the problem of audience boredom that early producers identified). This distance can empty the image into a banal disinterested flatness or can "make it come into 'presence'". Filming and presenting an image in unbroken time has the effect of creating a sustained detachment which can even out signification. Gidal gives the example of a leaf, which filmed in this way, keeps out ready associative analogue, symbol or metaphor or allegory. The associations "conjured up by the image given, is something formed by past connections but at a very low key, not a determining or over-determining presence, merely a not high moment of meaning".[16]

Using these film phenomena and materials the image of a tree in the wind is an object of enigma—the tree is not a metaphor but is a tree, severed and exiled in its photographic and filmic strangeness—yet is an image of the ordinary, external world. This is the paradox of a haunting image—that it remains and belongs in the world while also being removed from it.

The uninterrupted flow of time reflects the continuity of the world. The image in unbroken time clings on in the present, holds on to the evidential—1 minute of film time = 1 minute of spectator's time—it refuses to enable the world to be shed. It is said that the use of 'real time' mitigates against the ideal (immersive) environment created by the fictional manipulated time of editing.[17] Yet as we have seen 'real time' is not fixed but is a plastic dimension which affects the moving image in varying ways. Gidal's subjective experience of time is a relativistic one in which "There is here no absolute value other than that of the interaction of film moment and viewer".[18] This is a filmic experience of time which "may but does not necessarily connect" with 'real time' and which, if there is a corollary in lived experience could be a subjective consciousness of time.[19]

Virilio refers to an example of this in 'picnolepsy'—a natural occurrence in children, when, unbeknown to them, they 'drop out' for brief but frequent lapses from the continuity of time. As we enter adulthood these experiences lessen and disappear and "absence ceases therefore to have a prime effect on consciousness".[20] And we begin to experience time as continuous.

> If you admit that picnolepsy is a phenomenon that effects the conscious duration of everyone.... the meditation on Time would not only be the preliminary job delegated to the metaphysician... anyone would now live a duration which would be his own and no one else's... and the picnoleptic onset would be something that could make us think of human liberty, in the sense that it would be a latitude given to each man to invent his own relations to time and therefore a kind of will and power for minds, none of which 'mysteriously, can think of himself as being any lower than anyone else'. E A Poe[21]

Perhaps the visionary moment is one such episode of the release from linear time.

"All is still."

The grove is lit by a strong sun, everything is quiet. The tree, strange in its whiteness, the close ups of grasses and shadows are almost still. The tension builds up as a result of the impression of something about to happen, in the present of the film. As well as Lucia, the girl visionary, there are other children here too, they can be heard running about playing, their voices reverberate in the silence. They are hushed. "What escapes from the universal

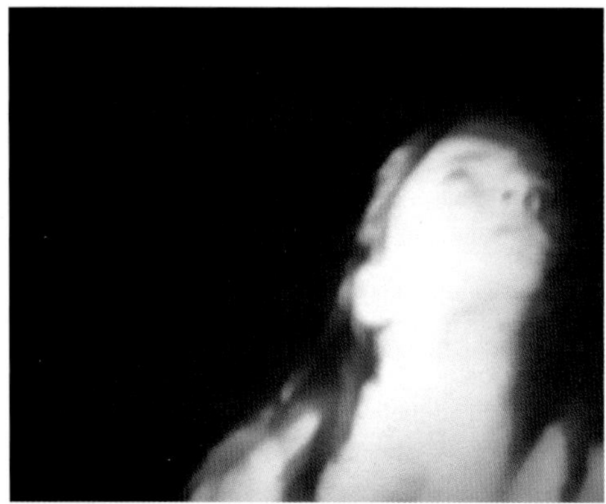

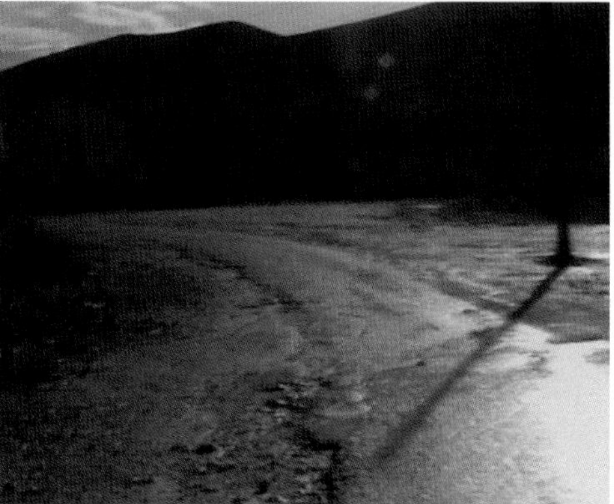

Temenos, 1998

and gives difference a context is the *epieikés*—that which pertains to a moment that is singular and, by definition, different."[22] Everything becomes quiet.

The apparition is a phenomenon which most often happens to children, perhaps because only children may be capable of accepting time as subjective. Reports tell us that for the visionary, the interruption from continuous time can be anything from 50 seconds to 45 minutes. "This visible communication is fleeting. It abolishes perception of the outside world in the same way as waking dismisses dreams."[23] The re-entry into the erosive time of the world brings to Bernadette a sense of sadness "I was well there in that place".[24]

Vistas open out as the camera pans slowly. The pace enables the creation of a 'calm' even atmosphere. The desire for stasis of course mitigates against loss. Things are shed in distance and time. A camera pan sweeps across the horizon of a stony wilderness, the sound of weeping cuts in on the sound track before the pan has ended, it cuts out and leaves the pan empty and the silence resounding.

Time shouldn't be filmed as merely passing—thereby allowing the image to fall into a record. Time is a physical dimension of film, a plastic material which creates space. The time demanded from each viewer, the time taken to represent small things not privileged in the hierarchy of dramatic images, time is a territory. The landscape changes, the seasons change, distance is travelled, space is claimed as time.

Quietness creates a space, it produces the auditorium in the cinema. In the quiet, the act of watching emerges, the experiencing of film and consciousness of other viewers watching yet absorption also takes place. Some viewers report that they 'lose' 20 minutes in the viewing of the film—that is that the film is experienced as shorter than it actually is. The viewer has been at least partially absorbed into the space of the film. The viewer experiences an absence, a disconnection from consciousness of time which has apparently been lost and is 'missing'.

There is subjective time, not through conventions which represent memory or point of view shots, e.g., hand held camera, slow motion or grain, but through absorption and the loss of self. The closing of the gap between viewer and viewed is a form of absorption. There is a sense of losing oneself through the narrative, which moves towards an increasing erasure and forgetting. "I don't remember any more". In the sequence "La Fin" a voice asks "What age does she have?" and the same voice replies "But monsieur she has no age".[25]

Perhaps what the children encounter is a different order of time, perhaps an encounter with an exit from time, or a suspension from time. Another name for the absence from time might be eternity. "Eternity is not like time where each successive moment blots out its predecessor, a state of perpetual erosion mitigated by memory."[26]

The journey of *Temenos* takes us through a cyclical time of seasons in which a bitter wind is heard and the birds cry out, followed by the spring breeze with the calls of the nomads, and summer heat returning us again to the northern wind across the white landscape.

At the end of the 75 minutes, a great distance has been travelled and left behind but we have also stayed in the same place. A voice interrupts us from an oneiric experience: "What time is it?" This leaving behind is also a form of shedding (the world is able to be shed) in the sense of oblivion: "What time is it?", but also an emptying of signification, yet remaining full of time and space for the viewer.

The last sequence is titled "The Virgin's Time", across a white indistinct landscape an unseen horizontal body is inscribed by a voice as if in a waking reverie which asks "What time is it?"

"What time is it?"

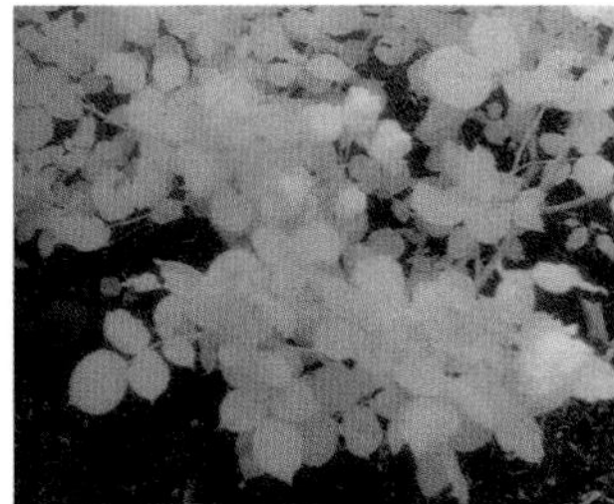

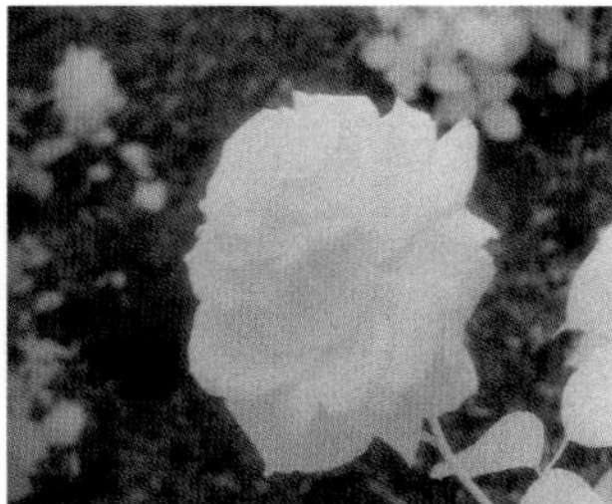

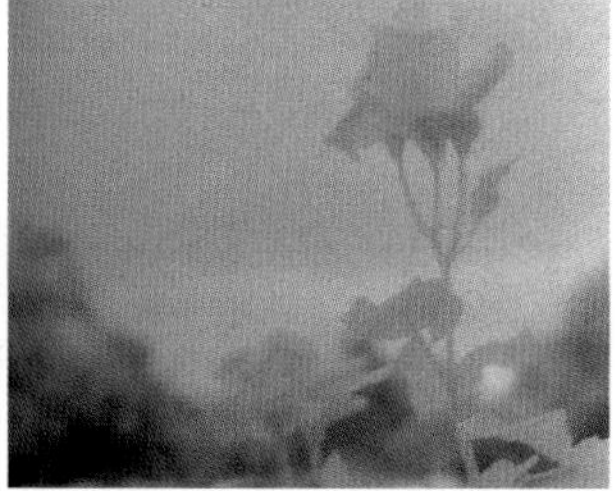

Temenos, 1998

Notes

1 Barthes, Roland, *Camera Lucida*, London: Vintage, 1982, p. 90.

2 Bellour, Raymond, "The Double Helix", *Passages de l'image*, Paris: Centre Georges Pompidou, 1990, p. 54.

3 Virilio, Paul, *Aesthetics of Disappearance*, New York: Semiotext(e), 1991, p. 35.

4 Laurentin, Rene, *Histoire authentique des apparitions*, vol. 1, Paris: P Lethielleux, p. 41.

5 Virilio, *Aesthetics of Disappearance*, quoting the painter René Magritte, p. 36.

6 Virilio, *Aesthetics of Disappearance*, quoting Edgar Allan Poe, p. 42.

7 Virilio, *Aesthetics of Disappearance*, p. 15.

8 Virilio, *Aesthetics of Disappearance*, p. 15. Refers to Méliès' stop trick photography which fulfilled this popular demand.

9 Bellour, "The Double Helix", p. 56.

10 Virilio, *Aesthetics of Disappearance*, p. 37.

11 *Temenos* script, 1997. Lucia dos Santos is the visionary of Fatima. Her autobiography and account of the apparitions at Cova da Iria is in *Fatima in Lucia's Own Words*, Fr Louis Kondor ed., Fatima: Postulation Centre, 1976.

12 Virilio, *Aesthetics of Disappearance*, p. 35.

13 Virilio, *Aesthetics of Disappearance*, p. 36.

14 Virilio, *Aesthetics of Disappearance*, p. 23

15 Virilio, *Aesthetics of Disappearance*, p. 37.

16 Gidal, Peter, "Theory and Definition of Structural/Materialist Film", *Structural Film Anthology*, London: British Film Institute, 1976, p. 8.

17 Gidal, "Theory and Definition", p. 9: "There is illusionistic time, time made to seem what it is not, such as in conventional and (it must be said) in much Eisensteinian editing.... either implying a linear thread of events with time compressed, or a simultaneity with time compressed."

18 Gidal, "Theory and Definition", p. 9.

19 Gidal, "Theory and Definition", p. 9.

20 Virilio, *Aesthetics of Disappearance*, p. 19

21 Virilio, *Aesthetics of Disappearance*, pp. 21-22.

22 Virilio, *Aesthetics of Disappearance*, p. 35. This quote is from Mario Perniola, "Logique de la séduction," *Traverses*, no. 18.

23 Laurentin, Rene and Henri Joyeux, *Scientific and Medical Studies on the Apparitions at Medjugorje*, Dublin: Veritas, 1987, p. 39.

24 Laurentin, *Histoire authentique des apparitions*, vol. 3, p. 100.

25 *Temenos* script, 1997.

26 Laurentin and Joyeux, *Scientific and Medical Studies on the Apparitions at Medjugorje*, pp. 38-39.

Opposite: Temenos, 1998

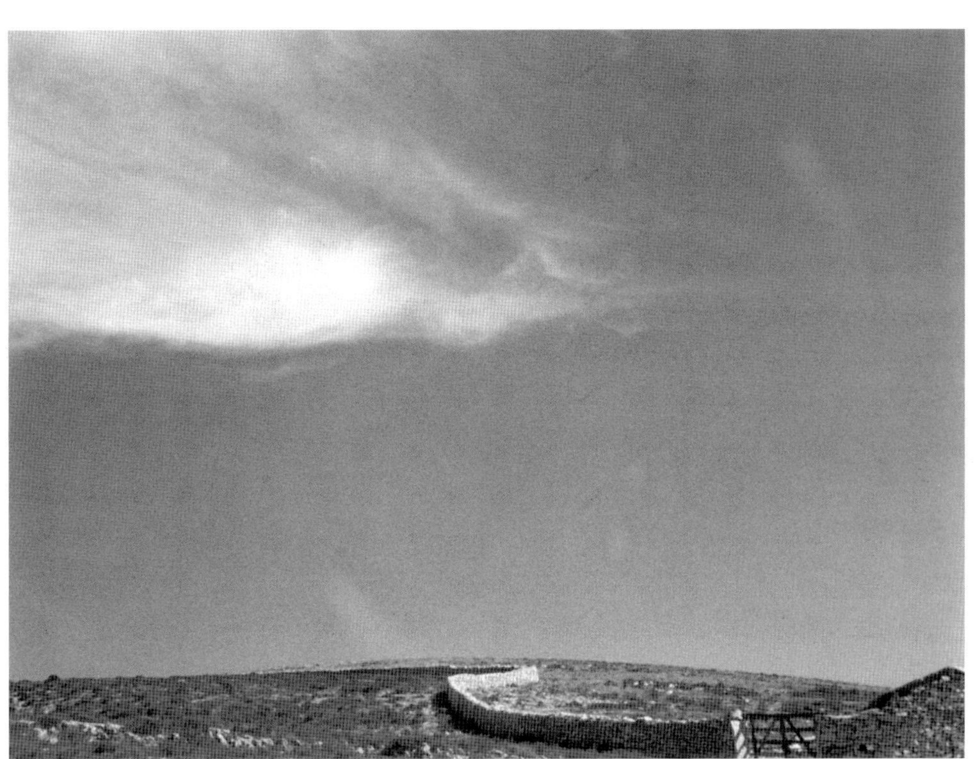

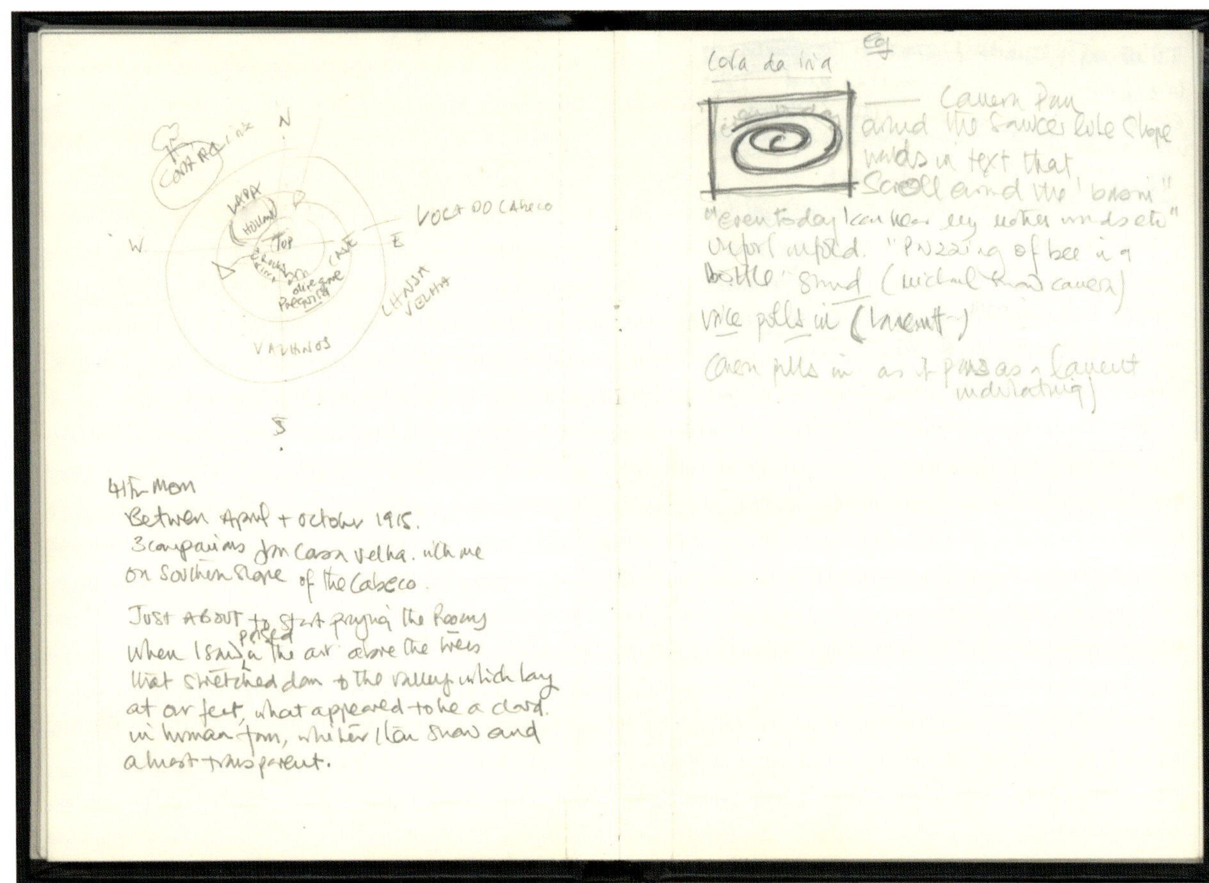

N
W
E
S
VALINHOS
Between April + October 1915.
3 companions from Casa Velha. with me
on Southern slope of the Cabeco.
Just about to start praying the Rosary
when I saw poised in the air above the trees
that stretched down to the valley which lay
at our feet, what appeared to be a cloud
in human form, whiter than snow and
almost transparent.
Cova da Iria
Camera Pan

Temenos, 1998

Filming notebook

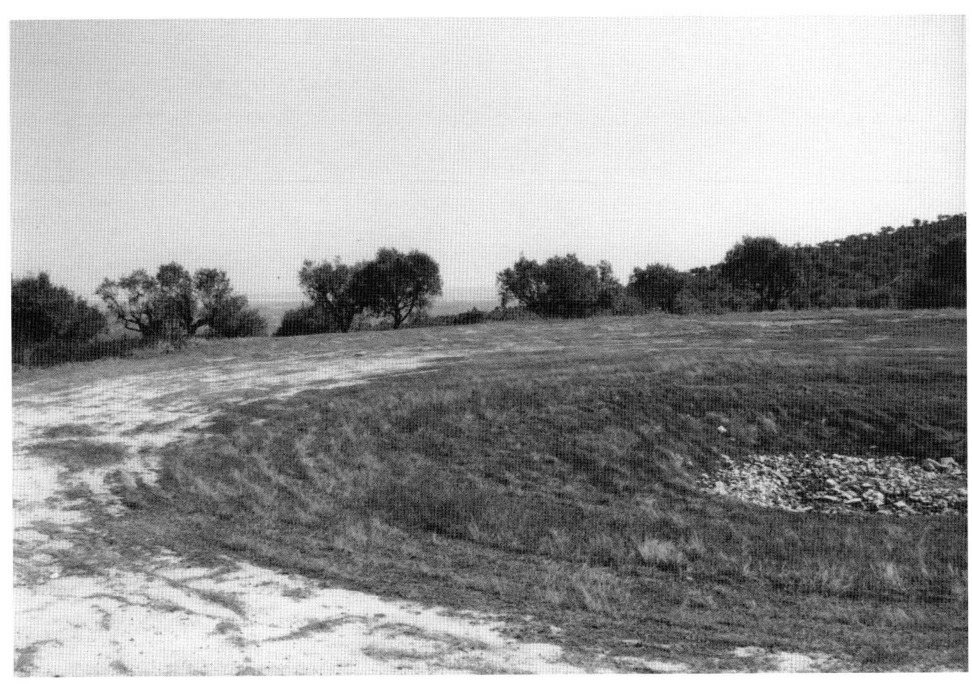

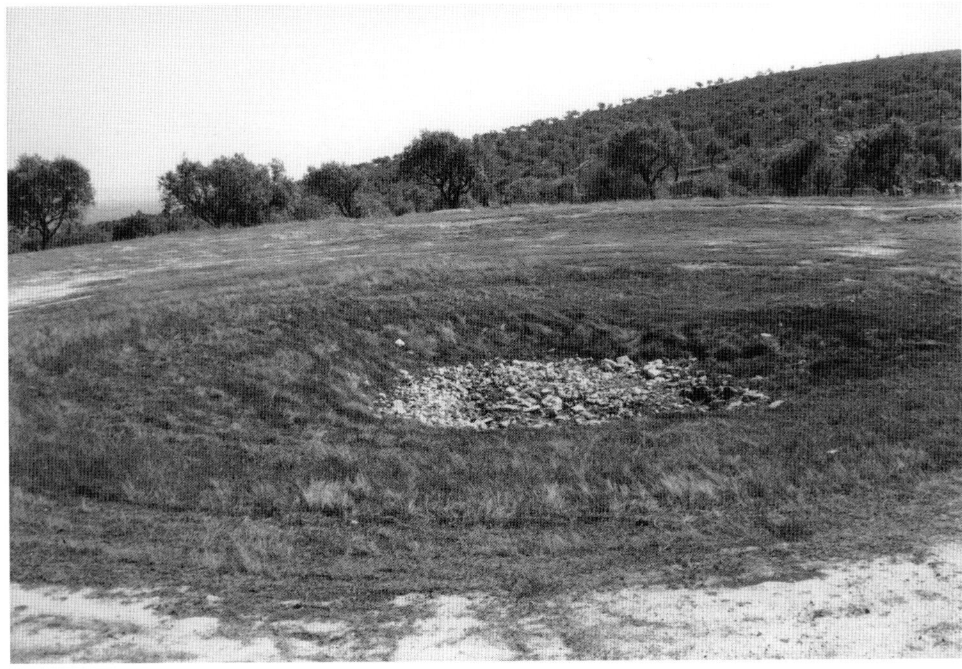

Temenos, 1998
Location photographs

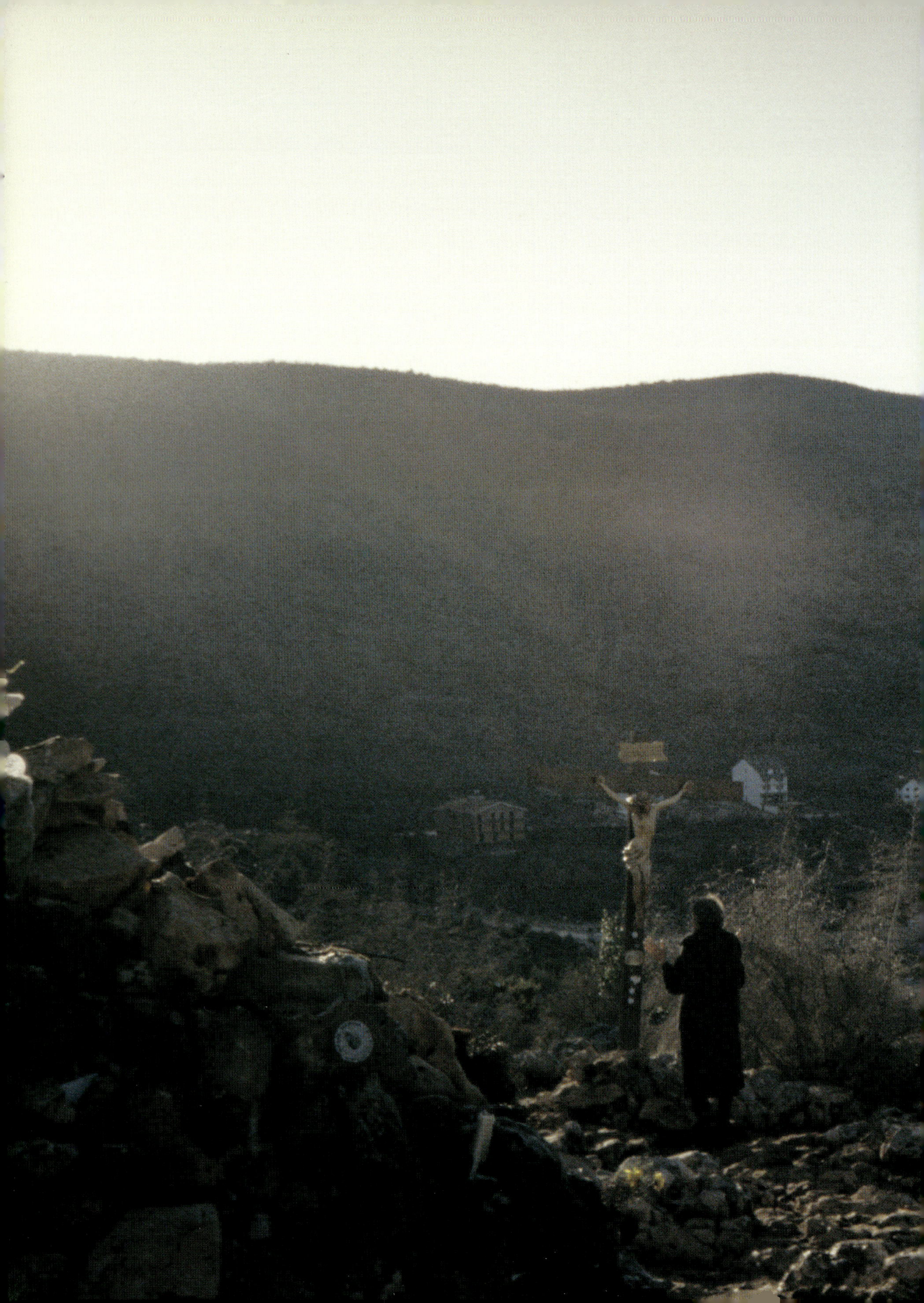

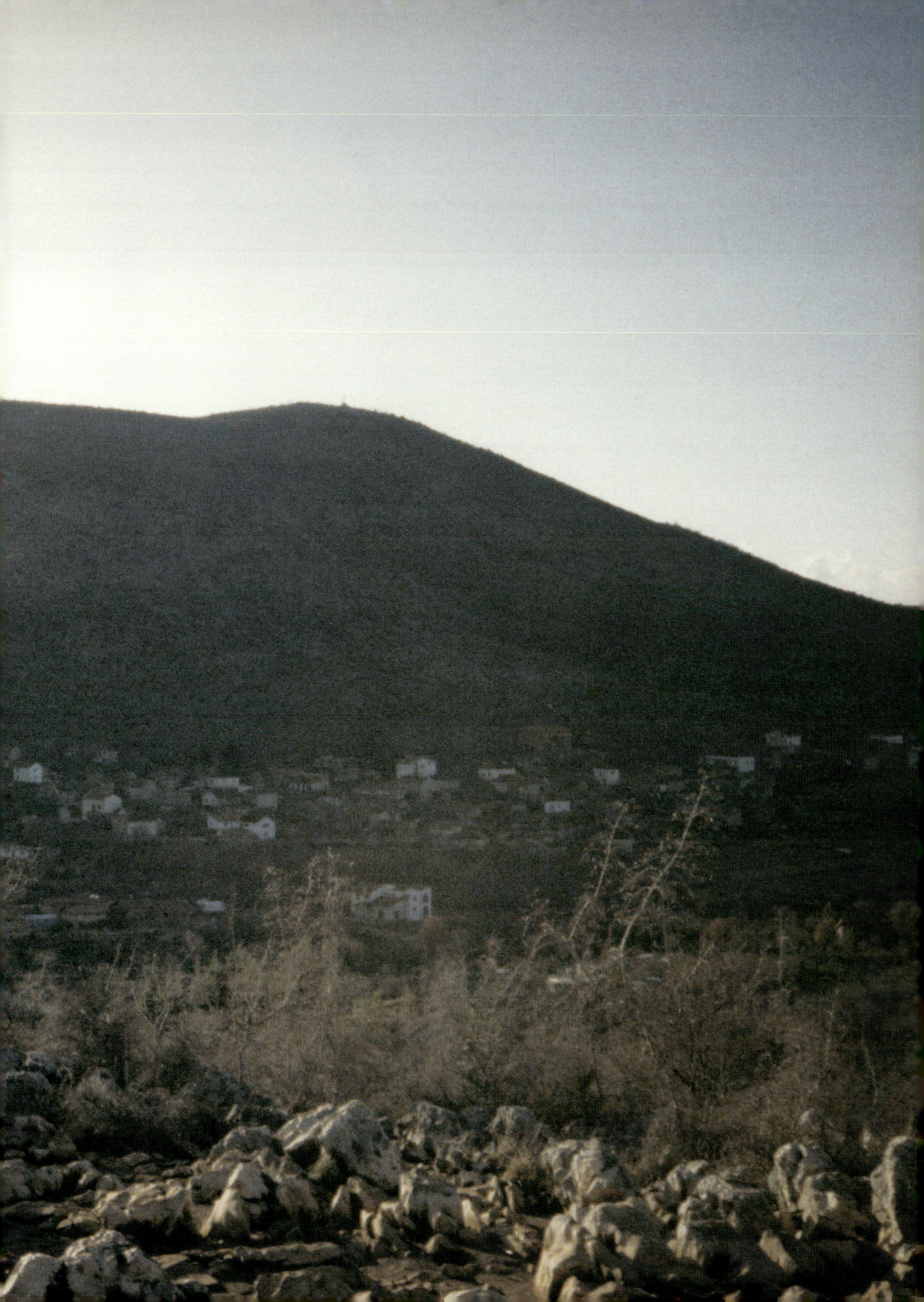

Filmography

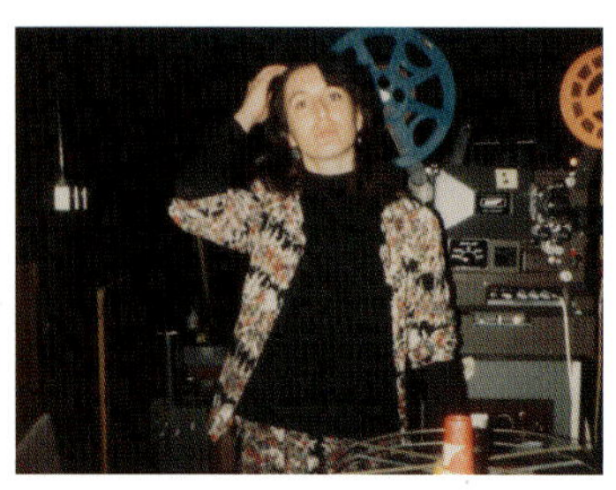

NINA DANINO

would like to invite you to:

1. Film: 'FIRST MEMORY'

   showing from 11th — 18th June
   at 3.30pm (except 15th and 17th June)
   and 6.00pm every day

2. Slide/Tape: 'FIRST MEMORY'

   showing at 3.30pm on the
   15th and 17th June

in

THE LECTURE THEATRE
(centre court)

LECTURE THEATRE

ROYAL COLLEGE OF ART
DEGREE SHOW 1981

Kensington Gore
London SW7

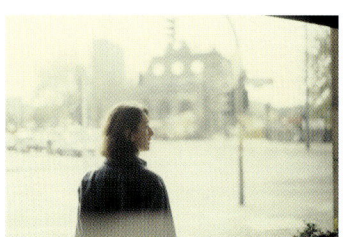

From top: Projection of *First Memory*, Royal College of Art (RCA), London, 1981, photograph taken by Patrick Keiller

Screening Invitation, *First Memory*, RCA, 1981

Nina Danino, location photograph, Berlin, 1983

First Memory 1980

Multi-Media Projection
Two screens, slide tape, Super 8 film, colour, sound, 27 mins 20 secs
Conceived, produced and spoken: Nina Danino
Slide photography and Super 8 film: Nina Danino
Audio-visual Technician: Alan Vallis
Recorded and produced at the Environmental Media Audio/Video Studio, Royal College of Art, London

First Memory 1981

16mm, colour, magnetic sound, 20 mins
Filmed on 16mm reversal film Kodachrome 40 from the original 35mm slides, opticals shot in-camera
Conceived, directed, edited and spoken: Nina Danino
Camera: Ian Duncan
Filming Assistant: Michael Raine
Audio-visual Technician: Alan Vallis
Production photographs: Mirta Alaggia
Dubbing Mixer: Graham Lawson
Produced at the Department of Environmental Media and School of Film and Television, Royal College of Art, London

Close to Home 1982-1985

16mm, black and white, sound, 28 mins
Filmed in Berlin and the Strait of Gibraltar
Conceived, directed, edited and spoken: Nina Danino
Camera: Arthur Howes
Additional camera, Berlin: Kai Glawe
Filming of projected footage: Belinda Parsons
Location photographer, Berlin: Mirta Alaggia
Photographs of Berlin monuments: Paul Donn
Enlargements of news photographs: John Daniel
Sound Dub: Glentham Studios
Loan of equipment and technical advice: Nicky Hamlyn, Michael Mazière, and Lucy Panteli
Thanks to: Walter Brun, Anthony Davis, London Filmmakers' Co-op Workshop
Produced with financial assistance from the Arts Council of Great Britain

Stabat Mater 1990

16mm, colour, sound, 8 mins
Original footage shot on Super 8 and optically printed to 16mm
Filmed in Gibraltar
Conceived, filmed, edited and spoken: Nina Danino
Singer: Elena Danino
Dubbing Mixer: Andrew Sears
Optical Printing: Nick Collins
Acknowledgements: James Joyce's *Ulysses* and Hélène Cixous' *La Jeune Née*
Thanks to Anthony Davis, Lucy Panteli, John Somerville-Large and London Filmmakers' Co-op Workshop
Financial assistance from the Arts Council of Great Britain

"Now I am yours" 1992

16mm, colour and black and white, sound, 32 mins
The Ecstasy of St Teresa filmed in the Cornaro Chapel in Rome
Conceived, directed, edited and spoken: Nina Danino
Voice performance and electronic compositions: Shelley Hirsch
Additional music: Diamanda Galás
Lighting Cameraman: Christopher Hughes
Light Camera: Nina Danino
Camera Assistant: Monica Zanolin
On-line Editors: Andrew Parker, John Sarson
Dubbing Editor: Andrew Thompkins
Dubbing Mixer: Dave Aston
Sound Engineer for Shelley Hirsch: Alan Lawrence
Voice recording and editing: David Hunt
Image post-production and graphics: John Chamberlain and Michael Lambourne
Film extract from *Teresa de Jesus*, Juan de Orduña. dir., 1961, courtesy of Estela Films, Madrid
Video footage: Latin Mass Video courtesy of Promotone BV, Amsterdam
Music: "Cris D'Aveugle" and "Deliver Me" by Diamanda Galás, courtesy of Mute Records
Acknowledgements: *The Works of St Teresa of Jesus* and *Works of Love* by Søren Kierkegaard
Special Thanks to: John Somerville-Large
Thanks to: Andrea Farci, Janet Marbrook, Chrysalis Television, Tangram Post-Production, Francesca D'Aloja, Steve Beresford, Anna Thew, Paco Aguirre, Barbara Matuska, Bianca Lepori, Em Kirkpatrick, The Community of St Hilda (Margaret Orr-Deas, Erica Dunmow), Peta Evelyn at the Victoria and Albert Museum
Real Biblioteca del Monasterio San Lorenzo de El Escorial, Madrid
Soprintendenza per i Beni Artistici e Storici, Rome
Financial assistance from the Arts Council of Great Britain and Channel Four

Programme Ten

Personalities, Sexualities, Identities

These films are expressions of sexuality and identity; investigating subversive positions of identification and desire.

Stabat Mater
Nina Danino UK 1990 16mm 8 mins
On one level **Stabat Mater** is a devotional piece, a short oracion. The songs at the beginning and end are the two pillars of the film - it is the voice of my mother singing two laments - a saeta - a type of song sung during holy week to the Mater Dolorosa. It is concerned to locate that which is lost, contained by the body but outside of objectification, absent and unnameable. *ND*

Traces
Barbara Meter Holl 1990 16mm 16 mins
Constructed out of personal images covering a period of almost twenty years. The film is an attempt to reconstruct a ('materialist') memory. The sound consists of political texts which comment on family, upbringing and relationships between men and women.

Walk
Christian Anstice UK 1990 16mm 8 mins
The subject creates the dynamic for his own anxieties: **Walk** studies the implications of the subject without object, paranoia, ensuing and cliched notions of self sacrifice, self questioning through the appropriation of other identities. One is left to question whether the new man is a form of apology or a narcissistic self appraisal: has guilt been previously delineated, is it always valid - finally can a tree be genderized? *CA*

Lilith
Tanya Ury UK 1988 video 12 mins
The filmmaker impersonates the biblical character in an attempt to explore the space of the female body within the Jewish tradition. *Rosemary Heather*

Claw Your Eye
James Carman Ger 1989 16mm 8 mins
This film is an invocation of the second sight. It tries to engender an ontological transformation in the viewer by allowing him/her to enter into another realm of consciousness beyond the threshold of normal perception. *JC*

One, and the Other Time
Sarah Turner UK 1990 16mm 5 mins
An exploration of the dynamics between intimacy and violence, in the context of one's continual desire to reconcile psychical and external reality, that is, the nearer one gets to that essentiality, the further one is literally pushed away from it. *ST*

Promtion
Lisa Hurley UK 1990 16mm 5 mins
A literal promotion. Fleeting glimpses of women with cropped hair in black leather darkly intimate the charms of a forbidden culture. *Rosemary Heather*

Let's Play Prisoners
Julie Zando US 1988 video 22 mins
Let's Play Prisoners is about how power is exchanged between females. It suggests that any struggle over love is modelled after the mother/child relationship. Their relations create a paradigm of need and dependency versus power and control. The tape suggests that this same power dynamic established between mother and child is transferred onto friends and lovers.

Stabat Mater
Walk
27

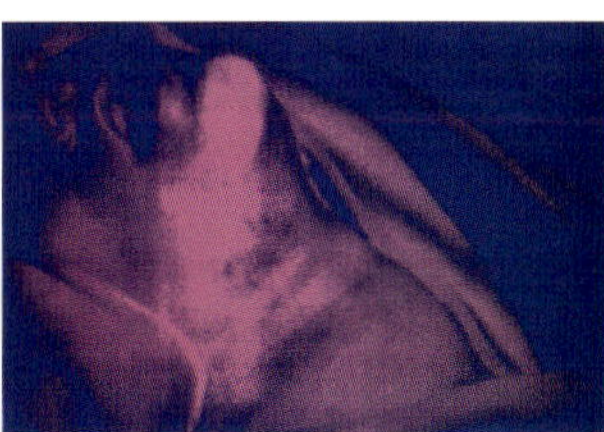

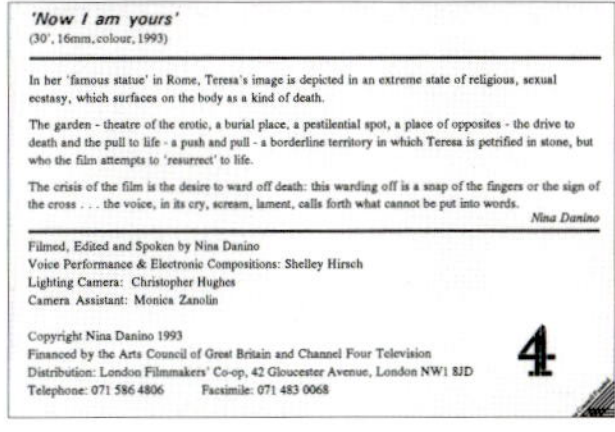

'Now I am yours'
(30', 16mm, colour, 1993)

In her 'famous statue' in Rome, Teresa's image is depicted in an extreme state of religious, sexual ecstasy, which surfaces on the body as a kind of death.

The garden - theatre of the erotic, a burial place, a pestilential spot, a place of opposites - the drive to death and the pull to life - a push and pull - a borderline territory in which Teresa is petrified in stone, but who the film attempts to 'resurrect' to life.

The crisis of the film is the desire to ward off death: this warding off is a snap of the fingers or the sign of the cross . . . the voice, in its cry, scream, lament, calls forth what cannot be put into words.

Nina Danino

Filmed, Edited and Spoken by Nina Danino
Voice Performance & Electronic Compositions: Shelley Hirsch
Lighting Camera: Christopher Hughes
Camera Assistant: Monica Zanolin

Copyright Nina Danino 1993
Financed by the Arts Council of Great Britain and Channel Four Television
Distribution: London Filmmakers' Co-op, 42 Gloucester Avenue, London NW1 8JD
Telephone: 071 586 4806 Facsimile: 071 483 0068

4

From top: *Stabat Mater*, London Film Festival Programme, 1990

"Now I am yours", Preview Invitation, 1993

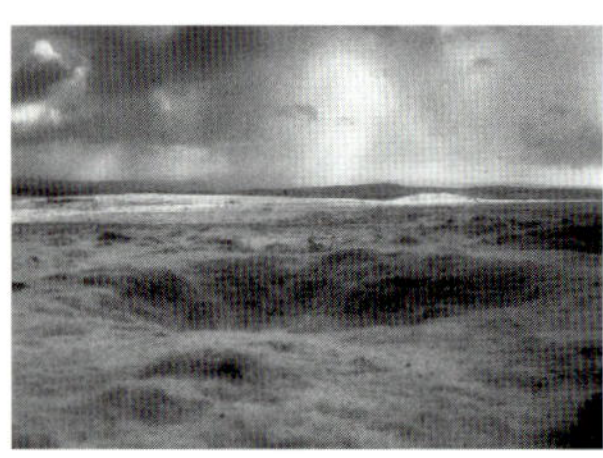

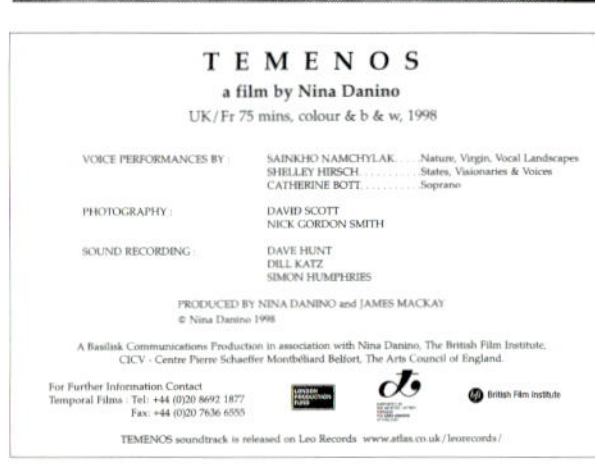

TEMENOS
a film by Nina Danino
UK/Fr 75 mins, colour & b & w, 1998

VOICE PERFORMANCES BY: SAINKHO NAMCHYLAK.....Nature, Virgin, Vocal Landscapes
SHELLEY HIRSCH..........States, Visionaries & Voices
CATHERINE BOTT..........Soprano

PHOTOGRAPHY: DAVID SCOTT
NICK GORDON SMITH

SOUND RECORDING: DAVE HUNT
DILL KATZ
SIMON HUMPHRIES

PRODUCED BY NINA DANINO and JAMES MACKAY
© Nina Danino 1998

A Basilisk Communications Production in association with Nina Danino, The British Film Institute, CICV - Centre Pierre Schaeffer Montbéliard Belfort, The Arts Council of England.

For Further Information Contact
Temporal Films: Tel: +44 (0)20 8692 1877
Fax: +44 (0)20 7636 6555

British Film Institute

TEMENOS soundtrack is released on Leo Records www.atlas.co.uk/leorecords/

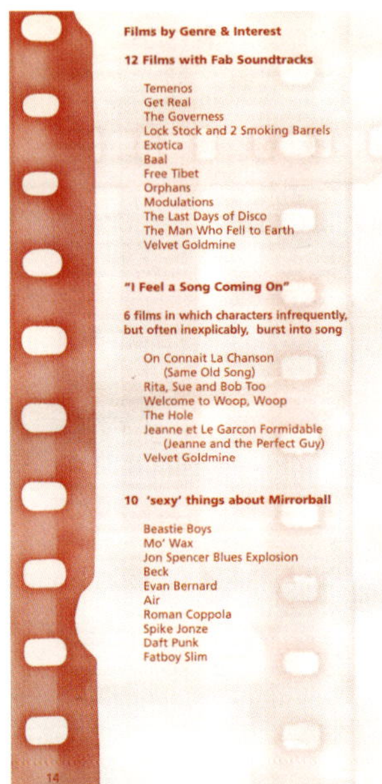

Films by Genre & Interest

12 Films with Fab Soundtracks

Temenos
Get Real
The Governess
Lock Stock and 2 Smoking Barrels
Exotica
Baal
Free Tibet
Orphans
Modulations
The Last Days of Disco
The Man Who Fell to Earth
Velvet Goldmine

"I Feel a Song Coming On"

6 films in which characters infrequently, but often inexplicably, burst into song

On Connait La Chanson
(Same Old Song)
Rita, Sue and Bob Too
Welcome to Woop, Woop
The Hole
Jeanne et Le Garcon Formidable
(Jeanne and the Perfect Guy)
Velvet Goldmine

10 'sexy' things about Mirrorball

Beastie Boys
Mo' Wax
Jon Spencer Blues Explosion
Beck
Evan Bernard
Air
Roman Coppola
Spike Jonze
Daft Punk
Fatboy Slim

14

From top: *Temenos*, Preview Invitation, 1998

Edinburgh Film Festival, Book of Lists, "12 Films with Fab soundtracks", 1998

The Silence is Baroque 1997

16mm, colour, sound, 12 mins
Filmed in Granada and Seville, music from the Holy Week street processions
Conceived, filmed, edited and spoken: Nina Danino
Singer: Anonymous
Location sound recording: Paco Tejero
On-line Editors: Jaime Estrada, Graham McGuiness
Voice recording and editing: David Hunt
Dubbing Editor: Ian Wilkinson
Dubbing Mixer: Billy Mahoney
Thanks to: John Gulliver, Richard Lund, David Moss, Matilde Romero, John Somerville-Large and Monica Zanolin
Producer: Karel Doing, Studio één, The Netherlands

Temenos 1998

35mm/16mm/Beta SP, colour and black and white, sound, 75 mins
Filmed in Bosnia, England, France, and Portugal
Director, screenplay, editor, and music arrangement: Nina Danino
Soundtrack composed and performed by Sainkho Namchylak, Shelley Hirsch and Catherine Bott
Sainkho Namchylak: Nature, Virgin and Vocal Landscapes
Shelley Hirsch: States, Visionaries and Voices
Catherine Bott: Soprano
Pavlo Beznosiuk: Vielles
Photography: David Scott, Nick Gordon Smith
Camera Assistants: Aris Kyriakides, Candida Richardson
Lightworks Editors: Sadiq D Mohamed, David Lewis
Electronic Image and On-line Editor: Bernard Bats
Dubbing Editor: Martin Cantwell
Dubbing Mixer: Paul Hamblin
Location Managers: Paul Savonitto (France), Humberto Pereira (Portugal)
Production Coordinator: Yasmina Demoly (CICV, France)
Thanks to: Pierre Bongiovanni, John Somerville-Large, Steve Farrer, Slavko Barbaric, Leo Feigin, Steve Felton, VTR, Fernando Vendrell, Monica Zanolin, John Gulliver, Andy Powell, Ian Magowan, Antonio Fael, Gianmarco del Re, Valerie Le Cuen, Veronique Routin.
Archive footage courtesy of Richard Everson, USA and NODO, Filmoteca Española
Film Extract from *Il Vangelo Secondo Matteo*, Pier Paolo Pasolini, dir., 1964, courtesy of Compass Films
Executive Producer: Steve Brookes, British Film Institute
Produced by Nina Danino and James Mackay
Financed by The British Film Institute, CICV—Centre Pierre Schaeffer, Montbéliard, Belfort, France, The London Production Fund, National Lottery, The Arts Council of England

Location 2004

16mm, colour, silent, 1 min
Loop or linear projection
One shot of a time lapse of trees at dawn from the opening sequence
"The Virgin's Time", *Temenos,* 1998

CDs

1997 *States,* Shelley Hirsch, New York: Tellus, TE-C003/1997.
Tracks 13-18 from the films *"Now I am yours"* and *Temenos* performed and composed by Shelley Hirsch

2000 *Temenos,* film soundtrack featuring Sainkho Namchylak, Shelley Hirsch and soprano Catherine Bott, Leo Records CDLR3203

DVD

2004 *Temenos,* 1998, *History of the Avant-Garde* series, London: British Film Institute

Nina Danino's films are distributed by:
Lux Distribution: www.lux.org.uk
BFI: www.bfi.org.uk

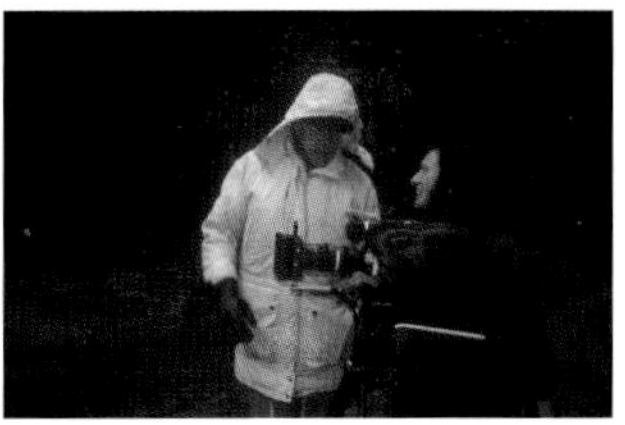

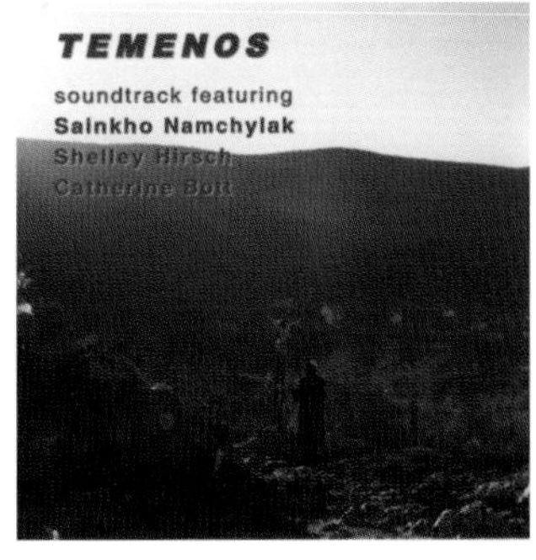

From top: *Temenos,* location filming with cameraman David Scott, 1997

Temenos, CD booklet cover, 2000

Biography and Bibliography

Born and educated in Gibraltar, Nina Danino studied painting at St Martin's School of Art, London, 1973-1977 and time-based media and film at the Department of Environmental Media, Royal College of Art, 1979-1981. Between 1980 and 1990 she was a member of the collective that produced *Undercut,* the journal of experimental film and video, as well as being the journal's co-editor. Her films have been shown nationally and internationally. She has taught extensively on visual art and film and is currently Lecturer in Fine Art at Goldsmiths College in London where she lives and works.

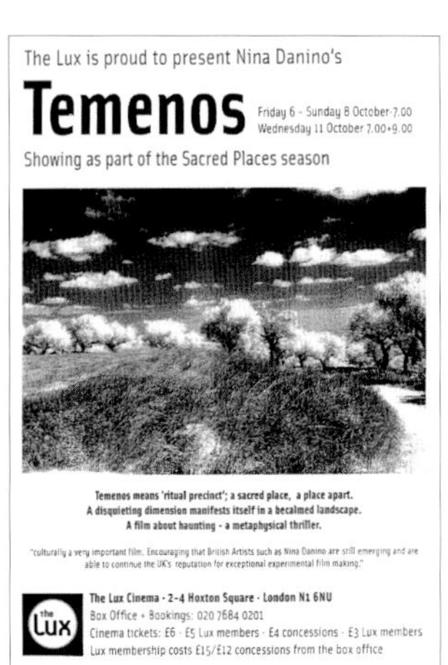

From top: Photograph of the filmmaker, 1979

Temenos in *Sacred Places,* Lux Cinema flyer, 2000

Selected Cinema Screenings and Exhibitions

2005 *Temenos* in *The Sacred and the Feminine: Image, Music, Text, Space,* AHRB CentreCATH, University of Leeds with ERCIF of the University of Bordeaux

2004 *Location* in *Light Reading,* no.w.here, London
First Memory, Stabat Mater, "Now I am yours", Temenos in *Experiments in Moving Image,* Old 'Lumiere' Cinema, University of Westminster, London

2002 *Stabat Mater* in *The Space of the Female Gaze,* TART Salon, London

2001 *Temenos,* Lux Cinema, London
Temenos and *"Now I am yours",* 291 Gallery, London
Temenos, Brighton Cinémathèque, UK
The Barn Cinema, Dartington, UK
Middle East Technical University, Ankara, Turkey

2000 *Temenos* in *Sacred Places,* Lux Cinema, London
Scratch Projections, L'Entrepot Cinema, Paris, France

1999 *Temenos,* Melbourne Cinémathèque, Melbourne, Australia
STUC, KunstenCentrum, Leuven, Belgium

1998 World Premiere of *Temenos,* Edinburgh International Film Festival
London International Film Festival, Lux Cinema, London
Hi-Lites from the LFF, Soho House, London
"Now I am yours" in *Bad Religion,* Lux Cinema, London

1997 *Stabat Mater* in *All that is Solid Melts into Air: 30 Years of the LFMC and the British Avant Garde, Pandaemonium,* ICA, London
World Premiere of *The Silence is Baroque* in the portmanteau feature film *Rainbow Stories,* Rotterdam International Film Festival, The Netherlands

1995 *"Now I am yours",* television broadcast on Kunst Kanaal TV, Amsterdam, The Netherlands and on *Eat Carpet,* SBS-TV, Australia
Retina, IV International Film and Video Festival, Hungary
Stabat Mater in *The British Avant Garde 1967-1990,* London Filmmakers' Co-op Cinema

1994 *"Now I am yours"* in *(S/T)extuality: Poetic Licence,* Pacific Film Archive, University of California, Berkeley, USA
Women in the Director's Chair, International Film Festival, Chicago, USA
IMPACKT Film Festival, Utrecht, The Netherlands
Psychoanalysis and the Image, ICA, London
Feminale, Frauen Film Festival, Koln, Germany
Avant-garde aus London—Films of Nina Danino, Freunde der Deutche Kinematek, Arsenal Cinema, Berlin, Germany
Scratch Projections, L'Entrepot Cinema, Paris, France
"Quelles Hystéries?", Galerie du Cloître, Ecole Régionale des Beaux Arts, Rennes, France

1993 *Stabat Mater* in *Mother Line,* London Filmmakers' Co-op Cinema
Premiere of *"Now I am yours"* in *Dreams, Visions and Rapture, Art and Experiment,* London International Film Festival, National Film Theatre, London
"Now I am yours", television broadcast on *Late Night Experiment,* Channel Four
Stabat Mater in "Imaging the Female", *Experimental Women,* Birkbeck College, University of London

1992 *Stabat Mater* in *Driving the Loop: New British Filmmakers,* Tate Britain, London

1991 *Stabat Mater* in *International Avant-Garde,* National Film Theatre, London
New British Work, Pleasure Dome, Toronto, Canada

1990 Premiere of *Stabat Mater* in *Personalities, Sexualities, Identities,* London International Film Festival, London Filmmakers' Co-op Cinema

1989 *Whitechapel Open,* Whitechapel Gallery, London

1988 *Close to Home* in *Silence in View,* London Filmmakers' Co-op Cinema

1987 *First Memory* in *Narrative Fragments,* London Filmmakers' Co-op Cinema

1985 Premiere of *Close to Home,* Edinburgh International Film Festival
Cambridge Dark Room, Cambridge, presented by Penny Webb
Labyrinths, London Filmmakers' Co-op Cinema

1984 *First Memory* in *Women in Film,* Brewery Arts Centre, Cumbria

1983 *First Memory* in *Word and Image,* London Filmmakers' Co-op Cinema

1982 *First Memory* in *New British Avant-garde Film,* Freunde der Deutche Kinematek, Arsenal Cinema, Berlin, Germany

1981 Premiere of *First Memory* in *New Contemporaries,* ICA, London
About the Pictures in this Room: Five RCA Environmental Media Artists, Seven Dials Gallery, London

1980 Premiere of *First Memory,* Multi-Media Projection in *About Time/ Women's Images of Men,* ICA, London

1976 *New Contemporaries,* International Arts Centre, London
Stowell's Trophy, Royal Academy, London

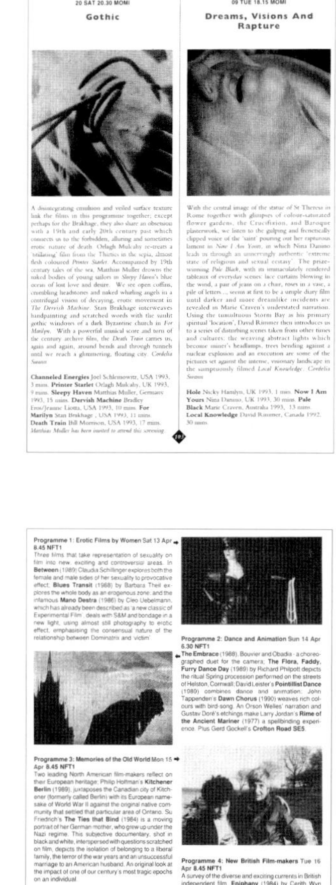

ART AND EXPERIMENT

20 SAT 20.30 MOMI

Gothic

A disintegrating emulsion and veiled surface texture link the films in this programme together; except perhaps for the Brakhage, they also share an obsession with a 19th and early 20th century past which connects us to the forbidden, alluring and sometimes erotic nature of death. Orlagh Mulcahy re-treats a 'titillating' film from the Thirties in the sepia, almost flesh coloured *Printer Starlet*. Accompanied by 19th century tales of the sea, Matthias Muller drowns the naked bodies of young sailors in *Sleepy Haven*'s blue ocean of lost love and desire. We see open coffins, crumbling headstones and naked whirling angels in a centrifugal vision of decaying, erotic movement in *The Dervish Machine*. Stan Brakhage interweaves handpainting and scratched words with the sunlit gothic windows of a dark Byzantine church in *For Marilyn*. With a powerful musical score and turn of the century archive film, the *Death Train* carries us, again and again, around bends and through tunnels until we reach a glimmering, floating city. *Cordelia Swann*

Channeled Energies Joel Schlemowitz, USA 1993, 3 mins. **Printer Starlet** Orlagh Mulcahy, UK 1993, 9 mins. **Sleepy Haven** Matthias Muller, Germany 1993, 15 mins. **Dervish Machine** Bradley Eros/Jeanne Liotta, USA 1993, 10 mins. **For Marilyn** Stan Brakhage , USA 1993, 11 mins. **Death Train** Bill Morrison, USA 1993, 17 mins. *Matthias Muller has been invited to attend this screening.*

09 TUE 18.15 MOMI

Dreams, Visions And Rapture

With the central image of the statue of St Theresa in Rome together with glimpses of colour-saturated flower gardens, the Crucifixion, and Baroque plasterwork, we listen to the gulping and frenetically clipped voice of the 'saint' pouring out her rapturous lament in *Now I Am Yours*, in which Nina Danino leads us through an unnervingly authentic 'extreme state of religious and sexual ecstasy'. The prize-winning *Pale Black*, with its immaculately rendered tableaux of everyday scenes: lace curtains blowing in the wind, a pair of jeans on a chair, roses in a vase, a pile of letters..., seems at first to be a simple diary film until darker and more dreamlike incidents are revealed in Marie Craven's understated narration. Using the tumultuous Storm Bay as his primary spiritual 'location', David Rimmer then introduces us to a series of disturbing scenes taken from other times and cultures: the weaving abstract lights which become miner's headlamps, trees bending against a nuclear explosion and an execution are some of the pictures set against the intense, visionary landscape in the sumptuously filmed *Local Knowledge*. *Cordelia Swann*

Hole Nicky Hamlyn, UK 1993, 1 min. **Now I Am Yours** Nina Danino, UK 1993, 30 mins. **Pale Black** Marie Craven, Australia 1993, 13 mins. **Local Knowledge** David Rimmer, Canada 1992, 30 mins.

103

Programme 1: Erotic Films by Women Sat 13 Apr **8.45 NFT1**
Three films that take representation of sexuality on film into new, exciting and controversial areas. In **Between** (1989) Claudia Schillinger explores both the female and male sides of her sexuality to provocative effect; **Blues Transit** (1988) by Barbara Theil explores the whole body as an erogenous zone; and the infamous **Mano Destra** (1986) by Cleo Uebelmann, which has already been described as 'a new classic of Experimental Film', deals with S&M and bondage in a new light, using almost still photography to erotic effect, emphasising the consensual nature of the relationship between Dominatrix and 'victim'.

Programme 2: Dance and Animation Sun 14 Apr **6.30 NFT1**
The Embrace (1988), Bouvier and Obadia - a choreographed duet for the camera; **The Flora, Faddy, Furry Dance Day** (1989) by Richard Philpott depicts the ritual Spring procession performed on the streets of Helston, Cornwall; David Leister's **Pointillist Dance** (1989) combines dance and animation; John Tappenden's **Dawn Chorus** (1990) weaves rich colours with bird-song. An Orson Welles' narration and Gustav Doré's etchings make Larry Jordan's **Rime of the Ancient Mariner** (1977) a spellbinding experience. Plus Gerd Gockell's **Crofton Road SE5**.

Programme 3: Memories of the Old World Mon 15 Apr **8.45 NFT1**
Two leading North American film-makers reflect on their European heritage; Philip Hoffman's **Kitchener Berlin** (1989), juxtaposes the Canadian city of Kitchener (formerly called Berlin) with its European namesake of World War II against the original native community that settled that particular area of Ontario. Su Friedrich's **The Ties that Bind** (1984) is a moving portrait of her German mother, who grew up under the Nazi regime. This subjective documentary, shot in black and white, interspersed with questions scratched on film, depicts the isolation of belonging to a liberal family, the terror of the war years and an unsuccessful marriage to an American husband. An original look at the impact of one of our century's most tragic epochs on an individual.

Programme 4: New British Film-makers Tue 16 Apr **8.45 NFT1**
A survey of the diverse and exciting currents in British independent film. **Epiphany** (1984) by Cerith Wyn Evans, is an early example of the film/video crossover using images reminicent of Rennaisance painting; **Sermon** (1987) by Nick Gordon-Smith is a visually spectacular meditation on stardom and mortality, showing a mastery of both film and video technologies; Nina Danino's **Stabat Mater** (1990) is a devotional piece responding to the song sung during Holy Week to the Mater Dolorosa; **Swamp** (1988) by Simon Cassell is a Kafkaesque and macabre black comedy.

11

From top: *"Now I am yours",* London Film Festival programme, 1993

Stabat Mater in *International Avant-Garde,* NFT Programme, 1991

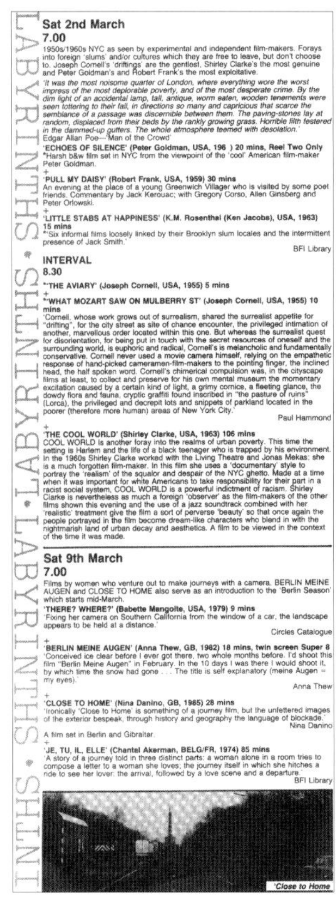

LABYRINTHS • LABYRINTHS • LABYRINTHS

Sat 2nd March
7.00

1950s/1960s NYC as seen by experimental and independent film-makers. Forays into foreign 'slums' and/or cultures which they are free to leave, but don't choose to. Joseph Cornell's 'driftings' are the gentlest, Shirley Clarke's the most genuine and Peter Goldman's and Robert Frank's the most exploitative.

'It was the most noisome quarter of London, where everything wore the worst impress of the most deplorable poverty, and of the most desperate crime. By the dim light of an accidental lamp, tall, antique, worm eaten, wooden tenements were seen tottering to their fall, in directions so many and capricious that scarce the semblance of a passage was discernible between them. The paving-stones lay at random, displaced from their beds by the rankly growing grass. Horrible filth festered in the dammed-up gutters. The whole atmosphere teemed with desolation.'
Edgar Allan Poe—'Man of the Crowd'

'ECHOES OF SILENCE' (Peter Goldman, USA, 196) 20 mins, Reel Two Only
*Harsh b&w film set in NYC from the viewpoint of the 'cool' American film-maker Peter Goldman.
+
'PULL MY DAISY' (Robert Frank, USA, 1959) 30 mins
An evening at the place of a young Greenwich Villager who is visited by some poet friends. Commentary by Jack Kerouac; with Gregory Corso, Allen Ginsberg and Peter Orlowski.
+
'LITTLE STABS AT HAPPINESS' (K.M. Rosenthal (Ken Jacobs), USA, 1963) 15 mins
*'Six informal films loosely linked by their Brooklyn slum locales and the intermittent presence of Jack Smith.'
BFI Library

INTERVAL
8.30

***'THE AVIARY' (Joseph Cornell, USA, 1955) 5 mins**
+
***'WHAT MOZART SAW ON MULBERRY ST' (Joseph Cornell, USA, 1955) 10 mins**
'Cornell, whose work grows out of surrealism, shared the surrealist appetite for "drifting", for the city street as site of chance encounter, the privileged intimation of another, marvellous order located within this one. But whereas the surrealist quest for disorientation, for being put in touch with the secret resources of oneself and the surrounding world, is euphoric and radical, Cornell's is melancholic and fundamentally conservative. Cornell never used a movie camera himself, relying on the empathetic response of hand-picked cameramen-film-makers to the pointing finger, the inclined head, the half spoken word. Cornell's chimerical compulsion was, in the cityscape films at least, to collect and preserve for his own mental museum the momentary excitation caused by a certain kind of light, a grimy cornice, a fleeting glance, the dowdy flora and fauna, cryptic graffiti found inscribed in "the pasture of ruins" (Lorca), the privileged and decrepit lots and snippets of parkland located in the poorer (therefore more human) areas of New York City.'
Paul Hammond
+
'THE COOL WORLD' (Shirley Clarke, USA, 1963) 106 mins
COOL WORLD is another foray into the realms of urban poverty. This time the setting is Harlem and the life of a black teenager who is trapped by his environment. In the 1960s Shirley Clarke worked with the Living Theatre and Jonas Mekas; she is a much forgotten film-maker. In this film she uses a 'documentary' style to portray the 'realism' of the squalor and despair of the NYC ghetto. Made at a time when it was important for white Americans to take responsibility for their part in a racist social system, COOL WORLD is a powerful indictment of racism. Shirley Clarke is nevertheless as much a foreign 'observer' as the film-makers of the other films shown this evening and the use of a jazz soundtrack combined with her 'realistic' treatment give the film a sort of perverse 'beauty' so that once again the people portrayed in the film become dream-like characters who blend in with the nightmarish land of urban decay and aesthetics. A film to be viewed in the context of the time it was made.

Sat 9th March
7.00

Films by women who venture out to make journeys with a camera. BERLIN MEINE AUGEN and CLOSE TO HOME also serve as an introduction to the 'Berlin Season' which starts mid-March.

'THERE? WHERE?' (Babette Mangolte, USA, 1979) 9 mins
'Fixing her camera on Southern California from the window of a car, the landscape appears to be held at a distance.'
Circles Catalogue
+
'BERLIN MEINE AUGEN' (Anna Thew, GB, 1982) 18 mins, twin screen Super 8
'Conceived ice clear before I ever got there, two whole months before. I'd shoot this film "Berlin Meine Augen" in February. In the 10 days I was there I would shoot it, by which time the snow had gone . . . The title is self explanatory (meine Augen = my eyes).'
Anna Thew
+
'CLOSE TO HOME' (Nina Danino, GB, 1985) 28 mins
'Ironically 'Close to Home' is something of a journey film, but the unfettered images of the exterior bespeak, through history and geography the language of blockade.'
Nina Danino

A film set in Berlin and Gibraltar.
+
'JE, TU, IL, ELLE' (Chantal Akerman, BELG/FR, 1974) 85 mins
'A story of a journey told in three distinct parts: a woman alone in a room tries to compose a letter to a woman she loves; the journey itself in which she hitches a ride to see her lover: the arrival, followed by a love scene and a departure.'
BFI Library

Close to Home in *Labyrinths*, London Filmmakers' Co-op programme, 1985

Publications by Nina Danino

2004 "Cinema without Cinema", *Experiments in Moving Image*, Jackie Hatfield and Stephen Littman, eds., Epigraph Publications

2003 "A Century of Artists' Film and Video—A Response to the Curational Rationale", *Filmwaves*, no. 22

2002 *The Undercut Reader: Critical Writings on Artists' Film and Video*, Nina Danino and Michael Mazière eds., London: Wallflower Press

2001 "British Experimental Film and Video", *Aesthetics and Art in the Twentieth Century*, Ipek Tureli ed., Ankara: SANART (Association of Aesthetics and Visual Culture)

1998 "Temenos and Other Places", *Filmwaves*, no. 5

1991 "The Object of Attention", *Reading the Glass*, Barber, Kivland and Leyser eds., London: Book Works

1990 "The Mother's Garden", photo essay, *Undercut*, no. 19
"A Decade of British Experimental Film and Video" special edition of *Undercut*, Nina Danino and Michael Mazière eds., *Undercut*, no. 19

1989 "East European and Soviet Avant-garde Film and Video", special edition of *Undercut*, Nina Danino and Michael Mazière eds., *Undercut*, no. 18

1988 "Cultural Identities", special edition of *Undercut*, Nina Danino ed., *Undercut*, no. 17

1985 "Almost Out by Jayne Parker", *Undercut*, no. 14/15

1983 "Interview with Laura Mulvey", Nina Danino and Lucy Moy Thomas, *Undercut*, no. 6

1981 "On Stonebridge Park a film by Patrick Keiller", *Undercut*, no. 2

Publications on Nina Danino

2005 Susanna Poole, "Film, The Body, The Fold—an Interview with Nina Danino on *"Now I am Yours"*", *Experimental Film and Video Anthology*, Jackie Hatfield and Steven Littman eds., London: John Libbey

2004 Nicky Hamlyn, "Film Location", "Public Places, Private Thoughts" and "Sense of Place, Evocation of Place", www.luxonline.org.uk
Mark Waller, "Kiss the Zombie", www.luxonline.org.uk
Helen de Witt, "The Persistence of Spirit", www.luxonline.org.uk

2001 Gill Addison, "Nina Danino at 291 Gallery", *Filmwaves*, no. 16

1999 A L Rees, *A History of Experimental Film and Video*, BFI: London

1998 Gianmarco del Re, "Cinema and the Sublime", *Contemporary Visual Arts*, no. 19

1995 *Directory of 100 British Film and Video Artists*, David Curtis ed., London: The Arts Council of England

1990 Jean Matthee, "On Wounds, Artificial Flowers, Orifices and the Infinite: A Response to the Films of Nina Danino", *Undercut*, no. 20 (Reprinted in *The Undercut Reader*, London: Wallflower Press 2002)

Media Interviews

2004 Radio discussion on *Experiments in Moving Image* with Nina Danino, Jackie Hatfield and Theo Prodromidis, Resonance FM, London

1998 *Cinepresa toccante*, documentary, Susanna Poole dir., on the body in the works of Nina Danino, Jo-Ann Kaplan and Sarah Pucill. London Guildhall University and Santalucia Produzione, featuring *"Now I am yours"*

1991 Radio Interview on *Stabat Mater, Third Opinion*, BBC3
Radio Interview on *Stabat Mater, Focus*, GBC Radio

Conferences and Talks (*published)

2005 *Stabat Mater* and talk in *The Sacred and the Feminine: Image, Music, Text, Space*, AHRB CentreCATH, University of Leeds with ERCIF of the University of Bordeaux

2001 "British Experimental Film and Video"*, *Retrospective: Aesthetics and Art in the Twentieth Century*, SANART, Ankara, Turkey

2000 *"Now I am yours"* and "The Image in the Visionary Experience of Teresa of Jesus" in *Space, Time and the Image*, Birkbeck College, Faculty of Continuing Education, University of London

1998 *Temenos* and "Film, Time and the Visionary"* in *Space, Time and the Image*, Birkbeck College, Faculty of Continuing Education, University of London.

1997 "Time and Black Film" in *Time and the Image*, Birkbeck College, Faculty of Continuing Education, University of London

1994 *Psychoanalysis and The Image*, ICA, London
Stabat Mater and talk in James Joyce International Symposium, delegation to Gibraltar from the University of Seville
Stabat Mater in *Time and the Image*, Birkbeck College, Faculty of Continuing Education, University of London
"Now I am yours" and talk for Hispanic Studies Film Seminar, Department of Spanish and Portuguese, University of Cambridge
MA Architecture and Critical Theory Film Seminar, Nottingham University

1993 "Speaking in the Dark: Film, The Voice and Teresa of Jesus' Speaking Texts"*, *Woman/Image/Text*, Sheffield Hallam University

Acknowledgments

I would like to thank all the artists, technicians and friends who have helped, collaborated with and supported me over the years.
Thank you to my artistic collaborators Shelley Hirsch and Sainkho Namchlyak.
For inspiring and stimulating conversations, for their films and art, for their interest in my work: Gill Addison, Mary Ball, Catherine Bott, Nick Collins, Mario Finlayson, the late Arthur Howes, Peter Kardia, the late Em Kirkpatrick, the late Sandra Lahire, Bracha Lichtenberg-Ettinger, the late Stuart Marshall, Jean Matthee, Barbara Meter, Anna Miszewska, Annabel Nicholson, Lucy Panteli, Susanna Poole, Sarah Pucill, Lis Rhodes, Gino Sanguinetti, Guy Sherwin, Anna Thew, Gary Thomas and Helen de Witt.
Thank you to all those who have given their time and technical expertise to my films, they are credited in the filmography. Without them it would not have been possible.
Special thanks to John Somerville-Large for his long standing support and to my mother Elena Danino.
At Black Dog Publishing, thank you to Catherine Grant for her editorship of this book, Emilia Gómez López for design, Oriana Fox for production and editorial assistance and to Duncan McCorquodale for his support.
Thanks to Alison Butler, Ellen Danino, Kathy Kubicki, Malcolm Le Grice and Marisia Lewandovska, who lent their support to the publication.
My thanks especially to Francesca Piovano for her visual advice as the book progressed.
Thank you to Louise Gray, S Brent Plate, Juan José Tellez and Helen de Witt, for their writing.
Thank you to Ivan Coleman and Jon Whitehall for digitisation of images for publication, as well as to Stefania Marangoni, John Panas, Mike Riley and Tolga Saygin at the Goldsmiths Department of Visual Arts, Research Laboratories.

Financial support for this publication has been given by the Arts Council of England and the Department of Visual Arts, Goldsmiths College, University of London.

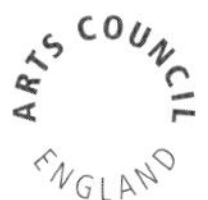

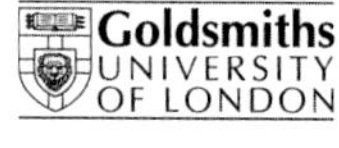

Picture Credits

All images are courtesy of Nina Danino except when otherwise stated

Mirta Alaggia, *First Memory*, production photographs, pp. 29, 40
Paul Donn, *Close to Home*, Berlin location photographs, p. 34
Aris Kyriakides, *Temenos*, location photographs, pp. 110, 112
John Somerville-Large, *Temenos*, location photographs, pp. 9, 116;
Stabat Mater location photographs, pp. 38, 108
Monica Zanolin, *"Now I am yours"*, location photographs, pp. 34, 67, 68, 70
Marguerite Duras, *India Song*, 1975, courtesy Jean Mascolo, p. 47
Film stills from Pasolini's *The Gospel According to St Matthew*, courtesy Compass Films, p. 47
Nikola Nedeljkovic, *"Now I am yours"*, installation photograph, courtesy the photographer, p. 78
Shirin Neshat, *Turbulent*, 1998, film still courtesy Barbara Gladstone Gallery, p. 91
Dagmar Gebers, photograph of Sainkho Namychylak, courtesy the photographer, p. 92
Michael Scheiner, photograph of Shelley Hirsch, courtesy the photographer, p. 94

Edited by Catherine Grant
Designed by Emilia Gómez López

Black Dog Publishing Limited
Unit 4.4 Tea Building
56 Shoreditch High Street
London
E1 6JJ

Tel: +44 (0)20 7613 1922
Fax: +44 (0)20 7613 1944
Email: info@bdp.demon.co.uk
www.bdpworld.com

British Library Cataloguing-in-Publication Data.

A CIP record for this book is available from the British Library.

ISBN 1 904772 07 2

Printed and bound in Italy by Printer Trento S.r.l.